Feminist Legal History

D1483839

Feminist Legal History

Essays on Women and Law

EDITED BY

Tracy A. Thomas and
Tracey Jean Boisseau

NEW YORK UNIVERSITY PRESS
New York and London

NEW YORK UNIVERSITY PRESS
New York and London
www.nyupress.org

© 2011 by New York University
All rights reserved

References to Internet websites (URLs) were accurate at the time of writing.
Neither the author nor New York University Press is responsible for URLs
that may have expired or changed since the manuscript was prepared.

Library of Congress Cataloging-in-Publication Data

Feminist legal history : essays on women and law /
edited by Tracy A. Thomas and Tracey Jean Boisseau.
p. cm.
Includes bibliographical references and index.
ISBN 978-0-8147-8719-9 (cl : alk. paper) — ISBN 978-0-8147-8720-5
(pb : alk. paper) — ISBN 978-0-8147-8721-2 (ebook)
1. Women—Legal status, laws, etc.—United States.—History.
2. Feminist jurisprudence—United States. I. Thomas, Tracy A.
II. Boisseau, Tracey Jean.
KF478.F46   2011
346.7301'34—dc22   2010047148

New York University Press books are printed on acid-free paper,
and their binding materials are chosen for strength and durability.
We strive to use environmentally responsible suppliers and materials
to the greatest extent possible in publishing our books.

Manufactured in the United States of America
c   10 9 8 7 6 5 4 3 2 1
p   10 9 8 7 6 5 4 3 2 1

Contents

PART II: WOMEN'S TRANSFORMATION OF THE LAW

Foreword

REVA SIEGEL

The impressive body of work collected in *Feminist Legal History* demonstrates that a new field is emerging in history and in law that speaks, at one and the same time, to audiences in the academy and beyond.

This is a book that alters our vision of American life and law. It revisits familiar terrain, and recovers long lost interactions between men and women at the root of this nation's defining commitments and institutions. We come better to understand how gender relations have defined spheres we have long recognized as gendered, such as suffrage, marriage, the military, sexual harassment, and reproductive rights law. And we encounter gender relations shaping spheres we do not conventionally conceive of as gendered, such as accident or poverty law. We learn of micro-choices that cumulatively produced and made reasonable a world in which men have power women lack. And we learn of micro-resistances, of how women's phenomenal agency and creativity have given defining shape to family, community, politics, and law.

The work collected in *Feminist Legal History* matters, both as it intervenes in particular institutions and policy choices, and as it demonstrates, again and again, why it pays to ask how gender matters. Narratives about the past illuminate not only past choices but future ones. They help us see more clearly who we are and how we live together—and to consider what is fixed, what is contingent, and what is open to re-imagining.

Preface

TRACEY JEAN BOISSEAU

The extent to which history is literally embedded in legal decision making even when dramatic departures from recent norms are being contemplated is revealed in the decision rendered by the U.S. Supreme Court in *Roe v. Wade*. Before addressing the claims made by legal counsel, Justice Harry Blackmun asserted in the 1973 majority opinion how desirable he felt it was to "survey, in several aspects, the history of abortion, for such insight as that history may afford us." Opening himself up to what would prove fairly devastating critiques of his representation and use of history, and the relative relevance of these particular traditions to present-day reproductive politics, the Justice cited ancient Greek law as well as historical common law practices as the foundation for the Court's decision establishing a new constitutional right for women to choose abortion. However flawed by an apparently idiosyncratic use of history, Blackmun's reasoning amply demonstrates the degree to which practitioners of the law inevitably use, misuse, invoke, and write their own versions of history—especially when women are centrally involved. This iconic moment in legal decision making, public history making, and women's history demonstrates a central precept animating this collection of essays: that the law comprises at once an engine of change and a buttressing of tradition, a view onto the past and a lesson in the significance and power afforded to history as it is conceived to shape the future.

Foundational to the thinking of the editors and contributors to *Feminist Legal History* is the idea that history—how it is imagined, who writes it, and how it is used—plays an integral role in the making and transformation of the law. No law is made or challenged or applied without reference, explicit or implicit, to an assumed past. Indeed, it could be said that the strategy of referring to a seemingly transparent (and deceptively so) past is perhaps most powerfully enacted by legal practitioners. What is considered reasonable or conventional is always determined so in light of a historical view of past practice. The more naturalized the categories and ideas at stake, the more this is true. Thus no arena of legal practice and lawmaking is more dependent upon references to the past than those legal decisions which explicitly center, or implicitly hinge upon, ideas about gender and women. As feminists we believe that the assumptions that animate such decisions are not natural; they come from somewhere. Our mission as feminists interested in legal change is to expose the way that legal practice constructs a history within which women and men emerge as distinct realities. History is being done—either poorly, without reflection, or carefully with great attention to the consequences of one's conclusions about the past—but, either way, in the assertion of legal practice and legal decision making, history is being produced through legal discourse all the time.

This volume is centrally concerned with not only how the law has changed but also how legal as well as extra-judicial discourse have—in the words of Reva Siegel, the keynote speaker for the October 2007 symposium held at the University of Akron that inspired this volume—"structured conversations between the public and the bench." Much the same way that the efforts of the lay lawyers, justices, and activists who are examined in this volume have influenced the legal decisions and decision makers in previous eras, writing our own feminist legal history is a strategy we employ to reshape our world.

The contribution of the professional feminist historian of law to our understanding of present legal practice lies in the confluence between the two classifications. What professional legal historians set out to do is to redirect our gaze in ways that serve to question widespread assumptions about the past—rather than reiterate them or blindly support their fortification as one might do lacking the historical perspective of a trained scholar. For *feminist* scholars of legal history, this mission to think counter-intuitively about the past takes on added significance. In addition to producing insights as to how, under what conditions, and through what mechanisms the law has been transformed, the interventions of professional feminist legal historians comprise a direct and purposeful assault on conventional thinking about the relationship between law, gender relations, and women's lives that is often directly undercutting what our legal system, stuck in a blind present, generally imagines to be natural or to have always been true.

Feminist Legal History is dedicated to just such illumination. This volume brings together those scholars of the law with distinct insights into historical ways that women have influenced and been shaped by law with those historians whose broad appreciation for the past brings new perspectives on what the law has meant to women within a larger context. By bringing the two disciplines together, we seek to contribute to the project of institutionalizing feminist history, feminist views of history, and feminist ideas of women's legal roles and rights. In these ways we hope to contribute not only to a reconsideration of the past but also to the imagining of a more liberatory legal system and decidedly feminist future.

Introduction

Law, History, and Feminism

TRACY A. THOMAS AND TRACEY JEAN BOISSEAU

Feminist Legal History offers new visions of American legal history that reveal women's engagement with the law over the past two centuries. The essays in this book look at women's status in society over time through the lens of the law. The conventional story portrays law as a barrier or constraint upon women's rights. While law has and continues to operate as a restraint upon women's full participation in society, law has also worked as a facilitating structure. The overall picture gleaned from the snapshots in time offered in this book shows the actualizing power of the law for women. Women have used the law historically as a vehicle to obtain personal and societal change. Even more, women have used feminist theory to transform the law itself to incorporate an appreciation of gendered realities.

The essays here locate women at the center of a historical understanding of the past. In what has been called "engendering legal history," the works integrate the stories of women into the dominant history of the law and then seek to reconstruct the assumed contours of history.[1] The authors recover the women and their contributions that have been omitted from history, enabling a rewriting of the traditional historical narratives. The research fills in some of the missing pieces of legal history and goes further to offer alternative interpretations of the general discourse of law: "Things we thought we knew about American history turn out to be more complex than we had suspected."[2] The essays test familiar generalizations and challenge the social construction of gender. Using historical inquiry, the authors focus on the details and social context, rather than the legal rules, to better understand the meaning and impact of the law. The details are important to avoid overgeneralizations and superficial descriptions of how and why events occurred in the past. Such reexaminations of American legal history contribute to discussions of the law and policy decisions of today in ways that promote women's rights, women's interests, and women's empowerment.

This introduction provides the context necessary to appreciate the essays in the book. It starts with an overview of the existing state of women's legal history, tracing the core events over the past two hundred years. This history, though sparse, provides the common foundation for the authors, and establishes the launching point for the deeper and more detailed inquiries offered here. Following this history is an exploration of the key themes advanced in the book. In part I, "Contradictions in Legalizing Gender," the essays develop analyses of the law's contradictory response to women's petitions. The essays in this section provide evidence of how law operated as a barrier to limit women's power, and challenge the assumptions that such barriers have been eliminated today. Yet the essays in part I also present a more nuanced historical picture. They show the law's facilitation of women's agency and power, often based on the same gendered norms that elsewhere produced limitations. Part II of the book, "Women's Transformation of the Law," shows women's impact upon the law and illustrates how women changed the law to incorporate their own, gendered, perspectives. By "feminizing" the legal process and altering the substantive law to respond to women's needs, women were able to shape the law in their own image.

The introduction concludes with an overview of feminist legal thought. An appreciation of such theory and methodology is important to understanding the lens through which the authors and advocates over time approached the problems presented. *Feminist Legal History* is not just a collection of stories about women. Instead, it is a feminist inquiry of the historical record, in which feminist theory illuminates the positions and motivating beliefs of women over time.

Women's Legal History Thus Far

The history of women in the law is still a work in progress. The existing narrative of women's legal history is somewhat skeletal, which is not surprising given that the field is relatively new.[3] The research, however, shares a common foundation, even as that history is being re-imagined by ongoing scholarship. The conventional story in law tells of women's linear progress from oppression under the law to equal opportunity in modern times. History is viewed as a series of small steps, as women slowly eradicate the legal barriers to their full empowerment. This collection shows that such incrementalism did not prevail in the law and that existing historical accounts of women's legal rights are one-dimensional.

The popular notion of women's history is often expressed as first-wave and second-wave feminism. The first wave spans the seventy-five years when demands for suffrage were prominent, beginning with Elizabeth Cady Stanton's *Declaration of Sentiments* in 1848 up to the adoption of the Nineteenth Amendment to the Constitution and women's right to vote in 1920. "Second-wave feminism" refers to the women's liberation movement of the 1960s and 1970s, often symbolized in mass media representations by Gloria Steinem—the quintessential liberated "career woman"—and Betty Friedan, the iconic middle-class housewife who documented the dehumanizing effect of her experience in her influential book, *The Feminine Mystique* (1963). The feminism that emerged in the 1960s and 1970s, however, was composed of a more complex and diverse set of political, social, and cultural challenges to a patriarchal order than could be adequately represented by either Steinem or Friedan. And the nineteenth-century campaigns for the rights of "woman" were rent with racial and class tensions that remain hidden when recounted only from the point of view of Cady Stanton. Despite significant focus on these contentious issues in the scholarship produced by historians of women's social history, official histories of law and women often continue to put white, middle-class women with professional ambitions and economic privilege—whether living in the nineteenth or twentieth century—at the center of their analysis. Yet, it is important to recognize the intricacies of the way that race and class tempers and shapes gender inequities as well as hinders cross-race and class alliances among women in order to appreciate the complexities of women's activism and legal situations over time.

Conventional legal histories of women tend to begin in the period before the first feminist wave, with studies of coverture and women's legal invisibility inherited from English common law. From the earliest times of American law, married women were "protected" by the law of coverture, which provided that a woman was covered legally by her husband and thus "relieved" of rights to property, wages, child custody, or suffrage. The English treatise writer, William Blackstone, summarized the existing common law. "By marriage, the husband and wife are one person in law: that is, the very being or legal existence of the woman is suspended during the marriage, or at least is incorporated and consolidated into that of the husband: under whose wing, protection, and cover, she performs every thing."[4] In practice this meant that a married woman could not own or control her own property or earnings, devise property by will, enter into contracts, have custody of her children, be liable for her own debts, or sue or be sued in court. A husband was permitted to provide physical correction or "domestic chastisement." The law allowed, even obligated, the husband to control his wife since he was liable both for her civil debts and criminal misdemeanors. Blackstone explained that the legal disabilities of coverture were "for the most part intended for her protection and benefit. So great a favorite is the female sex of the laws of England." Historians, however, have found evidence of women's autonomy during these early times. As Mary Beth Norton demonstrated in her book, *Founding Mothers and Fathers*, women exercised social and legal power in colonial America as midwives and on women's juries constituted for paternity determinations.

The dominant gender ideology of the late eighteenth and early nineteenth centuries evolved into one of separate spheres for men and women. The law embraced the popular cultural notion that women were relegated to the private sphere of home and family, while men dominated the public spheres of work and politics. Women's political role as a citizen of the new republic was cast in terms of domestic responsibility. Under this view of republican motherhood, women were entrusted to educate their sons as virtuous republican citizens. Linda Kerber, in her classic book *Women of the Republic: Intellect and Ideology in Revolutionary America* (1980), wrote of the ways women took advantage of their duty to raise civically responsible children by learning to read and taking seriously their role as educators of the young. This domestic role was intensified and sentimentalized in the first half of the nineteenth century by the promotion of a "cult" of domesticity. "True women," according to the "cult," focused all their efforts on the home and were protected from public responsibilities. In Barbara Welter's often cited delineation, in addition to domesticity they evinced piety, purity, and submission to the men of their family and community. This ideology, of course, was neither an accurate description of women in general nor was it an attainable ideal for any but the small strata of white middle-class women in this rapidly industrializing period. It was an aspiration applicable only to those women who did not have to labor at farm work, enter into commercial relations at market, work as servants in other family's homes, or work for remuneration outside their homes—for example, in the burgeoning textile industry. Though the ideology was full of contradictions, it was widely remarked upon and worked to justify and endorse the lack of political rights for women in the public sphere by presumably elevating them as the treasured "angels" of the private sphere.[5]

Challenges to this idea of women's need for protection, embodied in the law of coverture, began with the Married Women's Property Acts in the 1840s. These acts changed some of the express legal restrictions on women's rights to property and limited husband's prerogatives over that property. The first series of enactments barred husbands' creditors from seizing the property of married women. Later acts allowed married women to retain their personal property and earnings, sign contracts, and sue and be sued. The acts were motivated as much by the credit crises and wealthy fathers protecting their daughters as by feminist motivations to reform the law. The new statutes were also part of the larger codification movement, which sought to restrict the discretion of judges by reducing common law rules and equitable practices to express statutory terms. Most of this legislation was limited in scope. It did not, for example, provide wives with joint ownership of all property accumulated during marriage. Nonetheless, the reforms were the first steps toward recognizing women's economic and familial status.[6]

Women's demands for equality in the family sometimes extended to claims for political rights. On July 19 and 20, 1848, in Seneca Falls, New York, Elizabeth Cady Stanton presented her *Declaration of Sentiments* which contained eighteen demands for social, political, and legal equality. The first demand on the list of claims for equal property, custody of children, and employment was the right to vote. The movement for women's equal political and public rights became part of the nation's social discourse, led by Stanton and Susan B. Anthony's National Woman Suffrage Association and Lucy Stone's American Woman Suffrage Association. The organizations differed on the legal tactics for suffrage—the American pursuing a state-by-state approach and the National seeking federal action. They also disagreed about the involvement of men as officers (the American allowed) and on support for the Fifteenth Amendment mandating suffrage for black men but not women (the National opposed).

In 1873 in Rochester, New York, Susan B. Anthony tried to vote, arguing that the newly enacted Fourteenth Amendment granted women this right in federal elections. She was jailed and yet her sentence was stayed, thus prohibiting her from challenging the law on appeal. The following year, in *Minor v. Happersett*, Virginia Minor pursued the legal argument in the courts, arguing that the Fourteenth Amendment's protection for the "privileges and immunities of citizenship" guaranteed women the right to vote. The Supreme Court rejected her claim, narrowly interpreting the new amendment to hold that voting was not a privilege of citizenship and blocking women's juridical strategies to secure suffrage.[7] A suffrage amendment was introduced into Congress in 1878, and endlessly reintroduced, until it emerged from committee in 1914 and was quickly and easily defeated. A few states like Wyoming and Utah granted women the right to vote by the end of the century but, in the absence of a federal mandate, most continued to deny women this right until 1920.

In the late nineteenth century, the suffrage movement gained new traction with the additional support of socially conservative groups such as the Woman's Christian Temperance Union. These organizations, originally established to oppose the sale and consumption of alcohol, endorsed the ideology of "true womanhood" by reiterating women's purity and relative insulation from the amorality of the marketplace. They sought the vote for women on grounds that they were morally and spiritually superior to men and thus better suited to be the caretakers of society. They specifically argued that female leadership was best able to attend to social problems sparked by the increasing pace of immigration and urbanization, such as a rise in alcohol consumption which threatened the home as a protected haven for women and children. Applying the logic of "true womanhood" to promote women as "social housekeepers" was a powerful and effective new strategy of female reformers producing new roles, even professions, for women; nonetheless, it did not produce widespread acceptance of putting the vote in the hands of women.

The final impetus for women's suffrage would not come until after the turn of the new century. At that point more radical logic demanding women's political equality to men pushed aside conservative "true woman" ideology, and more subversive measures demanding women's right to vote finally won the day. In 1917, while Carrie Chapman Catt, as representative of the merged National-American Woman's Suffrage Association, engaged President Woodrow Wilson in discussion, Alice Paul, Lucy Burns, and other members of the National Woman's Party led silent pickets and protests in front of the White House. They continued these protests for six months—until they were jailed on the charge of obstructing the sidewalk. In prison, Paul led hunger strikes and endured forced feedings and inhumane treatment. The events triggered a public and political outcry sufficient to push the dormant suffrage amendment to the forefront. Meanwhile, additional congressional alliances were secured by recourse to racially divisive strategies that garnered the support of conservative southern congressmen happy to swell the ranks of white voters by adding white women to the rolls. In the immediate aftermath of the First World War, a combination of powerful rhetorics invoking modernity, democracy, and national and racial superiority tipped the scales in favor of woman suffrage.[8] The Nineteenth Amendment to the Constitution guaranteeing women's right to vote was finally passed in 1920.[9]

During this time women also sought access to other levels of power such as the right to practice law. A few women were benevolently granted admission to the bar and licensed to practice as lawyers. These included Arabella Mansfield in Iowa, in 1870, and Charlotte Ray, the first African American female lawyer, licensed in D.C. in 1872.[10] Other women—such as Phoebe Couzins, Emma Barkelo, and African American Mary Ann Shadd Cary—

succeeded in part when they were allowed to attend some of the newly emerging law schools. Most women, however, were refused access to the legal profession based on their sex. Myra Bradwell, a Chicago woman who worked in her husband's law office and published the *Chicago Legal Times*, sought admittance to the bar in 1869 after passing the state bar examination with honors. The Illinois Supreme Court refused to license her because she was a woman. In 1873 the U.S. Supreme Court in *Bradwell v. Illinois* affirmed that decision and denied women the right to practice law. In a concurring opinion that has become a classic reading in American history courses, Justice Joseph P. Bradley, with pointed reliance on "true woman" logic, wrote that women should be confined to their separate domestic sphere.

> Man is, or should be, woman's protector and defender. The natural and proper timidity and delicacy which belongs to the female sex evidently unfits it for many of the occupations of civil life. . . . The paramount destiny and mission of woman are to fulfill the noble and benign offices of wife and mother.[11]

Bradwell eventually worked to change the law in Illinois and was licensed to practice in 1890. Similarly Belva Lockwood was denied the right to practice in the U.S. Supreme Court—until she successfully petitioned Congress to change the law. The Supreme Court, however, subsequently denied her right to practice in the state courts of Virginia, citing states' rights and *Bradwell*.[12]

Despite the disempowering nature of protectionist ideology underlying much of nineteenth-century law, female labor reformers utilized the same theory to secure rights for women in the workplace. Progressive labor activists like Florence Kelley, head of the National Consumers League, believed that all workers needed protective legislation mandating minimum wages and maximum hours of labor. Kelley began with protections for women workers to gain a toehold for more general reforms. She strategized correctly that courts and legislatures would be more amenable to protecting "helpless" women than men.[13] The U.S. Supreme Court took this approach in the 1908 case of *Muller v. Oregon* to uphold protective legislation limiting working hours for women to ten a day. In view of women's disadvantage in the struggle for subsistence because of "physical structure and a proper discharge of her maternal function,"[14] Justice David Josiah Brewer wrote, Oregon was allowed to adopt such a rule. The Court was aided in its decision by the first "Brandeis Brief" presenting social science evidence of women's weakened status and need for protection. The brief, written and researched by Josephine Goldmark and Louis Brandeis with Kelley's influence, included medical evidence that women's blood and muscles had more water content than men's and noted that children of working women were injured by inevitable neglect. The brief explained women's need for more time than men outside of work:

> Free time is not resting time, as it is for a man. . . . For the working-girl on her return from the factory, there is a variety of work waiting. She has her room to keep clean and in order, her laundry work to do, clothes to repair and clean, and, besides this, she should be learning to keep house if her future household is not to be disorderly and a failure.[15]

Although this evidence accepted by the Supreme Court seemed limited to support for a gender-specific ruling, the Court subsequently extended its decision to men in *Bunting v. Oregon* by supporting hours restrictions for all "persons."[16] The Court backed away from these decisions in 1923 by invalidating a minimum wage law for women in *Adkins v. Children's Hospital* on freedom of contract grounds said to be applicable to both men and women.[17] Protective labor legislation returned to favor during the New Deal in *West Coast Hotel v. Parrish* (1937), when the Court upheld a law nearly identical to that in *Adkins*.[18]

After the passage of women's suffrage, disagreements resurfaced between Progressive activists focusing on women's differences and liberal feminists seeking equal treatment of women under the law. In 1923 Alice Paul first proposed the Equal Rights Amendment (ERA) to change the U.S. Constitution to provide that "equality of rights shall not be denied or abridged on account of sex." Though introduced into Congress, it was not passed by Congress and sent to the states for approval until 1972. The Amendment was defeated when it failed to obtain the necessary ratification by two-thirds of the states although many states amended their own state constitutions to include an ERA. The debate against the ERA was led by Phyllis Schlafly and the conservative organization she headed, Eagle Forum. Schlafly, a mother of six children and a full-time working lawyer and activist, demanded that women had the right to be treated like "ladies" and that social differences such as motherhood must be kept sacred. Schlafly claimed that the ERA would mandate abortion, require women to serve in the military, release men from obligations to support their wives and children, and require unisex bathrooms—issues that became hot button points of debate in the media, obscuring other issues more widely accepted in the public mind such as equal pay for equal work.

As the ERA debate unfolded, abortion became a linchpin issue for the women's rights debate. A woman's right to choose and control her body emerged as a central concern for many feminists. The twentieth-century feminist argument for abortion built upon arguments of earlier feminists. In the mid-nineteenth century, abortion, under the common law, was available from midwives and was legal prior to quickening (usually late in the fourth month of pregnancy), until an aggressive public campaign to criminalize abortions, led by doctors, rendered the practice risky and illicit. Between 1850 and 1880 most states outlawed abortions and restricted contraception, thereby reinforcing traditional power roles between men and women, and emphasizing women's social duty to bear children. The federal Comstock Act, enacted in 1873, classified information concerning contraception and abortion as obscene and prohibited selling or distributing contraception or abortion devices.[19] Nineteenth-century women's rights advocates did not often publicly endorse abortion or contraception—indeed, they most stridently avoided any association with the advocates of such. Nonetheless, many were outspoken about customs enshrined in law that denied a woman the right to control her own body and sexuality. These advocates supported "voluntary motherhood" by which they meant the right of married women to determine when and how many children they would bear by asserting their right to refuse their husband's demands for sex. Others, sometimes known as "free lovers," insisted on the right and obligation of wives (as well as husbands) to dissolve their marriages if love no longer motivated them to engage in intimate sexual acts. The idea that women ought to be free to choose motherhood as well as to indulge their sexuality (within marriage at least) at their own discretion and in accordance with their own personal feelings remained controversial until well into the twentieth century; it was clear, however, that the precepts of "true womanhood" were undergoing radical review even before the end of the nineteenth.

After the turn of the century, radical ideas about women's sexual freedom and right to birth control exploded onto the public consciousness. Women such as Emma Goldman—the "free lover" and anarchist—and Margaret Sanger—the progressive reformer, eugenicist, and nurse—helped expand the idea of voluntary motherhood by focusing their efforts on legalizing contraception. Goldman publicly flaunted local ordinances that reinforced the idea that women should present themselves as nonsexual beings. Sanger started the birth control movement by opening the first birth control clinic in New York in 1916. She was arrested for distributing birth control devices, although, in affirming her conviction, the New York Court of Appeals interpreted the law to allow doctors to prescribe contraception to prevent "disease." Sanger's clinic, renamed "Planned Parenthood" in 1942, went on to challenge the Comstock Act and other laws prohibiting contraception. In a series of cases culminating in the U.S. Supreme Court's decision in *Griswold v. Connecticut* in 1965, the Court recognized a constitutional right of privacy for contraception.[20]

Many early birth control advocates including Goldman and Sanger had personally favored a woman's freedom to choose abortion, but they expediently suppressed that issue in the campaign for contraception laws. Although Goldman and Sanger may have agreed upon this tactic, they approached the broader issue of birth control from widely differing perspectives, particularly regarding immigrant and poor women. Goldman, an immigrant herself, championed the rights of laboring women and embraced radical political critiques of capitalism. Sanger's eugenic outlook colored her appeals for birth control as well as sterilization as mechanisms that might succeed in inhibiting poor, disabled, and criminalized women from reproducing—as if poverty, disability, or criminality were signs of racial degeneration. Half a century later, demands to legalize abortion would no longer be motivated by such eugenic visions. By the early 1970s large numbers of women and doctors allied together to advocate for the availability of medically safe abortions for all women. This alliance grew to encompass a majority of voters, many of whom would embrace a new "pro-choice" movement in the 1980s.

Yet it was not at the ballot box but in the courts where abortion first gained traction as the primary feminist issue. In 1973, in *Roe v. Wade*, the Supreme Court held that a woman had the right to choose an abortion in the first trimester of a pregnancy.[21] Using historical information on the permissiveness of abortions prior to quickening, the Court relied upon the constitutional right to privacy, rather than the right to equality, as a basis for affirming women's reproductive rights. Thirty-four years later, in 2007, the Court restricted this right to abortion in its decision in *Gonzales v. Carhart*, upholding bans on late term or "partial-birth" abortions. In that decision the Court referenced an idea reminiscent of the nineteenth-century protectionist ideology that surrounded court decisions concerning women; only this time the state sought to protect women against themselves, citing the unintended emotional consequences of sadness and remorse which the Court believed abortion produced in women.[22]

Throughout this period the equality movement gained momentum in the courts and legislatures in ways that went beyond the issue of reproductive rights for women. One of the first successes was Title VII of the 1964 Civil Rights Act prohibiting race and sex discrimination in employment. The sex classification has sometimes been believed to have been added to the bill in an attempt to defeat its passage.[23] In theory it worked to expand the legislation to include key issues that specifically impinged upon women's lives. Enforcement of the new law, however, was weak. The Equal Employment Opportunity Commission (EEOC) focused its attention on the enforcement of race claims. It showed a lack of serious concern about sex discrimination in employment by deciding, in 1965, that sex segregation in job advertising through the use of male-only help-wanted ads was permissible. This outraged Betty Friedan and other women who, in 1966, responded by founding the National Organization of Women (NOW). NOW quickly organized to support women's equality by challenging the EEOC to take forceful actions against workplace sex discrimination under Title VII.

The employment cases were most successful when stereotypes of women's lack of equal ability to perform certain types of work were debunked. Equality theory, however, sometimes floundered in pregnancy cases where the courts confronted physical differences between men and women. Different treatment because of pregnancy, the Supreme Court held, was not discrimination "because of sex." [24] Congress reversed this result by passing the Pregnancy Discrimination Act of 1978. The act relied on an equality theory requiring employers to treat pregnant employees similarly to other temporarily disabled employees. The sameness/difference debate continued over the issue of parental leave. When California passed legislation granting pregnant employees, but not all parents, four months of unpaid leave and a guaranteed return to work, the Supreme Court upheld the legislation on grounds of women's difference and their need for special protection. The Family Medical Leave Act of 1993 rejected this theory by guaranteeing twelve weeks of (unpaid) medical and child-care leave equally to both men and women.

One of the leading figures for sex equality in the courts in the 1970s was Ruth Bader Ginsburg, who directed the Women's Rights Project at the American Civil Liberties Union while a professor at Columbia Law School. She later became the second woman to serve as a Justice of the U.S. Supreme Court. Ginsburg was the chief architect of the strategy that built the foundation for contemporary sex discrimination law. The strategy of the Women's Rights Project was designed to attack gender stereotypes across the board. As Ginsburg explained it, they set out to attack separate spheres assumptions built into the law. "The objective was to obtain thoughtful consideration of the assumptions underlying, and the purposes served by, sex-based classifications."[25] She attacked the fundamental premise of the law's differential treatment of men and women—typically rationalized as reflecting "natural" differences between the sexes—that had historically contributed to women's subordination and their confined "place" in a man's world.

In challenging sex-based classifications across the board, Ginsburg attacked laws on many different subjects including those like alimony or survivor benefits that appeared to favor women. She opposed laws barring women from working as bartenders or serving on juries, as well as those preventing men from receiving alimony. As historian Linda Kerber demonstrated in her work, *No Constitutional Right to be Ladies: Women and the Obligations of Citizenship* (1998), the law denied women equality not only where they sought equal benefits but also where they sought equal obligations such as jury service. The Supreme Court first recognized women's right to equal treatment under the Fourteenth Amendment in *Reed v. Reed* (1971), when it struck down a state law that created a preference for men to serve as administrators of estates. The Court refused to accept the gender stereotype that women were not capable of financial management. Using *Reed* as a baseline, Ginsburg then encouraged the Court to adopt a heightened level of scrutiny for reviewing distinctions on the basis of sex. In *Craig v. Boren* (1976) the Justices adopted a form of intensive review, though not as rigorous as that used for distinctions on the basis of race. Twenty years later, when Ginsburg herself was on the Court, she wrote an opinion for the majority in the case of *United States v. Virginia* (1996) that seemed to apply an even stricter standard of scrutiny in striking down Virginia Military Institute's male-only admission policy.

The essays in *Feminist Legal History* both build upon and challenge this basic history to expand our understanding of women and the law. The authors pick up where the classic story of women's legal history leaves off, adding new events, providing new details, and suggesting alternative explanations for the traditional historical narrative. The stories told here are detailed and contextualized. By patiently fleshing out the specifics of legal events, the essays avoid oversimplification and provide opportunities to challenge existing generalizations about women, their treatment under the law, and traditional narratives of legal history.

Contradictions in Legalizing Gender

Part I of *Feminist Legal History* focuses on the law's effect on women. It begins with an examination of the uneven ways in which the law has responded to women's assertions of social power and demands for control over their own lives. The chapters in this section display the complex ways in which law recognized women's rights and the contradictory responses to women's claims to autonomy and power. This ebb and flow of women's empowerment contrasts with the conventional understanding of incremental, but linear, progress toward the eradication of barriers to women's empowerment. The historical inquiries offered in this book disclose a more complex and variegated relationship between women, law, and society—marked not by steady progress but by a variety of contradictions, inconsistencies, and tensions.

The opening chapters of this section show women using the law to achieve agency and control of their circumstances. These chapters show that when it was assumed that women did not have access to the courts, women were in fact able to achieve limited power and recognition of their legal rights. This came at a time when it was procedurally difficult for women to access the courts because laws of coverture denied women standing to sue as a plaintiff, prohibited women on juries, and often denied women the opportunity to testify as witnesses. The research here suggests that early judicial recognition of women's autonomy was based upon an assertion of gender difference. Difference and women's need for special protection was a basis for awarding privileges and benefits. The chapters by Richard Chused and Margo Schlanger illustrate that women's perceived difference was the basis for granting legal rights or control over their circumstances. The view of women as different underlies Chused's essay on the women's temperance movement in Ohio in 1873. Women considered themselves morally distinctive when they sat in bars calling for an end to consumption of alcohol and expressed reluctance to enter the male-defined sphere of the courts. Chused's work shows, however, that when women were forced into the courts after injunctions were sought seeking the end of their demonstrations, they organized to use the forums to their advantage and achieved a measure of social change. Schlanger reveals how late-nineteenth-century cultural assumptions about the fragile and emotional nature of women enhanced their tort recoveries for personal injuries in transportation accidents. In contrast to much of the conventional wisdom holding that women were erased from the standards of tort law by being subsumed into the male category of "reasonable man," Schlanger's work shows that courts treated gender as an important factor in assessing appropriate standards of care. They took women's experiences and capabilities into account in a way that was frequently, though not uniformly, friendly to women and their needs.

While obtaining benefits in some areas, women were denied rights in others. While courts empowered women through grants of agency in tort cases as Schlanger discusses, they also denied women's claims to equal employment as lawyers in *Bradwell*. Leti Volpp's chapter shows the inconsistent application of gendered power when race was a dominant force. She explores the intersection of race and gender in marriage by narrating stories of the way immigration laws functioned through the first third of the twentieth century to exile women citizens from the United States upon their marriage to noncitizens. The history of dependent citizenship and marital exile shows how notions of incapacity were foundational to racial and gendered disenfranchisement from formal citizenship. Such notions of incapacity, reflected in laws of coverture and race-based exclusion, were deeply connected to "true womanhood" ideals which were assumed to be unattainable by Asian women. In exploring the historical practices of exclusion from the nation, Volpp offers some broader lessons about the gendered and racialized nature of American citizenship.

This inconsistent response to the needs of women continued through the second half of the twentieth century and into the present moment. Cases still arise in which gender serves as a legally significant basis upon which to deny women rights and autonomy. The remaining chapters of part I take up themes about difference as subordination by focusing on stories about the military and abortion. During the 1970s the staunch conservative advocate Phyllis Schlafly infused these two issues into the debate over constitutional sex equality during the battle to obtain ratification of the Equal Rights Amendment. Schlafly turned the debate over constitutionally guaranteed equality into emotionally charged arguments about abortion and mandated military service. Jill Hasday and Melissa Murray take up the issue of women and the military. Hasday explores how military service by women has been a lightning rod in the debate over gender equality. Women are still excluded from military registration, draft eligibility, and some combat positions. This record of women's legal status in the military, Hasday asserts, provides important counterevidence of the prevalent assumption of formal sex equality in the law. Yet she shows how many extrajudicial actors—such as Congress, the executive branch, the public, and the military itself—have changed their views to be more supportive of women's role in the military. Extrajudicial transformations have shifted the norms that shape the constitutional equal protection and rendered the Supreme Court's constitutional interpretations denying equality in the military less plausible over time.

One often overlooked consequence of women's exclusion from equal opportunity in the military is explored by Melissa Murray in her chapter on the GI Bill after World War II. The bill is often seen as one of the most successful laws of the modern age that offered returning World War II veterans an unprecedented array of educational and economic opportunities. Murray complicates this inherited narrative by showing the gendered impact of the bill. She argues that the bill was part of the New Deal's gendered legacy that was explicitly structured to facilitate the wage-earning capabilities of returning male veterans. This structure further entrenched the understanding of men as wage earners and women as their home-bound dependents. The resurrection of the GI Bill following the Iraqi War renews the concern over the gendered consequences of these laws.

Maya Manian takes the discussion about using difference theory to deny rights to women up to the present day by focusing attention on the Supreme Court's decision on abortion in *Gonzales v. Carhart* (2007). In *Carhart* the Court upheld restrictions on partial birth abortions citing women's emotional frailty and inability to appreciate the future emotional harm they might suffer as a result of abortion. Viewing women as in need of protection, the Court denied women access to medical procedures. The Court used perceptions about gender differences and the weakness of women to deviate from the usual rule supporting a patient's right to make informed health-care decisions. In these cases of abortion and the military, the Court resurrected coverture-like assumptions about women's inherent inferiority and need for protection without reference to the intervening cases affirming gender equality or the historical examples of difference as a basis for empowerment.

Taken together, the chapters in part I show the spotty legal pattern affirming women's agency sprinkled throughout the case law over two hundred years. Early women's history was not as constrained as the conventional narrative suggests. Glimmers of empowerment shine through in areas like marriage, tort, and temperance. Nor is the recent past as empowering as many suppose, given continued restraints on women's right to control key aspects of their personhood such as medical care and employment. In these cases we see the law operating as a barrier working to block women's access to social and legal rights.

Women's Transformation of the Law

Part II explores how feminists were sometimes able to remake existing legal norms and transform the law itself. The careful examinations of women's engagement with the law show how women used their own experience to transform gendered legal norms. At times they marshaled feminist theory to remake the law. Women's legal activism altered traditional legal concepts and reconceptualized basic notions of fairness and justice. This transformation shows that feminists understood law as more than just a fence to knock down. Law was not just a barrier to equality but also a tool that could be remade to incorporate the reality of gender.

This second section begins with an essay by Tracy Thomas on Elizabeth Cady Stanton and her use of the law to develop the notion of a legal class of gender. The notion of an identifiable social group of *women* was a categorization that became crucial to the establishment of modern notions of equality jurisprudence under the law. Stanton used the law of coverture and domestic relations to illustrate the commonalities among women because of sex despite their different classes, races, and religions. The establishment of a concept of group identity provided a baseline for Stanton's subsequent work on legal reform and forged a critical component of modern sex discrimination law.

Essays that follow, by Gwen Jordan, Felice Batlan, and Mae Quinn, reveal how women changed the legal process itself in order to accommodate their visions of legal norms. Women at the turn of the twentieth century expanded legal advocacy into work for social causes using lawyers to represent the concerns of communities and advocate for social change. This new type of lawyering based upon women's experiences in the community expanded the types of problems redressed by the courts beyond the private law economic concerns of contract and property. Gwen Jordan traces the development of legal aid in Chicago. She focuses on the efforts of the Protective Agency for Women and Children, founded in 1886 to assist working women with their legal harms. She shows how the daily practice of the agency radicalized the activists and quickly transformed their core mission into an effort to force the legal system to recognize and redress the gendered harms suffered by women and girls. These efforts to use the law to secure justice for the gendered crimes against women endured constant and often overwhelming opposition.

Felice Batlan adds a new and important gloss to the history of legal aid bureaus. She challenges the existing narrative of male-dominated societies by making the radical claim that the concept of organized free legal aid for the poor grew out of women's work. Batlan shows how the sphere of legal aid was deeply feminized from the 1860s through 1910 in organizations in New York City, Chicago, and Philadelphia. The claims of women clients against employers and husbands dominated the legal aid work handled primarily by elite and middle-class women. Like Jordan, Batlan concludes that the women's strategic activities were broadly embraced and established a paradigm for cause lawyering and the proliferation of legal aid societies in the twentieth century.

The need to alter the legal process to match social realities also was seen in the courts as Mae Quinn explores in her essay on Judge Anna Moscowitz Kross and the auxiliary caseworkers she helped to train and organize.

Quinn examines how Kross sought to rethink the role and goals of criminal courts expanding their boundaries to permit community involvement in their operations in part through the use of female volunteer caseworkers and probation officers. She suggests that today's criminal justice reformers might take notice of Kross's judicial innovations that relied on private funding and citizen involvement in criminal court operations while also noting the potential dangers of such an approach.

The remaining essays in part II show how women continued this transformative effect to change the law itself. The essays by Lynda Dodd, Carrie Baker, and Eileen Boris document three instances in which women altered the terms and abstract rights embodied in the law. Women advocates reconceptualized the actionable harms to include injuries more common to women. Guided by feminist understandings of women's experience, advocates worked to alter the very terms of the law itself to force it to include the gendered realities of women.

Dodd details the petitioning efforts of Alice Paul and the National Woman's Party in early-twentieth-century efforts to pass the Nineteenth Amendment guaranteeing women the right to vote. Dodd explores how Paul's passionate political leadership style utilized more aggressive demonstrations and media measures outside standard judicial and legislative avenues in order to more effectively achieve legal reform. These efforts were the crucial steps that pushed a fifty-year-old idea to completion and enshrined a concept of gender equality in the U.S. Constitution. Baker's essay on the establishment of sexual harassment as an actionable claim also portrays the external and internal processes required to achieve legal change. Baker details the diverse group of plaintiffs, political groups, lawyers, and law professors who helped codify a common employment experience of women into a new cause of action. Creating law where previously there was none, women infused feminist theory and practical gendered experience into legal action. Boris's essay takes the recognition of women's transformative power of the law up to the present day. She details the evolution of women's equal pay claims and the Supreme Court's use of procedure to limit their impact. The transformation came with the first legislative act of Barack Obama's presidency when he signed into law the Fair Pay Act giving women sufficient time to bring pay discrimination claims. However, Boris illustrates the limitations of this change which fails to take account of class and race issues intertwined with equal pay that impact home-care workers and other women in traditionally female jobs.

Together, the chapters in part II demonstrate the ways in which women have changed the law. Their efforts to "feminize" the law were important to incorporating gendered experiences into the legal norms. Women, often acting intentionally and relying upon feminist theorizing of women's experience under the law, worked to transform the law to make it more responsive to their realities.

Feminist Legal Thought

An appreciation for feminist legal theorizing is vital to the historical analyses featured in this collection of essays. The authors in this book adopt a feminist lens through which to interpret and analyze past events. They are particularly attuned to the ways in which women have been denied power, equality, and self-determination. Before delving into the historical details contained in the following chapters, it is important to get a sense of the feminist legal theory driving these writings and the women advocates of the past.

There is significant disagreement among feminists as to what "feminism" is or what it should be. The term "feminist" itself first appeared in common parlance in the United States around 1913 and was used to describe an emerging women's social movement expanding beyond the contours of the suffrage issue.[26] The precepts of feminism, however, existed well before this time as evidenced by the philosophies and approaches of the earlier "woman's movement." Modern definitions include dry explanations of feminism as a "theory of political, economic, and social equality of the sexes," as well as more activist and transformative definitions of feminism as "sharing an impulse to increase the power, equality, and autonomy of women in their families, communities, and/or society."[27] At its core, feminism is based upon a concern for women combined with an opposition to their subordinate status in society.

Feminist legal theory, as an intellectual movement, emerged in law schools in the 1970s at a time when women began entering the academy in significant numbers. Feminist theorists share a core belief in the subjugation of women and the need for change. Feminist legal theory is premised upon the belief that the law has been instrumental in women's subordination in society. Feminist legal scholars start with the assumption that the law's treatment of women has not been fair or equal, and they are suspicious of legal standards. Feminist jurisprudence seeks first to explain the ways in which the law has played a role in creating discrimination against women. The inquiry describes the nature and extent of discrimination and then asks how and why women continue to occupy a subordinate position. Feminist theory then moves pragmatically to seek effective strategies to change women's status by reconceptualizing the law. Within this broader umbrella of feminist legal theorizing, legal scholars have commonly identified four distinct schools of thought: liberal, difference, dominance, and postmodern.[28] Each of these types of feminist thinking differs in its identification of the legal mechanism that causes women's subordination and in the type of legal change needed to eradicate gender discrimination.

Liberal or equality feminist thinking tends to emphasize the sameness of women to men. Equality theory is based on the premise that there are no legally relevant differences between men and women. Equality theory views the individual woman as a rational, responsible agent, who is able to control and maintain equality through her own actions and choices, if permitted. Liberal legal theorists are thus committed to allowing individuals to be free to choose their own style of life in the economic, political, and personal spheres. Liberal feminism seeks the removal of barriers and laws that treat women differently than men and demands equal access to public and private rights. Drawing from Aristotle's theory of justice, equality is defined as the equal treatment of women who are similarly situated to men. Liberal equality theory has dominated the law, both in advocacy and reasoned support of judicial decisions, by providing a seemingly objective and easy equation by which courts evaluate claims of gender inequality. For example, the Supreme Court's test for assessing equal protection violations under the Fourteenth Amendment is whether women are "similarly situated" to men. This theory of liberal feminism was advanced by nineteenth-century suffrage advocates such as Elizabeth Cady Stanton and Susan B. Anthony who sought the removal of legal barriers that denied women the right to vote based on the natural equality of men and women. Many second-wave feminists of the 1970s echoed these liberal equality theories in their renewed demand for an Equal Rights Amendment, which would have enshrined in the U.S. Constitution the guarantee against denial or abridgment of rights on account of sex.

In contrast to liberal feminism's focus on gender similarities, difference feminism tends to highlight the fundamental cultural—and sometimes biological—differences between women's and men's experiences of their bodies and their relations with others. Difference feminism underscores the limitations of equality analysis and its inability to "to take into account real sex differences between women and men, to recognize that gender is a social construct, to acknowledge differences among women, particularly with regard to race, and to take into account the gendered dimensions of legal and social institutions."[29] Legally relevant differences include those that are biological, such as pregnancy, or those that are socially constructed, such as primary child-care responsibilities. Difference feminism argues for legal accommodation of the realities of women's gendered lives in a way that does not reinforce women's unequal and inferior status.[30] Feminists operating under these precepts might seek special legal treatment for women's differences or they might critique facially neutral laws that affect women and men disparately. Difference theorists tend to recommend laws that ease the burdens which gendered expectations place on people, usually to the detriment of women. They also criticize the legal culture's failure to adequately recognize or compensate women's gender-specific injuries, such as domestic violence, sexual harassment, or date rape.[31]

Cultural feminism, sometimes affiliated with difference feminism, elevates the identifiable gender differences of relation and maternity to a level of celebration. Feminists who lean in this direction often focus on how "women's 'different voice'—with its concern for human relationships and for the positive values of caring, nurturing, empathy, and connection—could find greater expression in the law."[32] Modern cultural feminist theory, as articulated in the mid-1980s, based its belief in women's relational nature on findings found in scholarly texts such as Carol Gilligan's *In a Different Voice* (1982). Gilligan draws on her psychological research of stages of moral development experienced by boys and girls to argue against the notion that women should be encouraged to act and think more like men. She opposed undervaluing girls' relational approach to resolving moral dilemmas utilizing an ethic of care as compared to boys' approach to resolving dilemmas based on the abstract logic of rules. Cultural feminists see in Gilligan's work support for their elevation and idealization of women's culture. Cultural feminism refuses to concede to male standards of behavior and values by seeking out and valuing women's own voices and experiences. To promote and enhance women's cultural difference from men, they often celebrate women's maternal role and other traditional activities associated with women. Cultural feminism's celebration of women's separate culture and values has been well integrated into American popular culture and taken up by many contemporary women as a way to resolve essential dilemmas in their personal lives in ways that liberal feminism often seems to evade rather than resolve. Most scholars, as well as non-scholarly activists, appear to combine aspects of both cultural and liberal feminism into their general outlook on women. But clashes between the two somewhat opposing ideas have led to complex legal scenarios.

The tension surrounding the sameness/difference debate is illustrated in the classic case of *Equal Employment Opportunity Commission v. Sears*.[33] In *Sears*, the government challenged the absence of women in high-paying commission sales jobs at the Sears chain of stores. Sears argued that female employees lacked interest in these commission sales, because they involved products they did not like, required working on weekends, and involved aggressive sales tactics. The Court accepted expert evidence that women were differently situated with respect to job preferences and thus could be treated unequally by the commission and promotion policies of Sears. The company's expert, feminist historian Rosalind Rosenberg, testified that women dislike high-pressure sales, prefer working regular hours during the day when children are in school, and seek personal identification through relationships rather than employment.[34] The judge rejected contrary evidence offered by the plaintiff's expert, another feminist historian, Alice Kessler-Harris. She opined that, when given the opportunity, women, like the symbolic "Rosie the Riveter" of World War II, embraced high-volume, hard work requiring assertive behavior.[35] Feminists watched with dismay as two seemingly "pro-woman" perspectives pitted feminist historians and legal practitioners against each other.

While liberal and difference feminism dueled in the *Sears* case, legal feminist scholars from the dominance school of thought opted out of this conundrum altogether by relocating the problem away from women or the law's treatment of them and toward challenges to basic notions of power as historically enshrined in the law itself. Dominance theorists view the legal system as a mechanism for perpetuating male dominance. This systemic dominance denies women their agency and autonomy, and deprives them of their ability to actively control their own lives and circumstances. Dominance theory depicts women as victims of patriarchal oppression and therefore in need of systemic change in legal norms. The most notable proponent of the dominance theory for the last twenty-five years has been law professor Catharine MacKinnon. Sexuality is central to MacKinnon's dominance account.[36] She argues that women's sexuality is socially constructed by male dominance and women's subordination results primarily from men's sexual dominance over women. Dominance theorists recommend retreating from scrutiny of individual laws and social constraints, and moving toward reform of the entirety of the law and its use as a mechanism for women's dominance and subordination. MacKinnon applied her theory to advocate legal change in areas highlighted by sexual dominance—rape, sexual harassment, and pornography. MacKinnon's work with Andrea Dworkin on anti-pornography laws attacked one of the causes of male dominance—men's social construction of women's sexuality.[37] They initially met with some success at the local government level, helping to enact anti-pornography ordinances in Indianapolis and Minneapolis, but the laws were subsequently overturned by the courts as unconstitutional restraints on protected free speech.[38]

A crucial insight that dominance theorists contributed to feminist considerations of the law is the law's lack of objectivity and inherent maleness. Feminists identified legal norms as "male," by definition, infused with male bias and historically created by and for men. As MacKinnon asserted in her 1984 essay, *Difference and Dominance: On Sex Discrimination*, the law uses men as the measure of all legal rights.

> Under the sameness standard, women are measured according to our correspondence with man, our equality judged by our proximity to his measure. Under the difference standard, we are measured according to our lack of correspondence with him, our womanhood judged by our distance from his measure. Gender neutrality is thus simply the male standard, and the special protection rule is simply the female standard, but do not be deceived: masculinity, or maleness, is the referent for both.

The intellectual roots of dominance theory came principally from discourses outside the law, including the fields of women's studies, women's history, social history, and feminist scholarship in sociology, anthropology, psychology, and literary criticism. Another major influence was the Critical Legal Theory movement of the 1980s. Theorists associated with this school expanded upon the radical critique of the indeterminacy of the law. They demonstrated that the ability of the law to vary based on the distinguishing facts of each case called into question the objective abstraction of the rule of law. And they revealed the extent to which social and political bias and context rather than rules are the determinative factors in judicial decision making. Given these inherent problems with the law itself, some feminist critical legal scholars began to view legal reform itself as futile. They opted out of efforts to use the law as an avenue of feminist change, and focused instead on social and political action. Other feminist law practitioners, activists, and scholars continued in their efforts to change the law, armed with a greater understanding of the extent of the hurdles in their path as a consequence of the work produced by critical legal theorists.

Alongside and fueling the rise of critical legal studies, postmodern feminist theory emerged in the mid-1980s as a vibrant new academic school of thought that would prove influential to many disciplines key to the study of women and gender—though its reception among feminist legal scholars has been uneven. Like dominance theorists, postmodern legal feminists radically challenge the idea of an objective rule of law by revealing its underlying political functions. But unlike dominance theory, whose focus remains on the experiences of women set in opposition to men as a class of oppressors, postmodern theory questions the very classifications of "women" and "men." Postmodernists tend to question not only gender norms that aim to dictate women's role in society but the foundational idea that gender is a natural expression of an authentically and inherently sexed body. Rejecting a focus on women's experiences per se, these theorists aim to analyze and call attention to a seemingly infinite spectrum of ways of performing and embodying gender. For Judith Butler, a key theorist in this field, there is no essential truth to women's experience or to gender as a social reality. Rather there are many complicated, inter-related, and internally contradictory performances of gender emerging from political power struggles that are ongoing and unavoidable. Following Michel Foucault, many postmodern feminists view power as rooted in *discourse* (politicized systems of meaning which include the law). According to this notion of power, the gendered self is neither an agent nor a victim of power but a product of a field of gendered power relations which are, at times, expressed and produced juridically. Postmodern feminist theorists attempt to intervene strategically in the field of power by exploiting and exposing the inevitable contradictions in gendered (as in all) discourse.[39]

Significant opposition to postmodern feminist theory has emerged from all quarters of social science but particularly as it applies in law. The concern is that a disbelief in foundational truths about women, gender relations, and the nature of justice undermines the stark realities of advocacy to end the discrimination and subordination that women experience. Many feminists working within and outside the academy to achieve political and legal justice for women feel strongly that, in the absence of an acceptance of women as more than merely an illusory product of discourse, political change to improve women's status, particularly legal change, becomes more difficult to conceptualize and work toward.[40]

Despite these pragmatic concerns about postmodern feminist legal theorizing of gender, the anti-essentialist critique that lies at the heart of this theory has been taken up by many different kinds of feminist scholars with profound implications for feminist theorizing of the law. Honed most effectively within the body of work produced by womanists, feminists of color, and queer theorists publishing in the 1980s and 1990s—and bracketing some of the more abstract postmodern concerns regarding gender as an effect of power—anti-essentialist feminist theorizing of women's experience dismisses the claims of any one set of theories to explain or describe patriarchal oppression as much as it objects to the tendencies of liberal theories to reduce all women to one image of womanhood. Anti-essentialist feminist writings have mounted powerful challenges to an assumption embedded in much of liberal feminist theorizing that there is one universal or essential woman's voice and reject theories that reduce all women to one uniform group. These scholars, such as Kimberlé Crenshaw, Angela Harris, and Patricia Cain, criticized the work of previous feminist scholars and activists for basing their conclusions on the experiences of white, middle-class, heterosexual women. Their premise is that the lived experiences of women differ depending upon such factors as race, class, ethnicity, and sexual orientation—none of which can be separated out from women's experience of gender. Given this complexity, they reject the goal of devising one overarching feminist strategy and instead recommend considering legal policies from the perspective of multiple groups of women with multiple allegiances and identities. Like postmodern theorists more generally, and lending complexity to feminist legal analysis, anti-essentialist theorizing of women's experience rejects the idea that gender issues as expressed by and experienced in the law can or should be considered in isolation from other axes of identity within which all women actually experience discrimination and oppression.

This summary of feminist legal thought attempts to outline the major trends in feminist theorizing that currently thrive and hold particular salience for present-day scholarship on women and the law. But it does not account for the specificity of historical social movements within feminist activism. The "second-wave" alone boasted myriad forms of feminist organizing including Marxist-feminist (having a great deal of influence on the rising ranks of academic feminists and social historians of women in particular) and radical feminist (the Redstockings, for instance, bringing a new emphasis on consciousness-raising among women and attention to women's personal experiences under patriarchy as a political condition) who were active and vocal during the 1970s. Nor does it detail the intense conversations among womanists, feminists of color, third-world feminists, lesbian feminists, and queer feminists whose scholarship and activism came to the fore in the 1980s.

Even within the more dominant current strains of feminist theorizing, much contention and confusion exists between these various forms of feminist thinking about the law and about women's historical status. Yet this book maintains that although the debates among feminist legal theorists, women's historians, and legal historians are grounded in sharp differences over how to conceptualize power, gender identity, and women's experience under the law, there is a core methodology that feminists employ to analyze social and legal problems. "Thinking like a feminist" means thinking in a gender-conscious way.[41] It is relevant to the analysis whether the actors are male or female. Feminist legal theory "proceeds from the assumption that gender is important in our everyday lives and recognizes that being a man or a woman is a central feature of our lives." [42] To paraphrase a feminist adage popular since the 1970s, "the personal is *still* political." Feminists validate women's individual personal experiences as important political and legal issues, and this context is critical to their legal reasoning. The storytelling of personal narratives allows for the consciousness raising by which individuals derive collective significance or meaning from their experiences. Feminists working in the field of law commonly use the legal method of *deconstruction* to take apart the law as it appears on its face to look beyond the seeming objective legal rules in order to consider the deeper structures and values underlying those rules. Through deconstruction, feminists can reveal gendered assumptions and biases that contribute to the formulation of the rules of law. Feminists see that the underlying assumptions are infused with male bias. They work to "unmask the patriarchy." Laws have historically been made by and for men. The law has been, and in many cases continues to be, based upon male norms, with legal rights defined in male terms. Feminists see how male privilege and assumptions that fed the development of the law have been reinforced by the patriarchal structure of religion and society. A basic agreement on these underlying precepts permits us to engage one another in the analysis of women's real-life and historic experiences with the law. Rather than bemoaning the differences between us, these differences can been seen as providing a productive and creative space for expansive thinking about the law and women.

The full spectrum of feminist legal theory is evident within the chapters of this book. The authors and the women in their stories adopt differing strands of feminist legal theory to advance their claims. As Elizabeth Cady Stanton remarked in 1869: "It matters not whether women and men are like or unlike, woman has the same right as man has to choose her own place." She explained: "We started on [the equality] ground twenty years ago, because we thought, from that standpoint, we could draw the strongest arguments for woman's enfranchisement. And there we stood, firmly entrenched until we saw that stronger arguments could be drawn from a difference in sex, in mind as well as body."[43] As Stanton's frank admission reveals, a strong strain of pragmatism has long run through feminist legal advocacy as has an awareness of the need to utilize a wide range of feminist theories in order to persuade a policymaker or court of the merits of a claim. If there is any common link uniting the contributors and editors of this volume, it is a commitment to what might be called "pragmatic feminism." Pragmatic feminism claims that "rather than looking to one approach to solve all problems in all circumstances, we should regard the variety of approaches available today as a set of tools to be used when appropriate."[44] It may also be true that feminist legal theory is more holistic and integrated than the compartmentalization of thought suggests. The essays in this book support such a conclusion that feminism is more nuanced and complex than any one theory, and that each theory advances part of the larger reform of women's rights.

The essays collected in *Feminist Legal History* explore the interaction between women and the law, and offer a kind of applied legal history of feminist legal studies. Like other feminist legal theory projects the works contained here are concerned with the personal, private experiences of women, and are "born of the world, responding to real lives and needs, reflecting the law and society tradition of reasoning from the world to law."[45] This kind of applied legal scholarship seeks to make history directly relevant to modern legal discourse. "In essence, what we need is a useable past," as Alfred Brophy has suggested, calling for "a history of law—of court decisions, statutes, and the practices of law enforcement—that is both accurate and relevant to understanding questions we have today, giving rise to optimism that once people have facts they will think the same."[46] *Feminist Legal History* attempts to provide this type of useable past with the hope it will impact future changes in the law that are responsive to the lived realities of women.

NOTES

1. Felice Batlan, *Engendering Legal History*, 30 Law & Soc. Inq. 823 (2005).
2. Linda K. Kerber & Jane Sherron De Hart, Gender and the New Women's History, Women's America: Refocusing the Past 2–3 (6th ed. 2004) (adopting framework of Gerda Lerner, The Majority Finds Its Past: Placing Women in History 145–59 (1979)).
3. *See* Joan Hoff, Law, Gender & Injustice: A Legal History of U.S. Women (2d ed. 1994); Kermit Hall, Paul Finkelman, and James W. Ely Jr., eds., American Legal History (3d ed. 2005); Kerber & De Hart, *supra; see also* Mary Becker, Cynthia Grant Bowman, Morrison Torrey, eds., Feminist Jurisprudence: Taking Women Seriously 1–51 (2d ed. 2001).
4. William Blackstone, Commentaries, bk. 1, chap. 15, Of Husband and Wife (1765).
5. Nancy Cott, The Bonds of Womanhood (1982); Linda K. Kerber, Women of the Republic: Intellect and Ideology in Revolutionary America (1980); Barbara Welter, *The Cult of True Womanhood: 1820–1860*, 18 Am. Q. 151 (1966).
6. The work on coverture and the MWPAs provided some of the first work in the field of women's legal history. *See* Elizabeth B. Warbasse, The Changing Legal Rights of Mar-

ried Women, 1800–1861 (1987); Norma Basch, In the Eyes of the Law: Women, Marriage, and Property in Nineteenth-Century New York (1982); Reva Siegel, *The Modernization of Marital Status Law: Adjudicating Wives' Rights to Earnings, 1860–1930*, 82 Geo. L.J. 2127 (1995); Reva Siegel, *Home as Work: The First Woman's Rights Claims Concerning Wives' Household Labor, 1850–1880*, 103 Yale L.J. 1073 (1994); Richard Chused, *Married Women's Property Law, 1800–1850*, 71 Geo. L.J. 1359 (1983); Peggy A. Rabkin, *The Origins of Law Reform: The Social Significance of the Nineteenth-Century Codification Movement and Its Contribution to the Passage of the Early Married Women's Property Acts*, 24 Buff. L. Rev. 683 (1975).

7. 88 U.S. 162 (1874).

8. Rosalyn Terborg-Penn, African American Women in the Struggle for the Vote, 1850–1920 (1998); Marjorie Spruill Wheeler, New Women of the New South: The Leaders of the Woman Suffrage Movement in the Southern States (1993); Aileen Kraditor, The Ideas of the Woman Suffrage Movement, 1890–1920 (1981).

9. Ellen Carol DuBois, Feminism & Suffrage: The Emergence of an Independent Women's Movement in America, 1848–1869 (1978); Eleanor Flexner & Ellen Fitzpatrick, Century of Struggle: The Woman's Rights Movement in the United States (1959); Tracy A. Thomas, *Women's Suffrage*, 5 Encyclopedia of the Supreme Court of the United States 251 (David S. Tanehaus, ed. 2008).

10. *See* Virginia G. Drachman, Sisters in Law: Women Lawyers in Modern American History 37, 45 (1998); Gwen Hoerr Jordan, *Agents of (Incremental) Change: From Myra Bradwell to Hillary Clinton*, 9 Nev. L.J. 580 (2009); Women's Legal History Biography Project, http://www.law.stanford.edu/library/womenslegalhistory/profiles.html (last accessed Jan. 8, 2010).

11. 83 U.S. (16 Wall.) 130 (1873).

12. Jill Norgren, Belva Lockwood: The Woman Who Would Be President (2007); *Ex parte* Lockwood, 154 U.S. 116 (1984); Jordan, 619–20.

13. Nancy Woloch, Muller v. Oregon: A Brief History with Documents (1996); Felice Batlan, *Notes from the Margins: Florence Kelley and the Making of Sociological Jurisprudence*, in Transformation of American Legal History, Vol. 2 (Daniel W. Hamilton and Alfred L. Brophy eds., 2010).

14. 208 U.S. 412 (1908).

15. The Brandeis Brief in full is available at the University of Louisville Law Library, http://www.law.louisville.edu/library/collections/brandeis/node/235; see also Justice Ruth Bader Ginsburg, *Muller v. Oregon: One Hundred Years Later*, 45 Willamette L. Rev. 359 (2009).

16. 243 U.S. 426 (1917).

17. 261 U.S. 525 (1923).

18. 300 U.S. 379 (1931).

19. Linda Gordon, The Moral Property of Women: A History of Birth Control Politics in America 55–71 (2002); Leslie Reagan, When Abortion Was a Crime: Women, Medicine, and Law in the United States, 1967–1973 (1997); Reva Siegel, *Reasoning from the Body: A Historical Perspective on Abortion Regulation and Questions of Equal Protection*, 44 Stan. L. Rev. 261, 308–14 (1992).

20. 381 U.S. 479 (1965); *see* People v. Sanger, 118 N.E. 637 (N.Y. 1918); William N. Eskridge Jr., *Some Effects of Identity-Based Social Movements on Constitutional Law in the Twentieth Century*, 100 Mich. L. Rev. 2062, 2122 (2002); Ellen Chesler, Woman of Valor: Margaret Sanger and the Birth Control Movement in America 88, 231 (1992).

21. 410 U.S. 113 (1973).

22. 550 U.S. 124, 127 S. Ct. 1610 (2007).

23. The "sex" amendment was introduced, to laughter, by Howard Smith, a conservative Virginia representative who was a known opponent of the civil rights legislation and was thought, by many accounts, to be a means of obstructing the bill's passage. Smith, however, was a staunch supporter of the Equal Rights Amendment. *See* Cynthia Harrison, On Account of Sex: The Politics of Women's Issues, 1945–1968 (1988); Cindy Deitch, *Gender, Race, and Class Politics and the Inclusion of Women in Title VII of the 1964 Civil Rights Act*, 7 Gender & Society 183 (1993); Jo Freeman, How *"Sex" Got into Title VII: Persistent Opportunism as a Maker of Public Policy*, 9 Law & Inequality 163 (1991).

24. General Electric Co. v. Gilbert, 429 U.S. 125 (1976) (Title VII); Gedulig v. Aiello, 417 U.S. 484 (1974) (14th Amendment).

25. Justice Ruth Bader Ginsburg and Barbara Flagg, *Some Reflections on the Feminist Legal Thought of the 1970s*, 1989 U. Chi. Legal. F. 16.

26. Nancy Cott, The Grounding of Modern Feminism 3, 13–14 (1987). For a thorough discussion of the emergence in popular parlance of the term "feminist" in 1913, as well as the implications of the retroactive use of this term to describe nineteenth-century suffragists and other activists, in the United States as well as Europe, see Karen Offen, *Defining Feminism: A Comparative Historical Approach*, 14 Signs: Journal of Women in Culture and Society 119–57 (1988), and the dialogue that ensued between Offen and other scholars on this topic in multiple essays included in 15 Signs: Journal of Women in Culture and Society 1 (fall 1989).

27. Merriam-Webster Dictionary; Linda Gordon, The Moral Property of Women: A History of Birth Control Politics in America 367 (2002).

28. Martha Chamallas, Introduction to Feminist Legal Theory 12 (2d ed. 2006); Nancy Levit & Robert R. M. Verchick, Feminist Legal Theory: A Primer 36–39 (2006); Deborah Rhode, *Feminist Critical Theories*, 42 Stan. L. Rev. 617 (1990); Patricia A. Cain, *Feminist Jurisprudence: Grounding the Theories*, 4 Berkeley Women's L.J. 191 (1989–90).

29. Karen J. Maschke, ed., Feminist Legal Theories ix (1997).

30. Martha Fineman, *Feminist Theory in Law: The Difference it Makes*, 2 Columbia J. of Gender & Law 171 (1992); Martha Fineman, *Challenging Law, Establishing Differences: The Future of Feminist Legal Scholarship*, 42 Fla. L. Rev. 25 (1990); *see* Maschke, ix–x.

31. Robin L. West, *The Difference in Women's Hedonic Lives: A Phenomenological Critique of Feminist Legal Theory*, 3 Wis. Women's L.J. 81 (1987).

32. Chammallas, 27.

33. 629 F. Supp. 1277 (N.D. Ill. 1986), aff'd, 839 F.2d 302 (7th Cir. 1988).

34. Offer of Proof Concerning the Testimony of Dr. Rosalind Rosenberg, reprinted in *Women's History Goes to Trial: EEOC v. Sears, Roebuck and Company*, 11 Signs 757 (1986).

35. Written Testimony of Alice Kessler-Harris, reprinted in *Women's History Goes to Trial: EEOC v. Sears, Roebuck and Company*, 11 Signs 767 (1986); Alice Kessler-Harris, *Equal Employment Opportunity Commission v. Sears, Roebuck and Company: A Personal Account*, in Unequal Sisters: A Multi-Cultural Reader in U.S. Women's History 545 (Vicki L. Ruiz & Ellen Carol DuBois, eds.) (2d ed. 1994).

36. Catharine A. MacKinnon, Toward a Feminist Theory of the State (1989).

37. Catharine A. MacKinnon, Only Words (1993); In Harm's Way: The Pornography Civil Rights Hearings (Catharine MacKinnon & Andrea Dworkin, eds., 1997); Andrea

Dworkin & Catharine MacKinnon, Pornography and Civil Rights: A New Day for Women's Equality (1988).

38. American Booksellers Assn. v. Hudnut, 771 F.2d 323 (7th Cir. 1985), aff'd, 475 U.S. 1001 (1986).

39. Judith Butler, Gender Trouble: Feminism and the Subversion of Identity (1999); Jana Sawicki, Disciplining Foucault: Feminism, Power, and the Body (1991); Lois McNay, Foucault and Feminism: Power, Gender, and the Self (1992); Feminism and Foucault: Reflections on Resistance (Irene Diamond & Lee Quimby, eds. 1988).

40. Levit & Verchick, 36–39; Chammallas, 92–96; Gary Minda, Postmodern Legal Movements: Law and Jurisprudence at Century's End 141–48 (1995).

41. Levit & Verchick, 45–53; Chamallas, 12.

42. Chamallas, xix.

43. Elizabeth Cady Stanton, *Miss Becker on the Difference in Sex*, Revolution, Sept. 24, 1868.

44. Minda, 146 (quoting law professor Mary Becker).

45. Martha Albertson Fineman, *Gender and Law: Feminist Legal Theory's Role in New Legal Realism*, 2005 Wis. L. Rev. 405.

46. Alfred L. Brophy, *Considering Reparations for Dred Scott*, in The Dred Scott Case: Historical and Contemporary Perspectives on Race and Law 177–90 (David Konig, Christopher Bracey, & Paul Finkelman) (Ohio State University Press 2010).

Part I

Contradictions in Legalizing Gender

1

Courts and Temperance "Ladies"

—— RICHARD H. CHUSED ——————————

In 1873 and 1874 parts of southern Ohio were gripped by a remark-able string of marches, religious gatherings, and sit-ins by conservative, Christian, white women intent on shutting down the distribution of alco-hol in their communities. The immediate catalyst for the movement was a speech given by Dr. Diocletian Lewis, a believer in God, gymnastics, and temperance. He frequently gave orations urging women to pray at bars for the deliverance of intemperate souls, but he usually was politely received and ignored. On a few occasions his plan to use prayer to obstruct liquor traffic led to small and short-lived demonstrations. But his speech on "The Duty of Christian Women in the Cause of Temperance," delivered on December 23, 1873, before a group of women in Hillsboro, Ohio, led to an outpouring of temperance fervor. The resulting "Crusade" spread like wildfire across the country's midsection, choking off the flow of alcohol in more than 250 com-munities.[1] After the demonstrations ebbed and a sense of normalcy returned to the liquor trade, women active in the movement established the Wom-an's Christian Temperance Union—a group that became the largest suffrage organization in the country by the 1890s.[2]

Though these events have been well described by historians,[3] a fascinating series of issues relating to the use of legal institutions to control the demon-strative women arose during the Temperance Crusade in Ohio. Many women in Hillsboro opposed using available legal avenues to suppress the liquor trade, preferring strategies based on moral suasion. But, as with other major controversies in our history, aspects of the Temperance Crusade ended up in court despite the desires of many to avoid such forums. When liquor trade supporters sought injunctions against the sit-ins and marches, murmurs of discontent could be heard on the town's streets. But once the court hearings began, Crusaders worked together to protect their interests. They regularly occupied large segments of courtroom public-seating areas and participated in some aspects of the legal proceedings. Their entrance into the traditionally male judicial domain had a profound influence on the progress of the movement and the camaraderie of the women. Historians have noted that the Crusade had a transformative impact on some of the women participants.[4] It convinced them that public actions could alter social patterns and reconstruct cultural norms. A major part of that influence was first felt in the small town courts of Southern Ohio.[5]

Setting the Stage

The Temperance Crusade explosion did not appear without warning. Organized opposition to the consumption of alcohol was part of the American political landscape since shortly after the founding of the republic. Beginning with the creation of the first temperance organizations in Massachusetts during the 1820s, hundreds of thousands of Americans became involved in actions to reduce or eliminate the consumption of alcoholic beverages. Before the 1850s the vast bulk of activity involved moral and religious suasion. But the gradual breakdown of tight-knit, small-town life in developing towns and cities, the movement of men to the frontier, the economic and social dislocations caused by the Panic of 1837 and later monetary crises, and the arrival of large numbers of immigrants ruptured many of the links between social or religious disapproval and civic behavior. Groups seeking total prohibition of alcohol emerged by the mid-century. During the 1850s women pouring alcohol from smashed containers in bars became a fairly common activity. But the intensity and breadth of the Temperance Crusade in Southern Ohio, the spread of the movement to many other parts of the country, and the active public role played by large numbers of conservative women differed from any prior events.

The women who took to the streets of Hillsboro, Ohio, were not the sorts typically involved in organized, public, political movements with mass participation. They came, according to Charles Isetts, from the upper crust of town society—mostly women from white, wealthy, religious families of long standing in the community.[6] He discovered that families with members in the Crusade owned the bulk of Hillsboro's wealth, were virtually all white and native-born, and had male household heads with white-collar jobs or successful skilled craftsman positions. Only 5 percent of the Crusaders were immigrants. Perhaps the class and ethnic differences between the Crusaders and those they sought to stop fueled the stunning intensity and fervor of the Crusade. J. H. Beadle, the most frequent commentator in the *Cincinnati Commercial* on the demonstrations, certainly thought so. Several months into the movement he wrote that it was pitting Catholic against Protestant and native-born against German, as well as one political faction against another.[7] The Crusade was a culture clash.

The leader of Ohio's early temperance movement, Samuel Cary, was among the first to popularize prohibition. In 1847 he published a pamphlet, *Cary's Appeal to the People of Ohio*, staking out the then growing belief that "moral appliance alone cannot arrest the traffic" in alcohol.[8] In part because of Cary's influence in the state, Ohio's 1852 Constitution barred the granting of licenses to sell alcoholic beverages by localities, making it the responsibility of the General Assembly to "provide against the evils resulting" from the sale of liquor. The burgeoning Prohibition movement in the state, like those in many other areas of the country, was given an added boost by the adoption of the nation's first prohibition law in Maine in 1851.[9] Large petition drives surfaced in Ohio as part of a campaign to have Prohibition written into the new state constitution then being drafted. When that effort failed, campaigns to elect legislators willing to follow Maine's example emerged.

Growth of the Prohibition movement was particularly important for women. They participated in circumscribed ways in church- or social service–based temperance activity through the mid-nineteenth century. But their inability to vote and the social stigma attached to their participation in political agitation led to a reduction in their role in the main national temperance organizations when their strategies shifted from working through churches and social organizations to seeking legal prohibition. Some women, including many in Ohio, remained comfortable using traditional methods of social pressure and continued their work outside the growing Prohibition movement. But more activist temperance and suffrage women found themselves cast aside from major Prohibition organizations.

The intensity of Prohibition activity continued to grow during the years before the Civil War and quickly reemerged when the fighting stopped. Immigration patterns and the growth in beer consumption clearly helped fuel the fire. The scale of German immigration before and after the war was enormous. Just over five hundred thousand immigrants arrived in the United States from Germany between 1852 and 1854—43 percent of all those finding their way to these shores in that short span.[10] For the twenty years following the Civil War, Germans also were the largest national immigrant group. Many moved to the Midwest. Alcohol consumption patterns changed dramatically with their arrival. Beer, previously a minor beverage in America, began to be sold in large amounts after 1840. Sales grew dramatically after the Civil War.[11]

The large growth in beer sales and the opening of large numbers of saloons, especially in places like southern Ohio where many German immigrants lived, exacerbated women's fears that alcohol was affecting their home environments. The issue was not so much that more alcohol was being consumed, although more beer certainly was, or that only immigrants or blacks were doing the consuming. Both rich and poor were drinking.[12] The problem was a sense that the practice was decentralizing and disrupting normal methods of social control. Hard liquor could easily be kept on hand at home. No special storage methods were required. If male drinkers had to be controlled, women could put the bottles under lock and key. But beer required special storage and dispensing facilities not typically available in households. Men drinking outside the home became much more common. Saloons, as many drinking establishments came to be known in the 1850s, proliferated and emerged as distinctly male domains.[13] Stories of men drinking in town, coming home drunk, wasting money, and beating up their families, while always present in cultural lore,[14] became much more common and believable.

The final straw for the women of Hillsboro, Ohio, may well have been anger and frustration. Sale of liquor by the drink had been barred in Ohio since at least 1854,[15] the same year that families obtained the authority to sue liquor dispensers for damages caused by their drunken relatives.[16] But owners of saloons, drug stores, beer gardens, and other establishments selling alcohol routinely claimed that their payment of federal taxes and receipt of a federal tax stamp legitimated their trade. Ohio's law, and similar laws in other jurisdictions, went largely unenforced by public authorities. Ballot initiatives in some towns made them legally "dry," but saloons continued to do business.[17] The failure of elected officials to take actions against those distributing alcohol led to substantial anger and frustration.

Some spectacular events began to occur. During the 1850s women in dozens of scattered communities formed bands to invade saloons and destroy their stocks of alcohol. They often obtained the tacit, and sometimes public, support and blessing of local religious leaders and male temperance societies. The war interrupted such actions. But the return of men, habituated to drinking during military service, to their prewar communities, the use of alcohol or beer as part payment of wages in many factories, the postwar onset of large-scale beer production, and the opening of many new saloons exacerbated the situation. Women who led wartime temperance activities sometimes were pushed aside as hostilities ended, adding to the level of discontent. When the major, male-dominated political parties showed little interest in temperance during the 1872 election and Ohio prepared for a constitutional convention in 1873, the moment was ripe for an activist women's Prohibition movement to surface. All that was needed was a catalyst. Diocletian Lewis filled the bill.

Women in Men's Domains: Setting the Tone

Typical nineteenth-century courtrooms, like the saloons that peppered the nearby landscapes, were not women's territory. After the Civil War women appeared as trial witnesses or attended public court sessions from time to time, and they joined the legal profession in very small numbers.[18] But the vast bulk of those present in courthouses across the nation—judges, jurors, court personnel, attorneys, and spectators—were men. There were exceptions, however, and at least two of them played an important role in the emergence of Hillsboro, Ohio, as the epicenter of the Crusade. One began some years before the Crusade in the nearby town of Greenfield, Ohio. A group of women in that town organized to shut down the liquor trade. As they marched in 1865 a woman whose son had been killed during a gun-toting saloon brawl became particularly incensed in front of the drinking establishment where the fight occurred. Her cries incited the women to use axes and other implements to destroy the saloon, as well as other taverns in town. Bar owners sued the women, and a trial commenced in Hillsboro early in 1867. There "the 'first ladies' of Hillsboro met the defendants when they arrived in town . . . 'and escorted them to private homes, for generous entertainment during their stay . . . [and] also took seats with them during the trial, and in every possible way gave demonstration of the morality of the case.'"[19] After a four-day trial Judge Albert S. Dickey ordered the women to pay $625 in damages.[20] But the proceeding was a precedent for women mobilizing to publicly support the most radical prohibition activities. Perhaps it was not an accident that the women of Greenfield were among the first to join the Crusade after it began in Hillsboro.

The second court proceeding was more remarkable. Suffragist Miriam Cole, in a letter she wrote puzzling over the public displays of temperance sentiment by women in Ohio,[21] recalled a trial in Springfield, Ohio, that occurred just shy of a year before the Crusades erupted. It was a case brought under a dram shop act commonly known, in Ohio, as the Adair Law—an old statute amended as temperance activity intensified in 1870 to allow any person to sue bar owners and sellers of liquor to recover damages caused by an intoxicated buyer.[22] "A woman whose husband had reduced his family to utter want by drunkenness, entered a suit against the rum seller," Cole recalled. After the local paper published an appeal for help from the plaintiff to the women of Springfield, "a large delegation of the most respectable and pious women of the city came into the court." After a week-long adjournment, "the excitement had become so great that when the trial came on the court-room was full of spectators, and the number of ladies within the rail was increased three-fold." And most surprising of all to Cole, a woman— Mrs. E. D. Stewart—made the closing argument for the plaintiff.

Mrs. E. D. Stewart was not a lawyer but a well-known Ohio temperance advocate. Popularly known as "Mother Stewart," she made something of a career showing up as an advocate in Adair Law cases and was a principal player and frequent speaker during the Hillsboro Crusades. Stewart's advocacy is a revealing portrayal of the way gender roles could be used to influence male behavior in late-nineteenth-century America. She began the central argument of her closing by noting that the plaintiff's husband, "when not under the influence of liquor, was a kind husband and father." He provided "for the necessities of his family . . . [and] even when occasionally giving way to his appetite it had been proven that he was able to earn from $6 to $9 per week." "But . . . the influence of drink," Stewart argued, made him "so worthless and incompetent that the wife and mother, besides her regular domestic duties, was obliged to labor to earn the means of support for her family." Powerful rhetoric followed, focusing on the stigma and suffering of the drunkard's wife and children. Finally, Stewart closed the rhetorical vise, asking the jury to "deal with this woman as they would that others should deal with their wife or daughter. And as they dealt with her, might God deal with them." Stewart described the response of the defense attorney: he gesticulated vehemently, declared it was "infamous to bring a female in to influence the court and jury." Mrs. Stewart should be ashamed to come into court, he exclaimed. "She had much better have been at home attending to her legitimate duties." The jury, however, "brought in a verdict of $100 and costs."[23]

Stewart knew how to pluck the heartstrings of the male jurors. Recognizing their role as protectors of wives, daughters, children, and grandchildren, she dared them to turn aside from their God-given obligation to provide for their families and kin. Even as she crossed traditional boundary lines to enter and then control the atmospherics of a courtroom, she asked the men before her to make sure that they met their own social obligations. When reading her story, you can visualize the discomfort she caused men unaccustomed to hearing articulate women speak, imagine the nervous twitches of opposing counsel, and sense the male jurors' recognition that they could not resist Mother Stewart's appeal for help. Stewart took her judicial experience with her to Hillsboro the following year and used it to school her peers there on the importance of ensuring women's presence in generally male bastions—courtrooms as well as saloons.

Events Giving Rise to Litigation in Hillsboro

Legal events took on major importance in Hillsboro very shortly after the Temperance Crusade began. The town buzzed with chatter about the operations of a grand jury investigating illegal sales of alcohol and the possibility that citizens might be called to testify.[24] Residents also reacted with surprise and some consternation to the posting of a notice by Dr. William Henry Harrison Dunn threatening legal action if the demonstrations in front of his Palace Drugstore continued. J. H. Beadle, in an article dated January 30, 1874, reported on a speech by Judge John Matthews delivered to a gathering of Crusaders at the Methodist Church in Hillsboro the night before and noted the disapproving audience reaction to the judge's comments on the use of law to further the Crusaders' goals. Matthews' remarks, Beadle reported, "were received with great favor, till he reached this passage: 'We all hold . . . [moral suasion] to be the best method. But we are trusting in God, and we must not dictate methods to Him. We had not intended to appeal to the law, but God works by means, and it may be that He has determined we shall make use of the law of Ohio!' At this ingenious attempt to smooth the way to legal proceedings there was quite a titter among the irreverent, and the ladies near me showed decided signs of disapprobation." Beadle noted, "Of the nine saloons (including three hotel bars) five have closed; whether permanently, and whether because of the ladies or the grand jury, is not known. The ladies are earnest in their repudiation of legal measures, and do not fail to protest whenever the matter is broached in their meetings."

It made little difference in Hillsboro, it turned out, whether such protests arose from traditional women's reluctance to leave the path of moral suasion, or from the conviction that God would provide a pathway to success, or from a desire to avoid the male judicial domain, or, simply from frustration at the failure of politicians and prosecutors to pursue illegal drinking establishments. On the morning of January 29, 1874, residents awoke to find a "Notice to the Ladies of Hillsboro" from Dunn posted throughout the town.[25] He called upon Mother Stewart and seventy-eight other women, as well as twenty-five men, "who, although not directly participating in your daily proceedings, are, nevertheless, counseling and advising you in your unlawful proceedings by subscriptions of money, and encouragement in the commission of daily trespasses upon my property" to cease the demonstrations in front of his store. Dunn complained that "my legitimate business has been obstructed, my feelings outraged, and my profession and occupation sought to be rendered odious, by reason of which I have suffered great pecuniary damage and injury." "Cherishing no unkind hostility toward any one," Dunn wrote, "but entertaining the highest regard for the ladies of Hillsboro, distinguished heretofore, as they have been, for their courtesy, refinement and Christian virtues, I feel extremely reluctant to have to appeal to the law for protection against their riotous and unlawful acts." But, he concluded, "if such action and trespasses are repeated, I shall apply to the laws of the State for redress and damages for the injuries occasioned by reason of the practices of which I complain."

Dunn sought legal redress and obtained temporary injunctive relief on January 31, a result that, according to Beadle, initially split the movement.[26] But Dunn's actions "had the effect to bring out a large number to the morning meeting" of the Crusaders who voted unanimously to continue their work. A delegation was sent to the mayor and construction began on a "Tabernacle" in the street in front of Dunn's store. The move to court, it seems, convinced most of the demonstrating women that they had to confront the new environment with political action as well as prayer and devotion.

Judge William H. Safford

Judge William H. Safford issued the Hillsboro temporary injunction. After promulgating the order barring the Crusaders from demonstrating in front of Dunn's business, Safford declined to seek another term as judge. He then became Dunn's attorney and handled the case for him during a hearing on whether to make the temporary injunction permanent! Less than two weeks after the initial court hearing, he gave an enlightening interview to "Amber," which was published in the *Cincinnati Commercial*.[27] When Amber asked what he thought of the Crusaders, Safford responded that the women were the finest of citizens but were not really in control of their actions. "I am personally acquainted with some of these ladies, and have accepted of their hospitality," Safford began. "For intelligence and refinement, and all the female graces and Christian virtues they are not excelled in this or any other State." "Many of these were in affluence and [from] distinguished and cultivated families," he continued. "They have appreciated and patronized learning and the arts; they have had the advantages of two, and part of the time three of the best female colleges in the State, conducted by the most successful and experienced teachers in the West."

But after making this polite bow to the elite women in town, Safford refused to give them much credit for the power of their demonstrations. "When the Yankee peddler of patent temperance societies explained their virtues," the plan of moral suasion pleased their views and gave promise of success," he opined. "Neither moral nor legal coercion was dreamed of in the commencement. It was intended to use mild and persuasive measures to induce the cessation of the liquor traffic," Safford continued. But, he complained, "having started in the enterprise, what with the aid of ministers and the encouragement of the male portion of the community, their zeal in the case increased. In the meetings at night they were stimulated by the flattering encouragement they received, and before they were aware of it had raised a whirlwind which they could not control." The women, in Safford's view, became the pawns of men. "They then became somewhat coercive and aggressive. They did not stop to make distinctions. Any one who sold liquors had to come down. If persuasion could not accomplish it, he was to be goaded and hectored into it," the judge bemoaned. "The spirit of conquest was aroused; and they fired prayers at his front door like hail. They gradually and unintentionally got into excesses." He concluded by arguing that the women lacked any control over their actions.

> I think that when matters had arrived at this point, the leaders of the movement would have gladly backed out, had it not been feared, if they did so, the whole thing would have fallen through. They, however, were in the whirl, and had to go with it. I can not believe that the leaders, or, I should say, prominent ladies, ever intended that matters should go so far.

Safford's statement presents a fascinating mix of politeness and disbelief that the refined, intelligent, well-educated, elegant, Christian ladies of Hillsboro possibly have unleashed such a storm of protest. Despite the obviously well-organized way in which daily demonstrations occurred, with prayer meetings followed by groups of women marching in an orderly fashion to bars, saloons, and drugstores, he found it difficult to believe that the women of Hillsboro actually desired to undertake such activity, intended to pressure their fellow citizens to join the Crusades, planned their course of action, and rejoiced at the power of their prayers.

The depth of his state of disbelief was demonstrated even more strongly a month later—after the judges who took over the *Dunn* case declined to make his temporary injunction order permanent—when Judge Safford gave a speech in Chillicothe.[28] He condemned the Crusaders in very strong language—as a "female commune" trespassing on legal rights, morally coercing citizens, and infringing on freedom of opinion. "Honest women," he exclaimed, are put forward by dishonest men who are cowards themselves. I will not say anything disrespectful of the mothers, wives, sisters and daughters engaged in this crusade. They have, a great many of them, God knows, reason for making every effort to suppress the whisky trade and we can say to them that we will lend you every aid to suppress it in a legal way.

Judge Safford's position that the women were "put forward by dishonest men who are cowards themselves" was a stunning misstatement of the Crusade reality. Such a denial that women were responsible for their own actions coursed through the public statements of those opposed to the demonstrations. The men making such statements could not fathom that women voluntarily would "place themselves in the purlieus of vice and immorality" and "be remarked upon by the rabble" supposedly inhabiting such places. Nor were they willing to accept women using "the ridiculous attitude of prayer" to coerce men, rather than soliciting help against the liquor trade from on high. It wasn't that prayer itself was ridiculous; it was the use of prayer as a way of controlling men that struck Safford as unsupportable.

These comments go to the heart of the public debate that unfolded about the Crusades as they occurred. In a perverse sort of way, they mirrored the thoughts of suffragists like Miriam Cole who also found it hard to understand why genteel, conservative ladies of rural America would place themselves in compromising positions to seek temperance while refusing to do the same to obtain the vote. Cole, who was a coeditor of the *Woman's Advocate* in Dayton, Ohio, was perplexed by the actions of "women who are so pressed with domestic cares that they have no time to vote; . . . who shun notoriety so much that they are unwilling to ask permission to vote; . . . [and] who believe that men are quite capable of managing State and municipal affairs without their interference." The traditional feminine virtues called upon by the Crusaders, according to Cole, were undermined by their actions. "Their singing," she protested, "though charged with a moral purpose, and their prayers, though directed to a specific end, do not make their warfare a wit more feminine, nor their situation more attractive. A woman knocking out the head of a whiskey barrel with an ax, to the tune of Old Hundred, is not the ideal woman sitting on a sofa, dining on strawberries and cream, and sweetly warbling, 'The Rose that All Are Praising.' She is as far from it as Susan B. Anthony was when pushing her ballot into the box."[29]

Both Safford and Cole were surprised that the women of Hillsboro violated social norms they previously had accepted. The actions offended them both. And that, of course, is just the point. The Crusaders took much of

American culture by surprise. Their persistence, despite the disapproval of significant segments of the body politic, led them to gain a deeper understanding of law and politics. That became very obvious at the Palace Drugstore injunction hearing.

The Permanent Injunction Hearing

The arguments before Judges S. F. Steele and T. M. Gray were on a demurrer filed by the defendants claiming that there was no legal basis for the suit and the issuance of an injunction. Mother Stewart's difficulties in getting women to attend an Adair Law trial the prior year were clearly overcome in the *Dunn* case. The men orchestrating the lawsuit and running the court were confronted with a sea of women. "A large and interested crowd, more than half of whom are ladies," it was reported, "were assembled this morning at the Courthouse . . . a large proportion of whom are some of the most respectable ladies in Hillsboro."[30] Because the women present were often defendants in the action, it was very difficult to criticize their presence. "The court-room today was again packed by a large crowd," another newspaper article reported, "the ladies, as usual, being in the majority, and a greater portion of them defendants in the case of Dunn against Scott and others."[31]

Despite the presence of so many women, the attorneys for Dunn—Judge William H. Safford, Mr. Ulrich Sloane, and Mr. Charles H. Collins—made some stunning critiques of the Crusaders' behavior. Sloane's comments must have been particularly irksome to the women present. "Singing is a very good thing, but like all other good things, it must be in its place, for Solomon says 'there is a time to sing, and there is a time to dance,'" Sloane argued. To laughter he continued, "I suppose these ladies would have danced before Dunn's door if they had thought they could have coerced him in that way." Demeaning the intelligence and worldly knowledge of the women sitting before him, Mr. Sloane embellished Judge Safford's theme that the Crusaders were not in control of their actions, adding that "ladies have no idea of their legal abilities," "do not know the components of a promissory note," and "lose that respect which should be paid them" when they "forget their woman's sphere." He ended his peroration with a volley of comments comparing the Crusaders to "Mahomedan" "dervishes" who go "before the door of the person and howl" to "extort" a desired result. Drawing laughter throughout his argument—presumably only from the non-Crusaders in the audience—Sloane not only declined to accept the women as instruments of their own fates, but he also belittled their behavior and demeaned their reputations. It is hard to believe that the women, though quietly listening, were not seething in their seats, storing their anger for use in the ongoing temperance agitation and, later, in the suffrage movement. Reading such material makes palpable the ways in which the male-dominated legal process could "radicalize" women and turn them into overt political actors.

Eventually, however, the use of humor and the atmospherics it created were far more complex than the remarks of Mr. Ulrich Sloane alone suggest. He was not the only person to poke fun in the proceeding. The rejoinder by one of the defendants' counsel, Mr. James H. Thompson, also had its laugh-provoking moments. "What is this drug store?" he asked. "They have admitted . . . that Dunn is a retail liquor seller," Thompson continued. But, he noted with laughter ringing through the courtroom, "he says that the ladies come to his place not to disturb him as a liquor dealer, but to prevent him from selling calomel and jalap . . . and sweet drugs for ladies. . . . He says 'they have come here to prevent me from selling paregoric.' . . . Give me Dunn's drug store and I can whip all the Modoc Indians in the country." To more peels of laughter, Sloane concluded, "He is a pirate, sailing under the black flag, and he comes here and says the ladies are injuring him in the drug business. Does any one suppose that the women here would go to Dunn's drug store to pray for him not to sell drugs? Such a thing would be ridiculous."

Although the women of Hillsboro were not the objects of Mr. Thompson's scorn, his jibes posed analytical problems. Were the women comfortable with this sort of argument? Did they appreciate Thompson's humorous use of the biblical character Miriam to critique Dunn's legal position and join in the laughter? Note that he took a very different approach than Mother Stewart in her previously described argument to the jury in the Adair Law case. Rather than playing on men's social obligations to protect "their" women as in Stewart's closing, Thompson focused on the hypocrisy of the saloon keepers. Did Thompson's statements, like those of the plaintiffs' counsel, suggest comfort about the male atmospherics of the courthouse even when women were present? Might it even suggest that somewhere in Mr. Thompson's soul he felt a degree of empathy for Mr. Sloane's strategy, if not his arguments? Did all this say something about men's willingness to use humor in public settings where the Crusaders would have abstained from such behavior?

There is no evidence of whether the women defendants were laughing or silent during various parts of the permanent injunction hearing. But the earnestness of their religious convictions, the steadfastness of their actions in the saloons of Hillsboro, and the strength of their belief in the wisdom of shutting down the liquor trade suggests a seriousness of purpose at odds with the courtroom mood they encountered. Such a culture clash appeared not only in legal settings but also in society at large. We certainly know that male humor was used as an acerbic critique of women who dared to enter the public political sphere. Many documents, pamphlets, and posters distributed during the Crusades and the subsequent prohibition movement portrayed women Prohibitionists in an unflattering light—as abortionists, prostitutes, and power seekers defiling their God-given roles as mothers and companions. Surely at some point the use of demeaning humor caused many if not all the women Crusaders of Hillsboro in attendance to sit uncomfortably in their seats as men made their arguments to the court.

The verbal repartee in the *Dunn* case was not all laced with jesting. In fact, the speeches went on for days, concluding on February 20, 1874. "One cannot help but be surprised at and admire," one article in the newspaper opined, "the patience with which the ladies sit and listen during the whole day to the dry arguments upon purely legal technical points in the case, which are probably not understood by one-fourth of them."[32] Judge Safford closed the arguments for Dunn with a five-hour oration on the 19th. Much of it dealt with aspects of nuisance law, whether the proper parties were named and the correctness of the procedures used. Near the end, Safford levied a final attack on the agency of the women present. "The ladies erected the booth right in the teeth of that notice of Dunn," Safford claimed. "I am not blaming them for it," he continued, "but unfortunately they had raised a whirlwind and could not direct it." Once again denying their agency, Safford explained, "I think they never intended to transgress laws, but it was brought about by meddlesome men, and for their own purposes, and they prostituted the holy services of the church to the accomplishment of their purposes. There is nothing in woman that is aggressive; they, more than all others, feel the effects of intemperance." After arguing that the traditional rules barring injunctions when damages can be determined, or when remedies at law are adequate, should not prevent the award of injunction relief in Dunn's case, Safford concluded, "You were fast becoming a village of slanderers . . . . In time of great excitement people must remember that the rights of individuals are to be protected and that the majority must respect the rights of the minority."

At the conclusion of the arguments, the court dissolved the injunction on grounds unrelated to nuisance law.[33] What tripped up the plaintiffs in the minds of Judges Steele and Gray was not the weakness of the allegations made against the women but a procedural problem. Nineteenth-century pleading and procedural law was rife with limitations on the use of court processes that have long since been discarded. Among them was a rule in Ohio requiring that when multiple parties joined together to bring a case, they all were required to have a valid cause against the defendants. In this dispute, the landlord Johnson was said not to have a valid claim. Access to relief in an equity court, the court noted, only was available when the remedies in a court of law were inadequate. In Johnson's case, the judges held, it would have been easy for a court of law to calculate the amount of any damages Johnson had suffered. Once the court concluded that Johnson could not seek injunctive relief, Dunn was shunted aside because of the procedural rule requiring that all plaintiffs have a viable equitable claim. The court therefore dismissed the case without deciding whether Dunn would have prevailed had he brought the litigation by himself. We can only wonder whether the presence of so many women in the courtroom had any influence on the result. It is possible, though totally speculative, that Judge Steele used a procedural rule to appease the women of Hillsboro without demeaning the social standing of any of the parties before him.

In general, efforts to use the courts to suppress the Crusades were not very successful. A result very much like that in the Hillsboro injunction case unfolded in Morrow, Ohio, about thirty-five miles to the northwest. As in Hillsboro, an outpouring of women appeared in the courtroom. Beadle reported, "The whole town of Morrow came over and emptied itself upon Lebanon. Forty women included in the list of defendants were among the crowd. These became the special guests of the Lebanon ladies, who gave them a public dinner." On the day the hearing began, "These forty marched from the church to the court-house in solemn procession. The excitement was intense in the town, and the case the only topic of conversation." The image of forty women and their supporters marching through Lebanon to the courthouse is a telling reminder of how wrong Judge Safford had been about the inability of the Crusading women to organize themselves, how important participation in legal proceedings was to their political education, and how important the court proceedings were as stimuli for camaraderie and political awareness among the women. After the court announced that the Crusaders were free to interfere with the operations of gambling and liquor sales that violated Ohio law, a band marched down the streets of Morrow, "followed by an immense throng of men, women, and children, shouting and rejoicing."[34] The results of the two cases in Hillsboro and Lebanon must have convinced the saloon keepers of southern Ohio that nuisance litigation was not going to help them very much. They, like the Crusaders, took up the mantle of politics instead.

Massive outbursts of public displeasure eventually ebb, and the Crusades were no exception. As liquor establishments closed and weariness replaced fortitude, the women and their male supporters returned to more normal lives, and most of the saloons reopened. But the impact of the Crusades was long-lasting. The Ohio State Constitutional Convention of 1873–74, whose imminence may have stimulated the Crusaders to take to the streets, was enlivened by vigorous discussions of Prohibition. Reports about the debates and public meetings on the liquor issue commonly appeared in the papers during the spring of 1874. As the constitutional convention unfolded, women's temperance leagues from all over the state gathered together, organized, and set the groundwork for founding the Woman's Christian Temperance Union.[35] The Crusaders' experiences in the churches, streets, saloons, and courthouses of Ohio dramatically broke through the cultural and social barriers that had previously limited their public roles in law and politics. They were no longer afraid to make their feelings known in places previously occupied only by men. The Woman's Christian Union eventually became the vanguard of a new suffrage movement.

Temperance to Suffrage

Today the entry of a group of women into an American saloon is almost universally viewed as a nonevent. It is difficult, therefore, to imagine how different the reactions were 135 years ago. Beadle provides accounts of two Crusade scenes involving interactions between men and women. These provide a sense of the impact that women dressed in their Sunday finery publicly praying for intemperate souls had on men. The first describes a saloon scene as women entered. A group of young men "had ranged themselves in the familiar semi-circle before the bar, had their drinks ready and cigars prepared for the match, when the rustle of women's wear attracted their attention, and looking up they saw what they thought a crowd of a thousand ladies entering." The highlight of the story involved customers who saw familiar faces. One saw "his mother and sister; another had two cousins in the invading host, and a still more unfortunate recognized his intended mother-in-law!" Envision the scene. "Had the invisible prince of the pantomime touched them with his magic wand, converting all to statues, the tableau could not have been more impressive. For one full minute they stood as if turned to stone; then a slight motion was evident, and lager beer and brandy-smash descended slowly to the counter, while cigars dropped unlighted from nerveless fingers." The tension broke when the ladies began singing a jaunty spiritual and the young men "escaped to the street, scared out of a year's growth."[36]

This is a remarkable scene. The women who entered the bar, finely dressed, perhaps toting prayer books or hymnals, carried a "space" with them. Prior to the Crusades such "spaces" were much more likely to be associated with a particular site—a church, a home, or the ladies car of a train—where some women could exercise a modicum of authority. The Crusaders broke such links between particular women's spaces and social control. The women discovered that the domestic authority they carried with them could be used not only to control domesticated space but also to alter behavior in previously male domains. It must have been a heady experience for those Crusaders who had never been socially active to walk into a saloon and see men scurry away with their tails between their legs.

The second, brief Beadle account is about a street scene fairly early in the Hillsboro campaign. "A fresh detail of women has just arrived, and after a lengthy prayer, are dealing out old 'Coronation' in heart-moving tones," he wrote. "The townspeople go and come their accustomed ways with little notice, but it is curiously comical to notice strangers and country people. They begin to step gingerly about a square off; as they get nearer steadily soften their steps, and finally take off their hats and edge their way slowly around the open-air prayer-meeting as one would pass a funeral."[37] In this tableau, the combination of public prayer and women's voices had a dramatic impact on those seeing the Crusade as a novel experience. Many town residents, however, by then inured to the sight of women kneeling in prayer on the streets of Hillsboro, went about "their accustomed ways with little notice." For them, the shock was gone. The risk of expanding the places where women moved and exercised their moral authority was that some stopped noticing or caring.

So it was, at least in part, at the Hillsboro Courthouse during the Palace Drugstore injunction hearing. The reactions of those men running the proceedings and arguing their points were not the same as the young "blood," slowly dropping his whiskey to the bar or the "strangers and country people" approaching the women praying on the street. They were perfectly willing to put the women back in their "proper place," at least verbally. As Ulrich Sloane noted in his argument on Dunn's behalf, "When . . . [the Crusaders] forget their woman's sphere they lose that respect which should be paid to them." But in a powerful way, it was that very reaction that may have convinced the women present that further steps were necessary to protect their interests; that intervening more often in public political spaces was required to make their influence meaningful; and, eventually, that seeking the ballot was central to the ultimate freedom they wished to exercise. Men flaunting their lack of concern about women's efforts to exercise moral authority led some women to alter their views about actively pursuing legal and political goals.

These women, drawn by the charismatic leadership of Frances Willard, gradually became the backbone of the Woman's Christian Temperance Union. Willard, who rose to the presidency of the Union in 1879, was a brilliant speaker, routinely melding the capacity of women for moral leadership with the need for substantial political and social reform. In her 1879 *Home Protection Manual*, Willard wove domestic violence, the temptations of alcohol, the power of familial love, and womanly virtue into a politically inspired argument for women's suffrage. The love of a woman's heart, she wrote, was a "magic lens." With "that powerful sunglass which we term the ballot, they shall all convert their power, and burn and blaze on the saloon, till it shrivels up and in lurid vapor, curls away like mist under the hot gaze of sunshine." Eschewing the egalitarian arguments made by Elizabeth Cady Stanton, Susan B. Anthony and other suffragists who grew up in the abolitionist movement, Willard relied upon much more traditional ideas about female domesticity, moral virtue, and familial obligation to support her call for the ballot. It was a deft move that resonated with the conservative Crusaders of Southern Ohio who founded the Woman's Christian Temperance Union and their peers across the country. Willard turned their belief in the capacity of women to lead men to new heights of virtue into a reason to join the suffrage cause.

In the long run suffrage was not achievable without such a shift in perspective by rural, conservative women and men. Neither western libertarians nor urban liberals could carry the day for suffrage when substantial numbers of Americans remained religious and conservative. Throughout the eras when temperance and suffrage were subjects of national debate, urbanites constituted a minority of the population. The 1920 U.S. Census was the first to show that a majority of Americans lived in urban areas.[38] Though women's suffrage first gained a foothold in the west, their influence in Congress was relatively low. The help of women like those who filled the streets of Hillsboro—and their political descendants—was necessary to alter the Constitution. Amendments to our national charter are never adopted without firm support from large segments of the entire political spectrum. Both Left and Right saw the Crusaders' successors as their darlings. Many Progressives on the left were descendants of longtime temperance advocates and suffragists. And conservative, religiously based movements saw both Prohibition and suffrage as paths allowing women to exercise their moral authority over the culture as a whole. It was no accident that the Prohibition and Suffrage Amendments were embedded in the Constitution at virtually the same historical moment.

An expanded version of this essay appeared as *Courts and Temperance "Ladies,"* 21 Yale J. L. & Feminism 339 (2010). My thanks go to New York Law School for supporting my research for this essay with a summer writer grant in 2008 and to my research assistant, Bryan J. Rush, New York Law School, Class of 2009. I also extend my thanks to members of the faculties of Georgetown University Law Center and New York Law School for their comments when portions of this paper were presented at workshops. Tracy Thomas and Tracey Jean Boisseau labored beyond the call of duty to make this volume a reality.

1. Ruth Bordin, *A Baptism of Power and Liberty: The Women's Crusade of 1873–1874*, 87 Ohio Hist. 393, 394–96 (1978).

2. Ruth Bordin, *Woman and Temperance: The Quest for Power and Liberty, 1873–1900*, 140 (1990).

3. The best works are the article and book by Ruth Bordin referred to above. *See also* Ruth Bordin, Frances Willard: A Biography (1986); Jack S. Blocker Jr., "Give to the Winds Thy Fears": The Women's Temperance Crusade, 1873–1874 (1985); Jed Dannenbaum, Drink and Disorder: Temperance Reform in Cincinnati from the Washingtonian Revival to the WCTU (1984); Charles Kynett Carpenter, The Origin of the Woman's Crusade and the W.C.T.U. (1949).

4. Bordin, The Women's Crusade, 402.

5. The relationships between the Crusading women in Ohio and legal institutions are most keenly revealed in a lengthy series of articles published almost daily in the Cincinnati Commercial.

6. Charles A. Isetts, *A Social Profile of the Women's Temperance Crusade: Hillsboro, Ohio*, in Alcohol, Reform, and Society: The Liquor Issue in Social Context 101–110 (Jack. S. Blocker Jr. ed. 1979).

7. Correspondence Cincinnati Commercial, Cincinnati Commercial, Mar. 18, 1874.

8. Dannenbaum, 86.

9. An Act for the Suppression of Drinking Houses and Tippling Shops, ch. 211, Acts and Resolves Passed by the Thirty-First Legislature of the State of Maine 210–18 (June 2, 1851).

10. Series C 89–119, Bureau of the Census, United States Department of Commerce, Historical Statistics of the United States: Colonial Times to 1970, at 106, 1975.

11. The data pattern displayed in publications from the late nineteenth century through today is consistent on this point. *See* Henry William Blair, The Temperance Movement: or, The Conflict between Man and Alcohol 35 (1887); Dept. of Health, Education and Welfare, First Special Report to the U.S. Congress on Alcohol & Health (1971); Harry G. Levine & Craig Reinarman, From Prohibition to Regulation: Lessons from Alcohol Policy for Drug Policy, http://www.drugtext.org/library/articles/craig102.htm (accessed Aug. 15, 2008). The same conclusions are reached in histories of beer. Maureen Ogle, Ambitious Brew: The Story of American Beer 151 (2006); Amy Mittelman, Brewing Battles: A History of American Beer 22, 34, 38 (2008). Data gathered by the Census Bureau confirm the pattern. Series P 231–300, Historical Statistics, 691.

12. Blocker, 97–113.

13. Thomas R. Pegram, Battling Demon Rum: The Struggle for a Dry America, 1800–1933, 53–56 (1998).

14. Martin, 46–53.

15. *An Act to Provide against the Evils Resulting from the Sale of Intoxicating Liquors in the State of Ohio*, Laws of Ohio, May 1, 1854.

16. James F. Mosher, *Dram Shop Liability and the Prevention of Alcohol-Related Problems*, 40 J. Studies on Alcohol 773 (1979).

17. *See* Blocker, 172.

18. Virginia G. Drachman, Sisters in Law: Women Lawyers in Modern American History (1998).

19. Dannenbaum, 204, quoting the Western Christian Advocate, Jan. 30, 1867.

20. Greenfield Historical Society, Greenfield, OH, Bicentennial 9 (2000).

21. Elizabeth Cady Stanton, Susan B. Anthony, & Matilda Joslyn Gage, eds. 3 History of Woman Suffrage 500–01 (1889). Jack S. Blocker Jr., *Separate Paths: Suffragists and the Women's Temperance Crusade*, 10 Signs 460, 469 (1985), reviews the responses of the suffragists to the Crusades.

22. An Act to Amend Sections Seven and Ten of an Act Entitled "An Act to Provide against the Evils Resulting from the Sale of Intoxicating Liquors in the State of Ohio," Passed May 1, 1854, Laws of Ohio (Apr. 18, 1870).

23. Mother Stewart, *Memories of the Crusade: A Thrilling Account of the Great Uprising of the Women of Ohio in 1873, Against the Liquor Crime* 35–37 (1888).

24. This article was signed "Beadle." *Woman's Whiskey War: The Hillsboro Battle,* Cincinnati Commercial, Feb. 2, 1874.

25. Beadle, *Correspondence Cincinnati Commercial,* Cincinnati Commercial, Jan. 31, 1874.

26. Id.

27. *Woman's Whiskey War: Judge Safford Interviewed; He Rises to Explain*, Cincinnati Commercial, Feb. 16, 1874.

28. *Judge Stafford's Speech at Chillicothe*, Cincinnati Commercial, Mar. 16, 1874.

29. 3 History of Woman Suffrage 500.

30. *The Temperance Injunction Case at Hillsboro,* Cincinnati Commercial, Feb. 18, 1874.

31. *The Women's Prayer Meeting Injunction Suit at Hillsboro,* Cincinnati Commercial, Feb. 20, 1874.

32. *The Injunction Case at Hillsboro,* Cincinnati Commercial, Feb. 19, 1874.

33. *Hillsboro Injunction case—Decision of the Court—Injunction Dissolved,* Cincinnati Commercial, Feb. 21, 1874.

34. J. H. Beadle, The Women's War on Whiskey: Its History, Theory, and Prospects 72–77 (1874).

35. *State Convention of the Woman's Temperance Leagues of Ohio: Between Two and Three Thousand Persons in Attendance*, Cincinnati Commercial, Apr. 23, 1874; *The Woman's Convention: Second Day's Proceedings*, Cincinnati Commercial, Apr. 24, 1874.

36. *Correspondence Cincinnati Commercial,* Cincinnati Commercial, Feb. 2, 1874.

37. Beadle, *Woman's Whisky War: The Hillsboro Battle,* Cincinnati Commercial, Feb. 2, 1874.

38. Bureau of the Census, Department of Commerce, Statistical History of the United States from Colonial Times to the Present 11–12 (1976).

2

Women behind the Wheel

Gender and Transportation Law, 1860–1930

MARGO SCHLANGER

Gender difference is only infrequently mentioned in recent negligence cases. To contemporary (mostly non-essentialist) eyes, gender difference seems to appear only mildly relevant to tort law's area of concern: care and harm to others and self. But in the early days of modern tort law, when gender differences loomed larger in the consciousness of American jurists, and unabashedly so, judicial opinions more frequently grappled with how negligence doctrine ought to take account of female difference. This chapter explores opinions published between approximately 1860 and 1930 that illuminate this issue in cases involving women drivers and passengers of cars and wagons.[1] The focus on transportation-related injuries reflects early tort law's similar preoccupation.

Many feminist scholars have argued that tort law historically subordinated women by simply omitting them from the developing objective standard of care. They point out that even as texts such as Holmes's *The Common Law*[2] or the famous British case of *Vaughn v. Menlove*[3] canonized the "reasonable man" standard, and simultaneously settled the way in which tort doctrine would deal with differences relating to intelligence, physical disability, mental disability, age, and other factors, women were simply left out. The claim is that tort law used to measure caretaking by a "reasonable man" standard which was not just linguistically but truly a masculine one—and that the construction was the once-unnoticed emblem of the legal system's substantive oppression and exclusion of women.[4] Recent feminist scholarship, however, rebuts charges of erasure. Barbara Welke, for example, writes of accident law from 1865 to 1920 that "taking the gender out of the law was something like taking the bounce out of a rabbit: unnatural, impossible, undesirable. . . . Men's and women's accidents were patterned by gender, generating legal rules which in effect were shaped by and directed toward women and men, but not both."[5] This chapter's examination of old accident cases likewise undermines the accusation that pre-feminist tort law consistently excluded both the category of gender and women themselves. Its contribution is to flesh out and complicate the account of just *how* gender and women were included.

As many other chapters in this collection note, the gender ideology in America ascendant in the mid-nineteenth century and still dominant, albeit with increasing ambivalence, well into the early twentieth century, was that of "separate spheres."[6] The division of the world into public and private, male and female worlds attached tension to women using any means of transportation, because transportation took place in a public, male space.[7] But ideology bent to convenience: women frequently, if less frequently than men, rode trains, streetcars, wagons, and cars, even if their use of these means of transportation ran counter to the separate spheres concept.[8] The cases in this chapter deal with women injured in wagons or cars, the most "private" and therefore the most acceptable conveyances for women. In the first set of cases, the injury victims were women drivers of wagons. Some nineteenth-century court decisions in this category acknowledged and treated a perceived gender difference—that women were inferior drivers to men. Others acknowledged but rejected that difference. Both types of opinions examined numerous doctrinal possibilities for the role gender should play but settled on none of them, showing that a particular shared understanding about gender could not answer the question of *how* gender should bear on the injured female tort plaintiff's right to recover.

In the second set of cases, women were injured as passengers in cars and wagons, usually when their husbands were driving. The opinions establish that judges' views of the gendered relationship of wife to husband were of central analytic importance to their legal assessments of a woman's right to recover against a third party who caused an accident. Although the cases display a relatively unchanging construction and presentation of the marital relationship—assigning the wife, at least in the public space of the roads, to a role subordinate to her husband's—between 1860 and 1930 the legal consequence of this assignment underwent a complete inversion. In the early part of the period, courts concluded from women's subordinate position in marriage that a female passenger could not recover against a third party if her husband's driving had negligently contributed to the accident. Around 1900, however, the results shifted, and courts concluded from the same subordination that a female passenger *could* recover in the same circumstances.

The most important point demonstrated here is that even a shared vision of actual and appropriate gender roles and abilities does not dictate case outcomes. Although the cases do evince judges' shared understanding that wives had less authority than husbands and, nearly as consistently, that women lacked competence in the public sphere of transportation, this chapter's presentation of the interplay of tort doctrine and ideas about gender demonstrates that judges varied enormously in their views of the difference gender should make for tort law.

Women Drivers

Late-nineteenth and early-twentieth-century women were more likely to ride in cars than to drive them. Nonetheless, there were female drivers, and they were sometimes injured in accidents. In the late nineteenth century resulting court opinions occasionally discussed gender, expressing a shared sense that women were not as capable drivers as men. A range of doctrinal options existed for a court confronting an accident involving a female driver and a claim that gender difference was relevant: women might be bound to take more care to compensate for their lack of skill; women might be held to commit contributory negligence simply by driving; women might be held to a standard of care that referenced only other women drivers (in practice, then, their perceived lesser skill could excuse what otherwise might be contributory negligence) or to a male standard of care or to a bi-gender standard of care; and defendants might be required to take more care to accommodate women's needs as drivers. There are opinions weighing each of these options, but no one approach appears to have prevailed. These cases demonstrate that even when courts share a view that women's abilities are not as developed as men's, gender politics can intertwine with doctrine in complex ways that produce varied approaches.

An 1860 Connecticut case provides an early example of the assumption that women were bad drivers, and how that assumption could operate within a personal injury case. In *Fox v. Town of Glastenbury*, the estate of Harriet Fox sued the town, arguing that the accident in which she died was caused by the town's failure to maintain a railing along the sides of a causeway. The jury had rendered a plaintiff's verdict, but the state supreme court vacated and remanded for a new trial, holding that although the town's failure to maintain a railing along the causeway was indeed negligence, Fox's attempt to pass across the causeway was contributory negligence. The court stated that "we think no person of ordinary discretion in their circumstances, and exercising ordinary prudence and discretion, would have made such attempt." This is a linguistically gender-neutral standard of care. But the court continued:

We are not unmindful of the fact urged upon our attention by the plaintiff's counsel, that these travelers were females. And in that fact, and in the timidity, inexperience, and want of skill which it implies, we can find an explanation of their injudicious and fatal attempt to turn around in the water, but no reason or excuse for the recklessness of their conduct in driving into it.

The court concluded: "if men of ordinary prudence and discretion would regard the ability of the party inadequate for the purpose without hazard or danger, the risk should not be assumed."[9]

It seems that in *Fox* the reviewing court merged two questions together: What would a reasonable person do, and what would a reasonable man expect the plaintiff to do? The opinion's "men of ordinary prudence and discretion" function not as models setting the standard for accident-avoidance, but as jury/blame-assessors. Thus members of the all-male jury are excused from deciding whether they themselves would have crossed the causeway. They are told, instead, to recall that women are bad drivers and to decide whether a woman driver should have crossed. To *neglect* to consider gender as a factor counting against the plaintiff is deemed inappropriate.

Other courts, however, took a more moderate approach. In *Daniels v. Clegg*, in 1873, as in *Fox*, the court believed that female sex equated to lack of driving skill but announced that femaleness could excuse lack of skill. Richard Clegg sued Calvin Daniels to recover the damage to his horse and buggy when Daniels collided with Clegg's daughter, who was driving. She was twenty years old and was driving quite fast, downhill, "being in great haste to find her father on account of the dangerous illness of a sister." After a jury verdict for Clegg, Daniels appealed, contesting several of the charges to the jury. The court had charged the jury that:

> In deciding whether the plaintiff's daughter exercised ordinary care in driving the horse, or was guilty of [contributory] negligence, the jury should consider the age of the daughter, and the fact that she was a woman. . . . [S]he would not be guilty of negligence if she used that degree of care that a person of her age and sex would ordinarily use.

The Michigan Supreme Court approved the charge as ultimately given, commenting:

> No one would ordinarily expect, and the defendant had no right to expect, from a young woman thus situated, the same amount of knowledge, skill,

dexterity, steadiness of nerve, or coolness of judgment, in short the same degree of competency, which he would expect of ordinary men under like circumstances; nor, consequently, would it be just to hold her to the same high degree of care and skill. The incompetency indicated by her age or sex—without evidence (of which there is none) of any unusual skill or experience on her part—was less in degree, it is true, than in the case of a mere child; but the difference is in degree only, and not in principle.[10]

Again, the injured female, at age twenty, a legal minor, is like a child; but this time she wins her suit rather than loses by that fact.

Tort law could have responded to perceptions of feminine incompetence with an onerous doctrinal rule that women committed contributory negligence as a matter of law simply by driving. This would have been enforcement of separate spheres ideology with a vengeance. But only one case was found that even urged such an approach, and the 1837 Maine Supreme Judicial Court there rejected the defendant's argument, holding, "There is no doubt but a woman may be permitted to drive a well broken horse, without any violation of common prudence."[11] Indeed, most opinions refused to ratify any notion that women and men made up different communities of drivers, whose conduct tort law should acknowledge as categorically different. In *Tucker v. Henniker*, the New Hampshire Supreme Court insisted that women were part of a bi-gender community of drivers by reference to which the ordinary standard of care was set. The plaintiff, injured while driving a horse and carriage, sued the town, arguing that defects in the repair of the road caused her accident. The town, in turn, accused her of contributory negligence. In the trial court, the jury had been instructed that the plaintiff was "bound to exercise ordinary care, skill and prudence in managing [her] horse, such care, skill and prudence as ordinary persons like herself were accustomed to exercise in managing their horses."

The New Hampshire Supreme Court reversed the plaintiff's verdict and remanded for a new trial, holding that the jury might have been misled into thinking that the phrase "ordinary persons like herself" meant that the plaintiff was to be held to a standard of care set by comparison to women, rather than the entire community. The court explained:

In a country where women are accustomed, as among us, to drive horses and carriages, there can be no doubt that the degree of care, skill and prudence required of a woman in managing her horse would be precisely that degree of care, skill and prudence which persons of common prudence, or mankind in general, usually exercise . . . in the management of the horses driven by them. Now the language of the charge in the court below might be construed as making the average care, skill and prudence of women in managing horses, instead of the average care, skill and prudence of mankind generally, including all those accustomed to manage horses, whether men or women, boys or girls, the standard. . . . As it may be doubtful whether this average would be higher or lower than that of mankind in general, and as it is not the precise standard prescribed by the law, and the jury may possibly have been misled by it, the instructions must be held to have been erroneous on this point.[12]

Although the opinions just discussed offered these varied analyses of gender's impact in women drivers cases, judges in such cases did not invariably address gender at all. This was probably not because late-nineteenth-century courts failed to consider the possibility of discussing gender in these circumstances. The cases discussed above were well known and frequently listed in treatises under gendered headings,[13] so the gender issues they raised were familiar to contemporaries. However, the cases' analyses of gender were rarely cited in other opinions. Moreover, as the twentieth century progressed, judges deciding woman-driver cases ceased addressing gender, whether the woman was driving a car or a horse-drawn vehicle. Again, and for the same reasons, it likely was not a case of unconscious erasure of gender but rather a considered decision not to include it expressly in the analysis. Perhaps the gendered analysis was unattractive because it was so inconclusive. Or perhaps the assumption of lesser feminine competence faded somewhat as horse-drawn vehicles were replaced by motorized ones.[14] Or perhaps the factual predicate of the cases became less frequent because many fewer women drove the early cars, which were difficult and dirty to start, than had driven horse-drawn vehicles.

Where courts *did* choose to address gender, the range of approaches taken in the women drivers cases shows that to know that courts considered gender important in a certain context—even when the reason gender was at issue was somewhat disrespectful of women's equality such as the assumption that women are bad drivers—is to know very little. When women were injured while they were driving, the category of cases was small enough, and the doctrinal possibilities wide enough, that the opinions do not yield a definitive approach. Rather, the cases highlight the pressure points of tort doctrine's interaction with gender, and reveal that those pressure points are not modern inventions.

Husband Drivers, Women Passengers

When the driver of a car involved in an accident was the passenger's husband, the issue frequently arose whether the husband's alleged contributory negligence should be "imputed" to his wife. As this section describes, before 1890 or 1900 the contributory negligence of a husband-driver typically was imputed to his wife-passenger, because she was subject to his control. Beginning about the turn of the century, however, the same ideas about marital hierarchy led to the precisely opposite results. Courts began to apply the nonmarital law of agency and to hold that because a wife did not have the right to control her husband, she was not responsible for his contributory negligence.

The doctrine of "imputed negligence" originated in the 1849 British case of *Thorogood v. Bryan*, a tort action seeking damages for the death of a man who had just gotten off one omnibus and was run over by another. The defendant was the owner of the second omnibus, who argued that the operator of the first omnibus should not have let off passengers at the point where it stopped and that his negligence in doing so should bar the action. The Court of Common Pleas agreed, attributing the contributory negligence of the first omnibus operator to the decedent passenger and reversing the plaintiff's jury verdict.[15] In its original application, assigning a common carrier's negligence to its passenger, most American courts were not receptive to the *Thorogood* imputed negligence rule.[16]

But while American courts became reluctant to uphold a fictitious identification of the passenger with the driver or conductor of a common carrier, for some years they were more willing to merge the identities of a wife-passenger and her husband-driver. Courts found support in the authoritative *Shearman and Redfield on Negligence,* which stated in its first edition, in 1869, that although "a passenger in a public conveyance . . . is not precluded from recovering" because of the contributory negligence of the driver of that conveyance, the rule was the reverse "where a wife suffers an injury while under the immediate care of her husband."[17] The treatise offered no explanation and ignored the fact that in the only case it cited, *Carlisle v. Town of Sheldon,*[18] the Vermont Supreme Court had expressly stated that there was "nothing in the marital relation" contributing to its analysis; the same result would obtain, said the court, for any passenger and any driver.

Nonetheless, a number of other courts agreed with *Shearman and Redfield* that a wife driven by her husband differed somehow from a passenger in other circumstances. In a few cases, courts analyzed this not as a question of *imputed* negligence at all but rather as a concomitant of coverture, which had "for centuries [given] husbands rights in their wives' property and earnings, and prohibited wives from contracting, filing suit, drafting wills, or holding property in their own names."[19] The husband's contributory negligence barred *his* action for personal injury to his wife; under coverture, she herself had no right to sue. Usually, however, courts in husband-driver/wife-passenger cases did not explicitly rely on the common law of coverture. Indeed, they could not, because most of the cases discussing the issue were decided *after* the passage of marital status reform statutes allowing women to hold separate property and bring their own lawsuits.[20] More typical was the analysis in an 1877 Illinois case, in which the court commented that because "plaintiff placed herself in the care of her husband, and submitted her personal safety to his keeping," any negligence on his part would be imputed to her.[21]

This "placing in the care" language does not, facially, explain why wives and husbands have any different relation for tort purposes than do passengers and common carriers. After all, the passenger on a train relies on the care of the conductor. Yet these decisions imputing the contributory negligence of a husband-driver to his wife-passenger were, generally, rendered despite the courts' simultaneous rejection of the *Thorogood* rule. The question is why. The exploration of the topic of imputed negligence found in a jury charge in an 1891 federal case provides some insight. The case concerned two adult siblings, driving together, who were in an accident; the sister-passenger was killed, and the question was whether the contributory negligence of the brother-driver would be imputed to her. The judge explained to the jury that no such imputed negligence would be allowed, and he contrasted the situation, in dicta, to the imputation of the contributory negligence of a husband to his wife, and other like circumstances:

> Now, there are certain circumstances, gentlemen, in which as a matter of law the negligence of a driver of a carriage . . . may be imputed to another person who occupies the vehicle with him; as, for instance, a father is driving, and has a child in the carriage, or a husband is driving, and has his wife there with him, or a guardian is driving with a ward that he has under his care. . . . [B]ecause . . . the one controls the other, and where ordinarily . . . we recognize the fact that the one trusts the other, and relies upon the other for protection; that is, a husband exercises protection, and the wife looks to the husband for protection.[22]

The charge indicates that when some courts said that a woman had "placed herself in the care of her husband," they meant far more than that she had trusted him to drive her safely, the meaning of the phrase for *Thorogood*. The phrase appears, instead, to have encapsulated the same theory of marriage that underlay the superseded common law doctrine of coverture. Indeed, Blackstone's 1765 explanation of coverture used language quite similar to this federal jury charge: "The husband and wife are one person in law [and] the very being or legal existence of the woman is suspended during the marriage, or at least is incorporated and consolidated into that of the husband, under whose wing, protection, and cover, she performs everything."[23]

In sum, in the earliest cases involving the contributory negligence of a husband-driver and his wife-passenger, the husband's negligence was frequently imputed to his wife, for the stated reason that she was subject to his control. The most persuasive explanation of the doctrine is that, although the rule was announced, technically, after the end of coverture, it drew on the common law understanding of marital status which subsumed wives' identities in the identities of their husbands.

But this early majority rule was quickly reversed, beginning in the 1890s.[24] Two historical developments are relevant to this reversal. The first was the growing impact of the Married Women's Property Acts enacted earlier. Both contemporary and modern observers have commented on the gradual expanding effect of coverture's end.[25] As Clare Dalton has commented, the logic of the Acts, if not precisely their language, undermined "the 'marital unity' ideology, endowing women with legal personality and capacity, and thereby recognizing their individuality."[26] Simultaneous non-doctrinal changes reinforced the point, as women undertook a variety of political campaigns for women's welfare,[27] and most pertinently for suffrage, emphasizing that their interests were not adequately represented by their husband's vote.[28] It seems likely that over time judges grew to understand and apply that logic to accident cases involving husband-drivers and wife-passengers. Indeed, one 1894 Georgia case acknowledged as much. The court cited the abundant authority for imputing a husband-driver's negligence to his wife-passenger but rejected the rule, commenting that, under Georgia law, she had a right to recover damages, which became her "separate and individual property, not subject to any debt or liability of the husband." The court called "indefensible" the "doctrine . . . that . . . would seek to charge a wife with the negligence of her husband simply because of the marital relation existing between the two," and emphasized that "the wife has distinct, individual legal rights."[29]

Growing juridical separation of husbands and wives created a kind of doctrinal vacuum in areas where decision rules had previously been based on marital merger. In the area considered here, a "control test" lifted from other areas of tort law promptly filled that vacuum. In the nineteenth century the rule of *respondeat superior* dictated that a "master" (i.e., employer) would be held responsible in tort for the negligent act committed by its "servant" (i.e., employee). Hirers of independent contractors, however, were not responsible for negligent acts committed by the contractors. The common law test that evolved to distinguish employees from independent contractors focused on whether the alleged employer had the right to control the alleged employee. Use of a "control test" to distinguish "servants" from "contractors" was announced in both the United States and Britain by 1850, but the test gained wide currency only in the following decades.[30] In the same time frame the right to control also became dispositive of liability under the law of the "joint enterprise," under which persons with joint rights of control over an instrumentality of harm are jointly liable for any harm caused by either of them.[31]

These doctrinal developments—by which one party answered for a second party's negligence only if the first party had a right to control the second's actions—took place in industrial contexts, with little similarity to the cases discussed here. In those settings the person or entity that was potentially vicariously liable was generally a defendant, not a plaintiff. Accordingly, the boundary on vicarious liability imposed by these rules generally worked to *limit* compensation to accident victims. But as the rules became dogmas of tort law rather than novel doctrines with limited application, courts began following their logic in nonindustrial settings as well, and the outcomes in the wife-passenger cases began to shift in favor of the female accident victims. As early as the 1890s,[32] and overwhelmingly in the first decades of the twentieth century,[33] courts found it no longer sufficient for defendants to argue that the negligence of the husband should be imputed to the wife by reason of the marital relation. Using either doctrinal label—*respondeat superior* or joint enterprise—the crucial issue for assessing liability was whether the injured passenger had the right to control the driver. If she did, then any contributory negligence of the driver would be imputed to her. Thus defendants accused of negligently causing injury to a wife-passenger, and seeking to avoid liability by accusing her of contributory negligence, now had to contradict contemporary gender norms and argue that the wife was the "master" of the "servant" husband or that they were engaged in a joint enterprise. As summarized in one court: "The negligence of the husband is not to be imputed to the wife unless he is her agent in the matter in hand, or they are jointly engaged in the prosecution of a common enterprise."[34] Another court emphasized the role of control: "Negligence on the part of a husband in driving an automobile, therefore, cannot be imputed to his wife who is riding with him, unless the parties are engaged in an enterprise giving the wife the power and duty to direct or to assist in the operation and management of the car."[35]

Doctrinally, then, the consequence of an unchanging understanding of the marital relationship was thus inverted. Where earlier the rationale for imputing a husband's negligence to his wife had been the wife's lack of control, now that very lack of control allowed her to win her case.

Courts implementing these doctrinal changes described very different types of moral intuitions than the courts that had held women to their husbands' care. In the very earliest case that refused to impute a husband's negligence to his wife, the court commented: "In our opinion, there would be no more reason or justice in a rule that would, in cases of this character, inflict upon a wife the consequences of her husband's negligence, solely and alone because of that relationship, than to hold her accountable at the bar of eternal justice for his sins because she was his wife."[36]

Success for defendants under the new doctrinal categories appears to have been rare, because it took unusual circumstances to create a joint enterprise. In a 1921 Wisconsin case, for example, the court stated: "In one sense husbands and wives in their journey through life are always engaged in joint enterprises, sometimes successful, sometimes disastrous. But the mere fact that they travel in the same car . . . does not constitute a joint enterprise within the meaning of the rule under decision."[37] But even though they had grown to recognize women's individuality, courts did not alter their views of women's limited authority. Judges simply were reluctant to entertain the idea that a wife controlled her husband, or at least his driving. The ideological component of such reluctance was brought out in an 1897 Kansas case:

> Say what we may in advocacy of the civil and political equality of the sexes, there are conditions of inequality between the same in other respects which the law recognizes, and out of which grow differing rights and liabilities. . . . By the universal sense of mankind, a privilege of management, a superiority of control, a right of mastery . . . is accorded to the husband, which forbids the idea of a co-ordinate authority, much less a supremacy of command in the wife. His physical strength and dexterity are greater; his knowledge, judgment, and discretion assumed to be greater; all sentiments and instincts of manhood and chivalry impose upon him the obligation to care for and protect his weaker and confiding companion; and all these justify the assumption by him of the labors and responsibilities of the journey, with their accompanying rights of direction and control.[38]

Even without this kind of express substantive theory of the proper relationship between husband and wife, the courts sometimes simply acted on their perception of social reality. For example, the Kansas Supreme Court said, in 1913:

> Common sense would dictate that when a wife goes riding with her children in a rig driven by her husband, she rightfully relies on him not to drive so as to imperil those in his charge. The law does not depart from common sense by requiring her under the circumstances shown here to impugn her husband's ability to drive and assume the prerogative to dictate to him the manner of driving. With one child on her lap, and another sitting next to look after, she might with human and legal fairness and propriety leave the driving in the exclusive care of the husband and father. . . . She frankly testified that she was "scrooched down," holding her baby, and "gawking around at things."[39]

Courts, then, refused to punish women passengers for acting as gender norms dictated, and leaving the responsibility for safe driving to their husbands.

Cases involving accidents that occurred where a wife was driving a car owned by her husband-passenger underscore the gendered nature of this analysis. A husband's car ownership, unlike a wife's,[40] seems invariably to have ensured that any contributory negligence his wife committed would be imputed to him. That the wife had direct control over the wheel simply did not suffice to outweigh the ideological imperative of male control. Thus, in 1923, the Arkansas Supreme Court held that the plaintiff's wife's negligence in driving his car would be imputed to him, because he "owned the automobile, and was in no sense a guest of his wife, so he had control, along with his wife, over the movements of the car."[41] The Kentucky Court of Appeals agreed, in a case in which the plaintiff, "who had been an invalid for some time, was riding in his automobile with his wife who was operating the machine." The court held that her contributory negligence was imputable to him, because she was "his agent in the operation of his automobile at the time of the collision."[42] Indeed, the same rule applied against a husband-owner when he was not even in the car, so long as he had authorized its use by his wife.[43]

Although the contributory negligence of a husband-driver was not generally imputable to his wife-passenger by 1890–1900, the issue of contributory negligence remained present. In cases involving husbands and wives, and other female passengers and male drivers, juries were asked to evaluate the passenger's actions to see if she had exercised ordinary care. This judgment, too, was imbued with gender-specific realities and assumptions. In order to recover, an injured woman had to negotiate a tricky rhetorical path. First she had to claim that she was not in control of the car, because that might suggest a joint enterprise or agency relationship and accordingly defeat recovery. At the same time, if she asserted too vehemently her own lack of control, she risked being judged to have trusted so completely to the care of the man driving as to constitute contributory negligence. The idea that a woman-passenger could be found guilty of contributory negligence for relying on her husband to take care acted as a check on the new recognition of wives' agency. In effect, a wife could forfeit her new legal claim to individuality by a complete failure to guard her own safety.[44]

More often, however, courts in female-passenger cases featured the rule that "the same degree of care is not required of a passenger riding in an automobile as is required of the driver of the car."[45] Occasionally courts made explicit the precise role that gender played in such cases. In an 1897 federal case involving a female passenger in a hack, the trial court, later affirmed on appeal, charged the jury:

> I am inclined to think that, if this plaintiff were a man suing for a recovery, I should be constrained to advise you that he could be no more relieved from the duty of looking out for the train than the driver of the wagon; but this plaintiff being a woman, a person who is not accustomed, or very much accustomed, to such places, and to going in this fashion from one depot to another, I think it is a matter fairly for your consideration whether she used the care and diligence which should be expected of a person in her situation, in going across this road.[46]

This case makes explicit the judicial expectation of women's cession of public spaces to men, and how such expectation influenced the analysis of contributory negligence.[47] Such cases etched the gendered ideology of separate spheres and the masculinization of public spaces into the law of personal injury in a way that benefited the actual female accident victims, making their compensation more likely.

Conclusion

This chapter has examined, in some detail, reported court opinions between 1860 and 1930 involving women injured in car and wagon accidents. The opinions show that common law courts, far from naively erasing gender by subsuming women into the male category of "reasonable men" or a purportedly neutral, but no less male, category of "reasonable persons," actually treated gender as an important factor in assessing appropriate standards of care, when perceived gender difference was highlighted. Ideas about women's autonomy and authority suffused judicial analyses of women's right to recover in tort. The opinions also establish the variety of responses available and taken even by jurists who shared a view of women's lesser authority and competence in the realm of marriage and transportation. The role of gender in these cases was not only unhidden, it was complex and mediated by other tort doctrines. Moving from the descriptive and historical to the normative, it is tempting—but unfair—to give these cases a failing feminist grade, concluding that they implemented an anti-female ideology of women's subordinate position in marriage and, more generally, in society. True, to acknowledge women's lesser authority or capability and embody that acknowledgment in, for example, a jury instruction could be seen as reinforcing a coercive and subordinating hierarchy by rewarding an accident victim's compliance with it. The accusation has particular force for the opinions that exhibited their authors' particular relish in women's subordinate role. But a more appropriate evaluation emphasizes that judicial refusal to recognize the social and ideological reality of women's lesser authority or skill would have imposed an unduly high standard of self-care on women—a standard that would have required them to rebel against the gender role strictures of society. Rather than coercing compliance with gender norms, the recognition of women's subordinate role simply avoided punishing individual accident victims for such compliance.

NOTES

1. This chapter is based on the much longer treatment in Margo Schlanger, *Injured Women before Common Law Courts, 1860–1930*, 21 Harv. Women's L.J. 79 (1998), which includes a third category of opinions involving cases of women injured while getting on and off trains.

2. Oliver Wendell Holmes Jr., The Common Law 86–89 (1881) (1963).

3. 132 Eng. Rep. 490 (C.P. 1837) (Tindal, C.J.).

4. Leslie Bender, *A Lawyer's Primer on Feminist Theory and Tort*, 38 J. Legal Educ. 3, 22 (1988); *see also, e.g.*, Robin L. West, *Relativism, Objectivity, and Law*, 99 Yale L.J. 1473, 1491 (1990).

5. Barbara Young Welke, Recasting American Liberty: Gender, Race, Law, and the Railroad Revolution, 1865–1920, at 96 (2001). I have argued with Welke's specific interpretation of opinions involving women injured getting on and off trains, in Schlanger, *Injured Women before Common Law Courts*, supra.

6. *See, e.g.*, Mary Ryan, Womanhood in America: From Colonial Times to the Present 113–19, 252 (3d ed. 1983); Linda K. Kerber, *Separate Spheres, Female Worlds, Woman's Place: The Rhetoric of Women's History*, 75 J. Am. Hist. 9 (1988).

7. *See, e.g.*, Virginia Scharff, Taking the Wheel: Women and the Coming of the Motor Age 1–7 (1991).

8. *See* Carol Sanger, *Girls and the Getaway: Cars, Culture, and the Predicament of Gendered Space*, 144 U. Pa. L. Rev. 705, 711 (1995); Patricia Cline Cohen, *Safety and Danger: Women on American Public Transport, 1750–1850, in* Gendered Domains: Rethinking Public and Private in Women's History 109 (Dorothy O. Helly & Susan M. Reverby eds. 1992).

9. 29 Conn. 204, 208–9 (1860).

10. 28 Mich. 32, 42 (1873).

11. 14 Me. 198, 199, 200 (1837).

12. 41 N.H. 317, 321–22 (1860).

13. *See, e.g.,* Charles Fisk Beach Jr., A Treatise on the Law of Contributory Negligence § 260, 391 (John J. Crawford ed., 3d ed. 1899); Seymour D. Thompson, 1 Commentaries on the Law of Negligence in All Relations §§ 319–320, 339 (2d ed. 1901).

14. Michael Berger, *Women Drivers: The Emergence of Folklore and Stereotypic Opinion Concerning Feminine Automotive Behavior*, 9 Women's Stud. Int'l Forum 257, 258 (1986).

15. 8 C.B. 115 (1848), *overruled by* Mills v. Armstrong (*The Bernina*), 12 P.D. 58, 13 App. Cas. 1. (1888).

16. *See* Chapman v. New Haven R.R., 19 N.Y. 341, 344 (1859); Little v. Hackett, 116 U.S. 366, 375 (1886). There were, however, scattered exceptions, chief among them Wisconsin and Montana (for a time), and Michigan (in non-common-carrier cases involving adults). For detailed discussions, see Schultz v. Old Colony St. Ry., 79 N.E. 873 (Mass. 1907); Cuddy v. Horn, 10 N.W. 32 (Mich. 1881); Mullen v. City of Owosso, 58 N.W. 663 (Mich. 1894); and Sherris v. Northern Pac. Ry., 175 P. 269 (Mont. 1918).

17. Thomas G. Shearman & Amasa Redfield, A Treatise on the Law of Negligence §46, 48–50 (1st ed. 1869).

18. 38 Vt. 440 (1866).

19. Reva B. Siegel, *The Modernization of Marital Status Law: Adjudicating Wives' Rights to Earnings, 1860–1930*, 82 Geo. L.J. 2127, 2127 (1994).

20. *See, e.g.,* Richard H. Chused, *Married Women's Property Law: 1800–1850*, 71 Geo. L.J. 1359 (1983).

21. City of Joliet v. Seward, 86 Ill. 402, 402–3 (1877); *see also, e.g.,* Yahn v. City of Ottumwa, 15 N.W. 257 (Iowa 1883); Nisbet v. Town of Garner, 39 N.W. 516, 517 (Iowa 1890); Gulf C. & S. F. Ry. v. Greenlee, 62 Tex. 344 (1884); Prideaux v. City of Mineral Point, 43 Wis. 513 (1878).

22. Lapsley v. Union Pac. R.R., 50 F. 172, 181 (C.C.N.D. Iowa 1891).

23. 1 William Blackstone, Commentaries on the Laws of England 442 (1765).

24. There was, however, no reversal in many community property states, where injured wife-passengers continued to be denied recovery for many years. *See, e.g.,* sources cited in Fleming James Jr., *Imputed Contributory Negligence*, 14 La. L. Rev. 340, 348 n.44 (1954).

25. The contemporary observation I have in mind is Letter from Elizabeth Cady Stanton to Gerrit Smith (Jan. 3, 1856), in Elizabeth Cady Stanton: As Revealed in Her Letters, Diary, and Reminiscences v. 2, 63 (Theodore Stanton and Harriot Stanton Blatch eds., 1969) (1922). I was alerted to this letter by Jacob Katz Cogan, Note, *The Look Within: Property, Capacity, and Suffrage in Nineteenth-Century America*, 107 Yale L.J. 473, 487 (1997). For examples of modern commentary, see, e.g., Reva B. Siegel, *"The Rule of Love": Wife Beating as Prerogative and Privacy*, 105 Yale L.J. 2117, 2142 (1996); Siegel, *Marital Status Law*, 2149–57; Bartrom v. Adjustment Bureau, Inc., 618 N.E.2d 1, 4 (Ind.

1993) ("[R]everberations from the lifting of coverture slowly resounded through the common law.").

26. Clare Dalton, *Domestic Violence, Domestic Torts and Divorce: Constraints and Possibilities*, 31 New Eng. L. Rev. 319, 327 (1997).

27. I thank an anonymous peer reviewer for emphasizing this point. *See, e.g.*, Kathryn Kish Sklar, Florence Kelley and the Nation's Work: The Rise of Women's Political Culture, 1830–1900 (1995).

28. *See* Eleanor Flexner and Ellen Fitzpatrick, Century of Struggle: The Woman's Rights Movement in the United States (1996).

29. Atlanta & C. Air-Line Ry. v. Gravitt, 20 S.E. 550, 556 (Ga. 1894).

30. *See* Shearman & Redfield, §§ 73–74, 76–79, 82–84, 85–92; Gerald M. Stevens, *The Test of the Employment Relation*, 38 Mich. L. Rev. 188, 189–94 (1939); Standard Oil Co. v. Anderson, 212 U.S. 215 (1909).

31. *See* Fleming James Jr., *Vicarious Liability*, 28 Tul. L. Rev. 161, 210–12 (1954), and sources there cited; Joseph Weintraub, *The Joint Enterprise Doctrine in Automobile Law*, 16 Cornell L.Q. 320 (1931); Gilbert K. Howard, Note, *Negligence—Driver's Negligence Imputed to Passenger in Suit by Third Party*, 1 Baylor L. Rev. 492 (1948–49).

32. Louisville, N. A. & C. Ry. v. Creek, 29 N.E. 481 (Ind. 1892); Reading Township v. Telfer, 48 P. 134 (Kan. 1897); Finley v. Chicago, M. & St. P. Ry., 74 N.W. 174, 174 (Minn. 1898).

33. As late as 1933 the issue was sufficiently live for the Supreme Court to treat the rule as open to question. *See* Miller v. Union Pac. R.R., 290 U.S. 227, 232 (1933).

34. Phillips v. Denver City Tramway Co., 128 P. 460, 464 (Colo. 1912).

35. Stevens v. Luther, 180 N.W. 87, 87 (Neb. 1920).

36. Louisville, N.A. & C. Ry. v. Creek, 29 N.E. 481, 482 (Ind. 1892).

37. Brubaker v. Iowa County, 183 N.W. 690, 692 (Wis. 1921).

38. Reading Township v. Telfer, 48 P. 134, 136 (Kan. 1897).

39. Williams v. Withington, 129 P. 1148, 1149–50 (Kan. 1913).

40. *See, e.g.*, Lucey v. Allen, 117 A. 539 (R.I. 1922); Southern Ry. v. Priester, 289 F. 945 (4th Cir. 1923); Virginia Ry. & Power v. Gorsuch, 91 S.E. 632, 633, 634 (Va. 1917).

41. Wisconsin & Arkansas Lumber v. Brady, 248 S.W. 278, 280 (Ark. 1923).

42. Standard Oil Co. of Kentucky v. Thompson, 226 S.W. 368, 369, 379 (Ky. 1920); *see also* Gochee v. Wagner, 178 N.E. 553 (N.Y. 1931).

43. Stickney v. Epstein, 123 A. 1, 4 (Conn. 1923).

44. *See, e.g.*, Fogg v. New York, N. H. & H. R.R., 111 N.E. 960, 962 (Mass. 1916); Whitman v. Fisher, 57 A. 895 (Me. 1904).

45. Waring v. Dubuque Elec., 186 N.W. 42, 43 (Iowa 1922) (per curiam).

46. Denver & R. G. R.R. v. Lorentzen, 79 F. 291, 292–93 (8th Cir. 1897).

47. *See also, e.g.*, Corn v. Kansas City C. C. & St. J. Ry., 228 S.W. 78, 82 (Mo. 1920); Denton v. Missouri, K. & T. Ry., 155 P. 812, 813 (Kan. 1916).

3

Expatriation by Marriage

The Case of Asian American Women

LETI VOLPP

In the United States the ritual of marriage is generally thought to reflect as well as enact citizenship. Indeed, it is precisely this positive relationship between marriage and citizenship that explains why marriage continues to be heterosexually policed. But marriage has not always served as a citizenship enacting institution. Marriage has also functioned to divest women from their citizenship. Feminist historians have written important work exploring the little-known fact that American women lost their citizenship for nothing more than marriage.[1] This chapter focuses that discussion upon Chinese and Chinese American women, to show how race unevenly shaped the gendered laws of citizenship.

Consider the story of Ng Fung Sing. Born in Port Ludlow, Washington, in October 1898 to Chinese parents, Sing was a U.S. citizen thanks to the U.S. Supreme Court's decision in *United States v. Wong Kim Ark*,[2] which held that under the Fourteenth Amendment of the U.S. Constitution Chinese born in the United States were entitled to birthright citizenship. At the age of five, Sing was taken by her parents to China, where, at the age of twenty-two, she married a Chinese citizen. After her husband passed away, Sing decided to return to the United States. When she arrived in Seattle in April 1925, she assumed she could, in the words of the Washington district court, "resume her 'American citizenship.'"[3]

But Sing was denied admission to the United States and found "ineligible for citizenship." Her marriage had divested Sing of her U.S. citizenship. Congress, in 1907, had mandated that any "American woman who marries a foreigner shall take the nationality of her husband."[4] Although the Cable Act of 1922 allowed some women who had lost their U.S. citizenship through marriage to rejoin the American body politic through naturalization, only women who themselves were "eligible to citizenship" were allowed to do so.[5] Although the court recognized that Sing "politically . . . was born a member of the citizenry of the United States," it noted that Sing was "Chinese" or, as the court clarified, of "yellow race." As such, Sing was barred from naturalization, since racial restrictions that remained in place until the mid-twentieth century prohibited Asians from naturalizing as U.S. citizens. Moreover, Sing was not permitted to enter the country; as a person of Chinese ancestry, she was also subject to immigration exclusion laws. If Sing had been white, she could have naturalized following widowhood; however, as a person of Chinese descent, she was precluded from doing so. Presumably Sing returned to China. The rest of her life is lost to history.

Legal history is often told as a story of the law acting upon people. But the cases here tell the story of women acting—taking pen in hand to inquire about their status, mounting legal challenges, and fighting to change the laws of marital expatriation. Their struggles afford insights into the way that gender and race together have shaped the legal concept of citizenship.

Race and Citizenship

Racial exclusion has constitutively shaped the acquisition of the legal status of citizen in the United States, whether granted through birth or through naturalization. The first federal citizenship statute, which Congress passed in 1790, limited naturalization to "free white" aliens.[6] This was amended after the Civil War to additionally permit naturalization of "aliens of African nativity or African descent."[7]

In 1878 a male Chinese national named Ah Yup brought the first case seeking to naturalize under the statute. The court denied his claim and held that the statute did not permit the naturalization of a member of the "Mongolian race."[8] The 1882 Chinese Exclusion Act subsequently contained a provision explicitly barring any state or federal court from allowing Chinese to naturalize as U.S. citizens. While Chinese were statutorily barred from naturalization, the ability of other nonwhites to naturalize was an open question and could be litigated in the courts. In 1923 the Supreme Court ruled twice on the matter within four months, first denying the naturalization of the Japanese-born Takao Ozawa, under the rationale that he was not "Caucasian."[9] Later that year the Court refused to authenticate the naturalization of the Punjabi Sikh Bhagat Singh Thind, who, according to the Court, was "Caucasian" but still failed to be "white."[10] Racial restrictions on naturalization were only selectively lifted in the twentieth century, starting in 1943 for Chinese, in 1946 in the case of Filipinos and Indians, in 1950 for Guamians, and in 1952 for everyone regardless of racial classification.

Racial exclusion was not only codified in the laws governing naturaliza-tion. The United States deviated from the common law rules inherited from England regarding birthright citizenship based on territory, since not all per-sons born in the United States were deemed citizens. Chief Justice Taney's opinion in *Dred Scott v. Sanford*[11] achieved this result in holding that free blacks born in the United States were not citizens. The first sentence of the Fourteenth Amendment was written to reject Taney's judgment. It provides that "all persons born or naturalized in the United States, and subject to the jurisdiction thereof, are citizens of the United States and of the State wherein they reside."[12] Racial exclusion of the Chinese was lifted, in a limited sense, by the Supreme Court's 1898 decision in *Wong Kim Ark*, which held that Chinese born in the United States were entitled to birthright citizenship.[13] Following the decision, immigrant inspectors required Chinese claiming citizenship, on return from overseas, to prove their "Americanness" through their familiarity with American geography and history, their adoption of American customs and dress, their English-language skills, and the attesta-tion of white witnesses to verify their claims.[14]

Americanization

Gender and Citizenship

During this same period the relationship between the formal legal status of citizenship and gender was shifting. At the advent of the republic and through the first half of the nineteenth century, the nationality of white women was not directly affected by marriage or coverture.[15] A white woman who immi-grated to the United States could naturalize to become a citizen, and marriage to a noncitizen did not deprive a female U.S. citizen of her citizenship.

But the relationship between marriage and nationality abruptly changed in 1855, when Congress passed a statute granting U.S. citizenship to any woman who had married or would marry a man who was a U.S. citizen. This enact-ment followed the logic of dependent citizenship: that all members of a family should have the same nationality, as led by the husband,[16] and upon the notion of coverture implicit in that idea.[17] Coverture transformed a married woman into a dependent, transferring to her husband her property and income.[18] One congressional sponsor of the 1855 Act, Francis Cutting of New York, asserted that "by the act of marriage itself the political character of the wife shall at once conform to the political character of the husband."[19] Thus marriage to a U.S. citizen husband was an act of political consent to the U.S. nation-state.

For many years after 1855 noncitizen women who married U.S. citizens acquired U.S. citizenship. However, these rules did not apply to women subject to the racial bars to naturalization. The 1855 law carefully included the proviso that the only women who could become citizens through marriage were those "who might lawfully be naturalized under existing laws."[20] This meant that until 1870—the year that the racial bar on naturalization was lifted for those "of African descent or nativity"—the only wives welcomed into the American polity were free white wives. The 1898 case of *Broadis v. Broadis* recognized the U.S. citizenship of Ellen Maria Broadis, who was "of African descent," through her marriage to her husband, James Broadis, described by the court as "a Negro, having been at one time a slave" and a U.S. citizen.[21] Although the court noted that it was unclear whether Ellen Broadis was born in Maine or Canada, it held that she was a citizen of the United States by virtue of the fact that she was married to a U.S. citizen. As the court wrote, "the political status of her husband was impressed upon her."

In 1888 Congress enacted legislation providing that American Indian women marrying U.S. citizens would thereafter acquire citizenship through marriage.[22] However, Asian women were still precluded from citizenship. The Supreme Court so held, in 1912, in *Low Wah Suey v. Backus*. Li Sim, married to a "Chinaman of American birth" with whom she had a child, could not naturalize, as she was a "Chinese person not born in this country." As a consequence of her lack of citizenship, she remained an alien and subject to deportation after she was found in a brothel. The Supreme Court rationalized the decision to deport her, writing that if Li Sim had engaged in "proper conduct," she would not have found herself in this situation, which was "of her own making."[23]

Congress extended the logic of dependent citizenship in the Expatriation Act of 1907 to U.S. citizen women who married foreign husbands. Because courts had determined that a wife took the nationality of her husband, U.S. citizen women—of any race—who married noncitizen men were stripped of their citizenship.[24] Thus the Expatriation Act created a striking gender disparity. When male U.S. citizens married foreign-born wives, their wives were welcomed into the national body, unless these women were racially barred from doing so. Meanwhile, female U.S. citizens who married foreign-born husbands were expelled from the nation.

Marital expatriation may have been designed to punish U.S. citizen women who married wealthy foreigners in order to "chase titles." In fact, the Expatriation Act was sometimes referred to as the "Gigolo Act,"[25] and one member of Congress charged that women who "married foreign dukes and counts . . . when there are enough Americans for them to select from" had only themselves to blame for their loss of citizenship.[26] But the impact of the Expatriation Act extended well beyond women of this social class.

The consequences of lack of citizenship bear explication. For women seeking admission to the United States, the lack of citizenship subjected them to grounds of exclusion (popular grounds of exclusion targeting noncitizen women were that they carried contagious diseases, engaged in prostitution, and were considered likely to become a public charge). Women already within the United States could be threatened with deportation as well. Women who lost citizenship also lost the ability to confer derivative citizenship to any children born outside the United States. In locations where women had voting privileges they lost that right. In addition, alien status prohibited the ownership of property in many states.

The constitutionality of marital expatriation was challenged before the Supreme Court by Ethel Mackenzie, a wealthy San Francisco suffragist, born in California, who had married the Scottish opera singer Gordon Mackenzie in 1909. When Mackenzie attempted to vote in 1913, her registration was refused by the Board of Election Commissioners of San Francisco on the ground that she had become a subject of Great Britain through marriage. Despite her argument that her citizenship was an incident to her birth and was a right, privilege, and immunity that could not be taken away from her other than as punishment for a crime, or through voluntary expatriation, the Court held, in *Mackenzie v. Hare,* that the language of the Expatriation Act was plain. The denial of her voter registration was upheld.[27]

Soon after the passage in 1920 of the Nineteenth Amendment granting women the right to vote,[28] the *Mackenzie* case led to significant suffragist activity on the question of expatriation. Newly enfranchised women voters focused great energy on the question of independent citizenship for married women. Both Republican and Democratic parties incorporated the concept of independent citizenship into their party platforms. This led Congress to pass the Cable Act of 1922, which partially repealed the 1907 Act.

The 1922 Cable Act

The Cable Act only ended the expatriation of white or black women married to white or black men; for these women, the Cable Act was a victory. Not so for Asian American women—or for any women married to "aliens ineligible to citizenship." In fact, for these women, the Cable Act was a defeat.

The Cable Act provided a means to restore citizenship to wives who had been expatriated, and it eliminated future marital expatriation for women so long as their husbands—and they themselves—were eligible to become citizens. In other words, the Cable Act allowed the white or black women who had been expatriated for marrying white or black noncitizen men to be re-naturalized. The Cable Act also guaranteed that any such future marriages would not lead to expatriation, unless such women chose formally to renounce their citizenship. These were the only positive effects of the Act. Its negative effects were manifold.

The legislation continued to take away U.S. citizenship from women who married a particular subset of noncitizen men. In fact, the Act went beyond the 1907 law in explicitly mandating such a loss of citizenship, stating that "any woman citizen who marries an alien ineligible to citizenship shall cease to be a citizen of the United States." Arguably women citizens of the United States most likely to marry Asian men were Asian American women owing both to the extralegal pressures against intermarriage and the legal prohibitions against it. But mixed marriages did exist, such as that between Mary Das, a Mayflower descendent, and Taraknath Das, probably the most prominent Indian independence activist in the United States.[29] He had naturalized successfully as a U.S. citizen in 1914, but this was revoked retroactively after the 1923 Supreme Court decision in *United States v. Thind*. Thus, suddenly, both Taraknath and Mary Das found themselves no longer U.S. citizens.[30] Her case was described in congressional testimony as follows:

One of these [Indian nationalists] has married an American wife . . . a member of an old American family from the South, of Revolutionary ancestry, a woman of wealth and prominence . . . . She married this particularly brilliant man because she is interested in the same line of work that he is. . . .

I found a letter . . . that the terrible blow had fallen, that this particular individual was likely to lose her American citizenship, that the Cable Act, which had passed unknown to this woman, had rendered her absolutely stateless. Because, under the system of Great Britain in her colonies she takes away citizenship from any one who applies for citizenship in another country; automatically they lose their British citizenship. . . .

She has no desire to divorce him to regain her citizenship, but she has the greatest desire to remain an American citizen. It has never been a question of title, or anything of that sort; she is one of the noblest of American citizens. . . .

She happens to live in a place where having lost her citizenship, it does not affect the holding of property. But there are other things that are very seriously menaced, particularly the humiliation and the thought of not being wanted as an American citizen.[31]

We can see here both the symbolic and practical implications of the loss of citizenship, as well as the strategic attempt to identify Mary Das as one who should be considered at the core of citizenship (an old American family from the South, of Revolutionary ancestry) and thus one whose expatriation would most shock the listener.

Emily L. Chinn was another white woman who faced expatriation because of her marriage to an "ineligible alien." She read about the Cable Act in the *Saturday Evening Post* in the summer of 1924 and wrote the Immigration Bureau to ask whether the citizenship of "an American born woman of naturalized father of the white race this woman having been married twenty years to a Chinese" was affected in any way by the new law. She asked, "Can you give me any information whether this woman mother of 4 children can regain her citizenship, without renouncing her husband?"[32] The response of Rore Carl White, Second Assistant Secretary, advised Mrs. Chinn that she had lost her citizenship upon her marriage and that she was also ineligible to proceed with naturalization to regain that citizenship, so long as she remained married.[33]

The Cable Act also precluded women who had been divested of their citizenship from regaining it if they were considered racially ineligible to naturalize, such as Ng Fung Sing, because only women racially "eligible to citizenship" could be naturalized. And thus the Cable Act created a new problem. The 1855 law had allowed alien women married to U.S. citizens to derivatively acquire U.S. citizenship. The Cable Act eliminated derivative citizenship and made a special compensatory provision whereby the fact of marriage gave a woman the right to be naturalized upon her own petition, "if eligible to citizenship." This shift had consequences for women with limited education who therefore faced difficulty naturalizing. Thus a handwritten letter written to President Roosevelt from an "American Citizen," forwarded to the Immigration and Naturalization Service in 1939, states, in part:

It is not only my wish, but the wishes of many in our United States, that a law that came into effect in the year 1922 *could be changed.* . . .

Dear President Roosevelt why not give these people a break, so long as they came to this country before this awfull depression started and were married, they realy *do deserve* a little consideration, for many have *reared familys* in *these United States. Why not change that law,* it is hard for them to school for citizenship, they have not much education, leaving school at 12 + 13 years of age and at the age most of them are now 40 + 50 ect, + with there worrys ect, they must be very tired of living. . . .

You are for the working class, but before your time expires try + help these hard working wifes or husbands by making them American Citizens through mariage by changeing that law of 1922.[34]

The Cable Act also created new problems for alien women who married Asian men. Section 5 of the Act provided that "no woman whose husband is not eligible to citizenship shall be naturalized during the continuance of the marital status."[35] Thus a woman like Mary Ann Montoya, an immigrant from Austria who had married a Filipino man, was precluded from naturalization so long as she remained married. Montoya immigrated to the United States in 1914 and married her husband in 1926. Even though there was "a law in Oregon forbidding marriage between whites and orientals, a marriage license was issued to [them] at the Court House." Montoya wrote the Director of Naturalization in June 1930, asking if she could take out her "first naturalization papers."[36] He forwarded her inquiry to the Commission of Naturalization, indicating in an accompanying letter that he assumed that Section 5 would bar her application, but requesting more guidance because although "Filipinos were . . . ineligible to citizenship," there was an "exception in the law."[37] The Commissioner responded that the only exception was for Filipinos who declared their intent to become citizens, enlisted in the U.S. Navy or Marine Corps, and after not less than three years of service were discharged honorably or with recommendation for reenlistment. Unless Mr. Montoya made himself eligible to naturalize in this manner, Mary Ann Montoya would be ineligible to become a citizen as well.[38]

The impact of the Cable Act on Asian and Asian American women was severe. Victor Houston, congressional delegate from the Territory of Hawaii, provided substantial testimony about the impact of the Cable Act on the residents of Hawaii. He clarified the urgent need for an amendment, given that about eighty thousand women belonging to the affected racial groups would be unable to re-naturalize after expatriation. Houston provided, as an example, the situation of a Yale Law School graduate:

I have in mind a young Chinese girl of American citizenship by birth, and of the second generation in her family, a graduate of Yale University Law School. She married a young Chinese by whom she has children. Because he was born in San Francisco before the fire, her husband is not able to prove his citizenship. The immigration authorities hold he is an alien and that she has lost her citizenship by such marriage, and can not recapture it.[39]

The testimony presented by Delegate Houston and additional lobbying by women's groups, including the National Woman's Party, and organizations such as the Chinese American Citizens' Alliance and the Japanese American Citizens League led Congress to finally amend the Cable Act. They did so, in a piecemeal fashion, starting in 1930 (simplifying the process through which women could be naturalized) and finally rescinding the racial barriers to citizenship that had disenfranchised women like Mary Das, Mary Ann Montoya, and Ng Fung Sing in 1931. In addition, Congress added two legislative fixes in 1932 (providing birthright citizenship to women born in Hawaii prior to 1900, regardless of race) and in 1936 (clarifying the proper treatment of women whose marriage had been terminated through death or divorce).[40]

Stepping back to consider this particular story in the context of broader historical dynamics helps show how race and gender intersected to both grant and deny citizenship. This intersection differed, however, for white women, Asian and Asian American men, and Asian and Asian American women.

The Citizenship of Republican Mothers

White women clearly enjoyed citizenship as a salient feature of their identity, in that they were considered foundational members of the national community. However, what this citizenship meant was limited by gender. For example, the Supreme Court, in the 1874 decision *Minor v. Happersett*, simultaneously recognized that white women were part of "the people" at the founding of the nation,[41] but held that women's citizenship did not encompass the right to vote. Women were denied citizenship as rights and citizenship as political activity and, through marital expatriation, were denied formal citizenship as well.

As scholars have argued, throughout U.S. history, access to citizenship has been gendered, and women's citizenship has been specifically shaped by their private roles and functions. Republican ideology and U.S. democratic discourse, descending from the Enlightenment and the French Revolution, were pervaded by binary assumptions about women and men.[42] Women's citizenship was mediated by husbands and sons who engaged in the public sphere, while women were occupied with the tasks of domesticity. Early in the republic, the ideology of "Republican motherhood" developed, offering a solution to the dilemma presented by classical republicanism, which posed the idea of equality, but excluded women from certain of its duties, such as bearing arms. Republican mothers were to inculcate their sons with civic virtues, but were only indirectly to have a connection to public life. Their presumptive disinterestedness in public life lent women a moral authority: they could not control property, so they were independent of the selfish motivations that ran the market. Their only role in society was to exert a pure influence on male family members.[43] As historian Linda Kerber has argued, this had certain effects: freeing women from civic obligations that men had to fulfill—that is, treating them as "ladies"—served to legitimate their disenfranchisement from rights such as voting.[44]

Despite the fact that from the earliest naturalization statute white women were able to acquire U.S. citizenship, the subsequent 1855 and 1907 Expatriation Acts aligned women's citizenship with their husbands, showing how marriage mediated women's relationship to the nation. While political activity in the form of suffrage was not conceived as a necessary right of women's citizenship, women's lack of political autonomy was used in a circular argument to deny them independent citizenship. Recall Congressman Cutting asserting in debates concerning the 1855 Act that "by the act of marriage itself the political character of the wife shall at once conform to the political character of the husband."[45] Since women had no independent political identity, there was no need for their citizenship to maintain its own integrity to the nation.

What of the relationship between gender and citizenship as a matter of identity? It has been argued that there is an inverse relationship between the prominence of female figures in the allegorizations of nation and the degree of access granted women to the political apparatus of the state—that it is precisely women's exclusion from political life that renders their images fit to represent the high cause of the nation for which men are willing to kill and be killed.[46] Thus, the fact that the figure of the woman frequently stands in for the nation should not be confused with the idea that women possess full citizenship: while women are called upon to emblemize the nation, they have been sidelined in the process of nation building. Nonetheless, white women enjoyed citizenship as a matter of identity, as they belonged to the national community, as expressed on the terrain of culture. Symbolically standing in for the nation both required and reproduced whiteness.

The Citizenship of Alien Citizens

Race has tremendously shaped the access to different forms of citizenship for Asian Americans. Although birthright citizenship was guaranteed to Asian Americans after 1898, the racial bar on naturalization was not completely lifted until 1952. The long delay in allowing Asians to naturalize as U.S. citizens was predicated upon the perception of Asian Americans as perpetual foreigners, disinterested in mainstream American democratic processes and incapable of participating in republican citizenship. The lack of formal citizenship status meant that many Asian Americans could not vote, serve on juries, or otherwise engage in the responsibilities of citizenship. Thus the lack of formal citizenship status severely constrained the ability of Asian Americans to engage in citizenship as political activity. Of course, that Asians could not naturalize not only reflected the racialization of Asian Americans as foreign, it helped fix it as such in the American imagination.

Those Asian Americans who were able to enjoy the formal status of citizenship were still, in the words of historian Mae Ngai, "alien citizens": persons with the formal status of citizenship as an immigration matter but without citizenship as a matter of identity. Perpetually suspected of maintaining dual loyalties, "alien citizens" were considered aliens, and not citizens, especially in times of war. This was evident in the incarceration of eighty thousand U.S. citizens whose citizenship status was nullified both rhetorically and in fact during World War II. American citizens of Japanese ancestry were labeled "non-aliens," as opposed to "citizens" in orders from the U.S. military directing "persons of Japanese ancestry, both aliens and non-aliens" to report to assembly centers for evacuation.[47]

The case of Japanese American internment most dramatically illustrates the fact that formal citizenship was no guarantee of citizenship as a matter of rights. Although African Americans stood as the paradigmatic "second-class citizens," Asian Americans also lacked full citizenship in the form of rights. The U.S. Supreme Court upheld the segregation of Asian American students in public schools in 1927[48] and the practice of operating "separate but equal schools" for Asians in California continued at least through the mid-1940s.[49] Racism "permeated many areas of public life," so that Asian Americans were banned from public recreational facilities and forced to sit in the back rows of movie theaters.[50]

That Asian Americans could be citizens formally but not enjoy other dimensions of citizenship exemplifies the contradiction posed by the purported universality of liberalism and citizenship. As inheritor to European ideals, the United States adopted problematic Enlightenment notions about temporal and spatial citizenship and civilization, so that the "savage," the slave, the woman, and the non–property-holding person were excluded from consideration as a subject of rights and democratic participation.[51] The slippage between a universal "we the people" and a particularized enjoyment of citizenship is evident in the historical racialized citizenship of Asian Americans.

Gender, Race, and Citizenship

The racial bars that white women only experienced through their interracial marriages were uniformly applied to Asian American women and men. In this way, race might appear to trump gender in shaping the experiences of Asian American women. However, understanding the position of Asian American women through the lens of race alone is insufficient. We can see this through analyzing the interaction between gender, citizenship, and the racial bars to immigration.

Asian American women and men maintained distinct relationships to the nation-state because of their gender. Men and women were treated differently by the immigration laws, which, like marriage and citizenship laws, also followed the logic of coverture.[52] Male citizens and resident aliens were given the right to control their alien wives' immigration status. A wife's immigration status depended upon her husband's, but the converse did not hold. Citizen or resident alien women did not have the same rights as their male counterparts to petition for their alien spouses. Men could not gain immigration status through accompanying their citizen wives. This relationship of coverture limited the ability of alien women to control their own futures and rendered them dependent.

We can trace how these restrictions shaped the immigration admission of Chinese women in the exclusion era. Historian Erika Lee documents that most Chinese women were admitted as the dependents (wives and daughters) of men either allowed entry as U.S. citizens or of men who were allowed entry as exempt from Chinese exclusion—merchants, in particular. Far fewer Chinese women entered as independent immigrants. When they did, for example, as students or teachers, they were not able to bring husbands as dependents.[53] Thus we can see that the racial experience of Asian American women and men diverged because of gender.

But race–or immigration status (utterly shaped at that time by race)—also altered the experience of Asian women relative to their white counterparts. Recall that the Cable Act sought to end the doctrine of dependent citizenship in the name of classifying women as independent individuals. The Act simultaneously ended marital expatriation as well as dependent citizenship for alien wives of U.S. citizens. But in a context of racial exclusion, the status of Chinese women as dependent upon their husbands had, in fact, been crucial to these women gaining admission to the United States. In 1900, in the case *United States v. Gue Lim*,[54] the Supreme Court held that the admissibility of a wife or child followed that of the husband or father. Thus, if a husband could prove that he was a merchant, his wife would be able to enter the United States through the dependent status of being his wife. Moreover, marriage to a U.S. citizen could grant a Chinese woman, although racially ineligible to naturalize, the right to remain in the United States.

The idea of independent citizenship signaled to the courts that the immigration status of wives could be considered separate from that of their husbands. But this rendered Asian women more vulnerable to exclusion and deportation.[55] Thus the very goal that suffragists had been fighting for—independence from husbands in the realm of citizenship—jeopardized the ability of Asian women to enter or remain in the United States because they relied upon a dependent relationship to husbands for recognition from the nation-state.[56] Race unevenly molded coverture.

Conclusion

This history tells the complicated tale of how gender and race worked together to divest thousands of women from citizenship, through laws importing the idea of coverture into both immigration and citizenship laws. In telling this story, this chapter has sought to foreground the stories of women languishing in dusty archives, struggling to make sense of the legal constraints they encountered. It closes with the story of an extraordinary woman who fought marital expatriation.

The testimony of Delegate Houston of the Territory of Hawaii as to the detrimental impact of the Cable Act on a young law school graduate referred to Sau Ung Loo Chan, a graduate of Yale Law School, class of 1928, who had been born in Hawaii of Chinese parents. While at Yale, Chan met a Chinese American man, then a student at Hamilton College, who had been born in San Francisco. After their marriage, the couple lived in Hong Kong for ten years, where their only child was born. They decided to return to the United States, at which point Chan was required to demonstrate her husband's U.S. citizenship. She was apparently so successful at doing so, marshaling witnesses and documentary evidence, that the Immigration and Naturalization Service offered her a permanent position. Chan accepted the position but resigned after she fell seriously ill and had to return to Hawaii to recuperate, where she became the first Asian American woman to practice law.[57]

In an interview, Chan told the following anecdote. After her first year at Yale, Chan traveled to Europe. Returning back through Canada, despite her U.S. passport, she was refused entry because of her Chinese ancestry and threatened with detainment. She said, "After having finished one year at Yale,

I knew just enough law to scream 'habeas corpus' at the immigration officials . . . and they finally let me in."[58]

Within Chan's narrative we experience a compelling contradiction. She was a Chinese woman threatened with exclusion and detention because of race, and threatened with expatriation because of marriage—one whom the state would position as an abject victim. Yet embodied in the same person we also find the ferocious sense of agency of the U.S. citizen trained as a lawyer at a prestigious law school. Sau Ung Loo Chan possessed formal citizenship, which allowed her to be free from immigration exclusion; a knowledge of the rights that correlated with that citizenship, which allowed her to shout "habeas corpus" and ultimately be heard; and an ability to serve as her own advocate, which allowed her to win her husband's citizenship case (and, derivatively, her own). Her story leaves us with a sense of both excitement and loss: excitement to see her beating the state at its own game but also loss to imagine the lives of unknown others silenced by this history. The story of Sau Ung Loo Chan stands as a powerful counter-narrative to that of her silenced double, Ng Fung Sing.

NOTES

This is a shortened version of a longer article that originally appeared as *Divesting Citizenship: On Asian American History and the Loss of Citizenship Through Marriage*, 53 UCLA L. Rev. 405 (2005).

1. See Candice Lewis Bredbenner, A Nationality of Her Own: Women, Marriage, and the Law of Citizenship (1998); Nancy F. Cott, Public Vows: A History of Marriage and the Nation (2000); Martha Gardner, The Qualities of a Citizen: Women, Immigration, and Citizenship, 1870–1965 (2005).

2. 169 U.S. 649 (1898).

3. *Ex parte* Ng Fung Sing, 6 F.2d 670, 670 (D.D.C. 1925).

4. Expatriation Act, ch. 2534, § 3, 34 Stat. 1228, 1228–29 (1907).

5. See Act Relative to the Naturalization and Citizenship of Married Women (Cable Act), ch. 411, § 4, 42 Stat. 1021, 1022 (1922).

6. Act of Mar. 26, 1790, ch. 3, 1 Stat. 103.

7. Act of July 14, 1870, ch. 254, § 7, 16 Stat. 254, 256.

8. *In re* Ah Yup, 1 F. Cas. 223 (C.C.D. Cal. 1878) (No. 104).

9. Ozawa v. United States, 260 U.S. 178 (1922).

10. United States v. Thind, 261 U.S. 204 (1923).

11. 60 U.S. (19 How.) 393 (1857).

12. U.S. Const. amend. XIV.

13. 169 U.S. 649 (1898).

14. Erika Lee, At America's Gates: Chinese Immigration during the Exclusion Era, 1992–1943, 106–8 (2003).

15. Nancy Cott, *Marriage and Women's Citizenship in the United States, 1830–1934*, 103 Am. Hist. Rev. 1140, 1455 (1998).

16. Until World War I the nationality laws of virtually all countries made a married woman's nationality dependent on her husband's nationality.

17. Cott, *Marriage and Women's Citizenship*, 1456.

18. Linda Kerber, No Constitutional Right to Be Ladies: Women and the Obligations of Citizenship 11–29 (1998).

19. Cong. Globe, 33d Cong., 1st Sess. 170 (1854).

20. Act of Feb. 10, 1855, ch. 71, § 2, 10 Stat. 604, 604.

21. Broadis v. Broadis, 86 F. 951 (N.D. Cal. 1898).

22. Act of Aug. 9, 1888, ch. 818, § 2, 25 Stat. 392, 392.

23. Low Wah Suey v. Backus, 225 U.S. 460, 476 (1912).

24. Expatriation Act, ch. 2534, §§ 1–5, 34 Stat. 1228, 1228–29 (1907).

25. *See* Rogers Smith, Civic Ideals: Conflicted Visions of Citizenship in U.S. History 457 (1997).

26. Congressman Dickstein responding to Statement of Emma Wold, Immigration and Citizenship of American-Born Women Married to Aliens: Hearings on H.R. 4057, H.R. 6238, and H.R. 9825, before the House Comm. on Immigration and Naturalization, 69th Cong. 18 (1926).

27. 239 U.S. 299, 305–12 (1915).

28. *See* Bredbenner, 70.

29. For a biography of Taraknath Das, see Tapan K. Mukherjee, Taraknath Das: Life and Letters of a Revolutionary in Exile (1997).

30. In an article in *The Nation*, Mary Das wrote: "I am an American-born woman. My ancestors came from England to America in the year 1700. By the existing double standard of the American Government, I am not only rendered alien, but a stateless alien." Mary K. Das, *A Woman without a Country*, 123 Nation 105 (1926).

31. Statement of Elizabeth Kite, *Immigration and Citizenship of American-Born Women Married to Aliens: Hearing on H.R. 4057, H.R. 6238, and H.R. 9825 before the House Comm. on Immigration and Naturalization*, 69th Cong. 22–28 (1926).

32. Letter from Emily L. Chinn, Baltimore, Maryland, to "Dear Sirs" (received Aug. 13, 1924) (National Archives and Records Administration, Record Group 85, Box 399, Entry 26, File 20/3).

33. Letter from Rore Carl White, Second Assistant Secretary, Bureau of Immigration to Mrs. George S. Chinn (Aug. 27, 1924) (National Archives).

34. Letter from an American Citizen to President Roosevelt (received by the Immigration and Naturalization Service Jan. 21, 1939) (National Archives, File 20/2).

35. Act Relative to the Naturalization and Citizenship of Married Women (Cable Act), ch. 411, § 5, 42 Stat. 1021, 1022 (1923).

36. Letter from Mary Ann Montoya to Director of Naturalization, Portland, Oregon (June 18, 1930) (National Archives, File 20/2).

37. Letter from V. M. Tomlinson, District Director of Naturalization, Portland, Oregon, to Commissioner of Naturalization (June 19, 1930) (National Archives, File 20/2).

38. Letter from Commissioner of Naturalization to Mary A. Montoya (July 19, 1930) (National Archives, File 20/2).

39. *Amendment to the Women's Citizenship Act of 1922, and for Other Purposes: Hearing on H.R. 14684, H.R. 14685, and H.R. 16303 before the House Comm. on Immigration and Naturalization*, 71st Cong. 19 (1931) (3d sess.) at 32.

40. For a detailed description of the organizing by women's groups and the repeal of the Cable Act, see Bredbenner, *supra*.

41. 88 U.S. 162 (1874).

42. *See, e.g.*, Cott, *supra*; Kerber, *supra*; Carole Pateman, *The Sexual Contract* (1988).

43. *See* Kristi Andersen, After Suffrage: Women in Partisan and Electoral Politics before the New Deal 22–23 (1996).

44. *See, generally*, Kerber, 8–15.

45. Cong. Globe, 33rd Cong., 1st Sess. 170 (1854).

46. Ruth Roach Pierson, *Nations: Gendered, Racialized, Crossed with Empire*, in Gendered Nations: Nationalisms and Gender Order in the Long Nineteenth Century 41, 44 (Ida Blom et al. eds., 2000).

47. Mae Ngai, Impossible Subjects: Illegal Aliens and the Making of Modern America 2, 175 (2004).

48. Gong Lum v. Rice, 275 U.S. 78 (1927).

49. *See* Theodore Hsien Wang, *Swallowing Bitterness: The Impact of the California Civil Rights Initiative on Asian Pacific Americans*, 1995 Ann. Surv. Am. L. 463, 471.

50. Sucheng Chan, Asian Americans: An Interpretative History 113 (1991).

51. *See* David Theo Goldberg, Racist Culture: Philosophy and the Politics of Meaning (1993).

52. *See, e.g.*, Janet M. Calvo, *Spouse-Based Immigration Laws: The Legacies of Coverture*, 28 San Diego L. Rev. 593 (1991).

53. Lee, 97.

54. 176 U.S. 459 (1900).

55. *See* Todd Stevens, *Tender Ties: Husband's Rights and Racial Exclusion in Chinese Marriage Cases*, 1882–1924, 27 Law & Soc. Inq. 271 (2002).

56. *See* Bredbenner, 8.

57. Chan was able to prove her husband's citizenship by locating his birth certificate in Sacramento and by the testimony of several witnesses who confirmed having known him as a baby and as an adult in San Francisco. Sucheng Chan, Called from Within: Early Women Lawyers of Hawai'i 176, 178 (Mari Matsuda ed. 1992).

58. *Id.*

4

Made with Men in Mind

The GI Bill and Its Reinforcement of
Gendered Work after World War II

MELISSA MURRAY

This chapter critically examines the GI Bill of 1944—perhaps the most well-known veterans' benefits program in American history. The GI Bill of Rights, signed into law by President Franklin D. Roosevelt, afforded enormous employment, educational, and financial benefits to veterans following World War II.[1] Predicated solely on military service, GI Bill benefits were seen as the logical entitlement of those who had served their country during World War II. Feminist scholarship has identified the gendered nature of veterans' benefits and preferences that privilege military service and, in so doing, disadvantage women, who as a group are less likely to have served in the military.[2] The disparate impact of veterans' benefits and preferences on women are only part of their gendered legacy. The relationship between work, gender, and military service in the post–World War II era presents a more disturbing picture.

Although veterans' benefits and preferences were facially gender-neutral, they were structured and implemented with particular gender roles firmly in mind, and were pursued with the intent of preserving and further entrenching these gender roles. Specifically the policies were aimed at helping veterans transition from their wartime role as soldiers to their civilian roles as workers. Because the military and the workforce were understood to be male institutions, these policies were socially understood to benefit men, who were expected to be economic providers for their wives and families. As such, veterans' benefits and preferences not only disadvantaged women— they reflected, reinforced, and further embedded traditional gender norms that positioned men as protectors and providers, and women as their homebound dependents.

Gender, Work, and the Construction of Citizenship

The relationship between the citizen and the state has been strongly influenced by gender and the understanding that men and women were relegated to separate roles and spheres within the polity.[3] According to the separate spheres ideology, men occupied the public sphere, participating in market work in order to provide economic sustenance for their families, and women were consigned to the private sphere. The gendered understanding of men as breadwinners and women as their dependents was not relegated to the nineteenth century. Indeed, as many scholars have argued, the ideology of work and dependence found full expression in the relief programs of the New Deal, many of which were either directly aimed at creating jobs for out-of-work men or providing meager assistance to those women who did not have a breadwinner to depend on.[4]

In this way the relationship between work and gender informed the relationship between men, women, and the state. An equally important aspect of this relationship, however, was military participation. In the antebellum United States, the relationship between citizenship and military service was clearly understood—with one's status as a citizen being dependent (at least in part) on one's ability and willingness to perform military service. In the 1857 case, *Dred Scott v. Sandford*, Chief Justice Roger Taney pointed to a 1792 federal law excluding black men from the militia to underscore his claim that African Americans, whether freed or enslaved, were not citizens.[5] Taney's view was reinforced during Reconstruction when calls for the enfranchisement of African American men were linked to that group's service to the Union during the Civil War. African American men argued (if only partly successfully) that because they risked their lives for the Union, they should be included as full members of the polity.

The same logic framed women's claims for political citizenship. Arguments for refusing women the franchise focused on the fact that women were ineligible for military service. A century later suffragists' appeals for the ratification of the Nineteenth Amendment emphasized women's auxiliary military service during World War I. Although they had not performed as soldiers in that conflict, women had assisted the military effort in important ways. These efforts, suffragists argued, favored including women in the polity as voters.

In order to understand the connections between men's work and military service in constituting a masculine ideal of citizenship—one that would continue to shape the post–World War II period in ways distinctly disadvantageous to women—it is important to recognize the way in which military service and the citizen-soldier ideal functioned as an amplified variant of the traditional male breadwinner role. The ideology of work and dependence posited men as breadwinners responsible for providing the household (and the dependent wives and children within) with economic sustenance and physical protection. The male obligation of military service was simply an extension of this role. Men were not only expected to provide for and protect their families and homes. In extraordinary circumstances, they were duty-bound to shoulder the burden of protecting the homeland (and the dependents within) from external threats. Not only did the social construction of military service coincide with the ideal of the male breadwinner and protector, it also relied on the trope of the dependent woman as a foil for the citizen-soldier. Indeed, the relationship between military service, work, and feminine dependence in constructing male and female citizenship became explicit during World War II, when gender roles were challenged in the military and civilian life.

The advent of World War II brought with it calls to fully incorporate women into the structure of the military—calls that would clash directly with ideas about the relationship between women and work.[6] During World War II the introduction of mechanized warfare created a new cadre of military positions like communications and code breaking that needed to be filled by military personnel. Staffing enlisted men in these positions diverted them from menial, but no less necessary, military jobs such as kitchen police duty, cooking, and clerical work. In order to accommodate the demands of twentieth-century warfare, some suggested expanding the Women's Army Auxiliary Corps (WAAC), which had been used successfully in World War I for administrative and clerical work, into a full-fledged military unit. With women to shoulder the drudgery of these support functions, male soldiers would be available for the battlefield and other military tasks.

Not surprisingly the effort to incorporate women in the armed forces was met with strong resistance. Entirely apart from the issues of women's ability to perform combat duty, the notion of women as soldiers and veterans challenged embedded gender norms that characterized men as breadwinners for, and protectors of, women. Allowing women to serve as soldiers, rather than as auxiliaries, would strip the citizen-soldier ideal of its masculine character and divest women of their dependent status, placing them instead on equal footing with men in the military and in civilian society. Worse, it would leave those male partners of women employed in the military in the humiliated position of being married to women who did not require their earnings or their protection. In this way the introduction of women to the armed forces was subversive precisely because it was at odds with the entrenched gender discourse that figured men as providers and protectors, and women as dependent helpmates.

To allay the broad fears about women in the armed forces, the military's Bureau of Public Relations tried to present the proposed changes in terms that would be familiar to the public and consistent with extant gender norms. Specifically they emphasized that the inclusion of women in the military would not dismantle gender norms. Even within the structure of the military, the male protector role and the female dependent-helpmate role would persist. Tasked with administrative and clerical tasks, and menial duties such as kitchen duty, enlisted women would support male soldiers, and most significant, make them available for more important duties like combat. Although they were paid for their service, women's military participation, as in the home, was not understood as independent "work," nor were they understood as independent workers. Instead, women's military service was organized around supporting men. Indeed, the women's support made it possible for men to do the "real" military work of defending the nation. In short, the subversive nature of including women in the military was undercut by the fact that these women would continue to occupy a traditional role rather than usurping a traditionally male role.

On Capitol Hill, where Congress was debating the bill that would incorporate women into the armed forces, the bill's proponents made similar claims. Enlisted women would do the work that male soldiers were too valuable to perform: clerical and administrative work and domestic tasks. Thus enlisting women would not disrupt the family or the military but, rather, would bolster both institutions. Male enlisted personnel would be free to pursue pressing military tasks rather than the minutiae of military administration. And enlisted women would perform work consistent with the traditional family role that they occupied in the civilian sphere. Indeed, military service could make women *better* wives and mothers upon their return to civilian life. As one War Department slogan exhorted, military life would make enlisted women "better postwar wi[ves]" because they would have a better understanding of the military experience than their civilian counterparts.[7]

Further, military regulations accompanying the integration of women into the armed forces ensured that the understanding of military service as a male endeavor would not be substantively disrupted. Women's enlistment was capped at 2 percent of military personnel, women with minor children were not permitted to serve, and women were not trained for combat roles.[8] Instead, women's military participation would be a temporary event animated by the exigencies of war and, most important, would dovetail with the traditional conception of the feminine role.

Critically the effort to integrate women into the military coincided with the Manpower Commission's attempts to recruit civilian women to jobs in heavy industry during the war. Mobilization, and the conscription and enlistment of working men, created a glut of available civilian jobs that had to be filled in order to sustain the industrial output necessary for the war effort. The Manpower Commission looked to women to fill the void and, in so doing, framed their appeals by explaining that this new foray into the workplace—a traditionally masculine space—was entirely consistent with the traditional feminine role. Relying on the emerging rhetoric of the "home front," which expanded conceptually the physical boundaries of the home to include the nation and its defense, the Commission made clear that even as women left the home to work, they were not venturing far from their prescribed roles at all. Their industrial jobs were encompassed in the broader domestic sphere of the home front—a point made clear by the frequent efforts to analogize industrial labor to household tasks—where women were protected and defended by men.

Thus, in a time of tremendous national crisis, gender norms were challenged but held firm. Although the war permitted women's inclusion in two traditionally male institutions—the military and the labor force—these changes did not dislodge the perceptions of work and military service as male enterprises. Instead, in the military and in civilian life, elaborate fictions were crafted to explain and normalize women's entry into these male institutions. As these fictions prescribed, the upheaval of war did not disrupt established gender roles but further embedded them. Men continued to perform their role providing security and protection for their families, and women continued to support these efforts at home and on the home front.

Understanding the relationship between gender, work, and military service provides an appropriate lens through which to examine the entitlements of citizenship—in this case, veterans' benefits and preferences. Although scholars have identified the way in which veterans' benefits and preferences have disadvantaged non-veterans, and women, in particular, these programs have been justified as a quid pro quo for military service and sacrifice.[9] However, in order to fully understand veterans' benefits and preferences, and their effects, it is important to recognize the degree to which the benefits served as a means of facilitating the veteran's reentry to civilian life and his role in civilian society. Put another way, veterans' benefits and preferences were more than just compensation for military service. They were purposefully structured to facilitate the veteran's transition from one traditionally male institution, the military, to another, the workforce. As such, these policies not only disadvantaged women in the postwar era, but they were constructed with an eye toward maintaining traditional gender roles that figured men as workers who provided for their dependent wives and children.

The GI Bill

Nearly fifty years after World War II political scientist Suzanne Mettler surveyed veterans about the GI Bill's impact on their lives. Although the Bill profoundly altered the lives of millions of male veterans, allowing them to attend college, seek job training, and purchase homes and businesses, women veterans were clearly not the intended beneficiaries of the Bill's largesse. As one female veteran survey respondent reported "we viewed it as a policy for the men. I mean, they really created it with the men in mind, didn't they?"[10]

The intuition that the GI Bill was created "with the men in mind" is perhaps surprising when one considers that the Bill was drafted to apply to *all* World War II veterans who had served at least ninety days in the armed forces and had been honorably discharged. Of course, the empirical reality of the military gives force to the intuition that the Bill was not intended for women veterans. During World War II women comprised, as noted, only 2 percent of the military population; men, comprising 98 percent of military personnel, were overwhelmingly represented in the veteran population.[11]

Women's negligible representation in the military resulted from the confluence of social forces and military policy. As previously discussed, military service was seen as a quintessentially male enterprise—so much so that the proposal to include women within the military's ranks prompted profound anxiety about the disruption of gender roles. The male character of military service was further underscored by military enlistment procedures. First, military administrative policies limited women's representation in the armed forces to just 2 percent, a requirement that persisted until 1968.[12] Women were also required to have higher military aptitude examination scores and references in order to be admitted to the enlisted and officer ranks. Women under the age of twenty-one had to secure parental consent in order to enlist. Finally, women with minor children were not permitted to enlist in the armed forces, a policy that clearly deferred to women's customary child-rearing role. None of these policies applied to men.

That women comprised a minority of military personnel partly explains why veterans' benefits like the GI Bill were understood to be "for the men." However, to explain fully why even women veterans did not believe that they were included within the Bill's intended beneficiary class, it is important to revisit the ideology of work and dependence, and consider the animating principles behind the GI Bill.

Today the expansion of home ownership and higher education are the foundations of the GI Bill's legacy.[13] This legacy, however, obscures the concerns and fears that animated the Bill's drafting. At its core the Bill was about work. Veterans were not just returning soldiers, entitled to a reward for their sacrifice; they were returning workers who had to be reintegrated into the civilian workforce. The end of the war, many feared, would inevitably lead to economic relapse and unemployment as industrial output slowed and returning veterans flooded the labor force. The prospect of unemployed veterans was particularly troubling. As recently as 1932 Washington, D.C., had been upended as angry, unemployed veterans stormed the capital to lobby for unpaid veterans' benefits.[14] Likewise, political leaders were mindful of recent events in post–World War I Europe, where unemployed and disaffected veterans fueled the rise of Nazism and Fascism.[15] With these recent historical precedents in mind, many politicians were keen to find a way to stabilize the postwar economy, while modulating the reentry of veterans— mostly men—to the workforce.[16] The GI Bill was part of a larger demobilization strategy intended to address these concerns.

The GI Bill directly addressed the question of veterans' postwar employment prospects and their ability to resume their roles as breadwinning workers. As an initial matter, the bill offered unemployed veterans a weekly twenty-dollar "readjustment allowance" to tide them over until they could secure employment commensurate with their skills and abilities.[17] To further support jobless veterans in their search for gainful employment, the Bill also established a job-counseling and employment-placement service.

But unemployment assistance was only one aspect of the Bill's efforts to stabilize the economy and facilitate veteran reintegration. Title III of the Bill provided veterans with access to low-interest, government-backed loans to purchase homes, farms, and business property. Armed with unprecedented access to capital, veterans began new businesses and purchased homes in record numbers.[18] The effect of this influx of capital was dramatic for the individual veteran and for the nation. New home construction pushed the boundary of American life past the city toward a new frontier: the suburb.[19] These new settlement patterns also were accompanied by new consumption patterns as families purchased new furniture, cars (to reach these suburban enclaves), appliances, and household goods.[20] The increase in entrepreneurship and new home construction, coupled with a robust consumer culture, fueled the post-war economy and kept the specter of the Great Depression at bay.

Maintaining economic growth, however, required a stable labor force. To prevent large-scale unemployment, veteran reentry to the labor market had to be carefully modulated. On this front, the GI Bill would leave an indelible mark. Title II of the Bill offered any veteran who had served at least ninety days of active duty and "whose education or training was impeded, delayed, interrupted, or interfered with" by entry into the armed forces was eligible to pursue college, graduate school, or vocational training on the government's dime.[21] Of the 15 million eligible veterans, about half availed themselves of Title II's educational benefits. By 1947 veterans constituted "half of enrolled college students, doubling the number of males registered in prewar times, and increasing overall enrollment by 75 percent."[22] Because of these unprecedented provisions, the Bill has been credited with expanding access to higher education in the United States.[23] However, at the time of the Bill's drafting, its generous investment in human capital was secondary to its role in diverting returning veterans from the labor force toward other pursuits, namely colleges, universities, and vocational training. Despite the lofty results, the Bill's educational and training provisions had a decidedly rudimentary goal: preserve the economy by preventing unemployment.

From Soldiers to Workers

Recognizing the central role that work (and the understanding of veterans as returning workers) played in creating the GI Bill provides fresh insight into the intuition that the Bill was made with men in mind. Not only was the Bill intended to serve the needs of those who comprised the overwhelming majority of the military population; it was specifically intended to enhance the postwar prospects of those veterans who were workers and breadwinners: men. In so doing the Bill was informed by, and further entrenched, the gendered worker-dependent dichotomy.

The GI Bill's orientation toward male soldier-workers is further clarified by military discharge procedures. Whereas male veterans were advised of their eligibility for education and training benefits in the course of discharge, women veterans often were not.[24] Similarly, while men routinely received vocational counseling when they separated from the military, women veterans reported that they rarely received such counseling. The military's failure to address these topics with departing women veterans could be easily dismissed as a mere oversight. However, even if it were simple administrative negligence, the oversight is revealing. Women were not expected to be workers in postwar civilian society and, accordingly, would not need such information. Indeed, providing this information to female military personnel would require contemplating the possibility of women as postwar workers, which in turn would require the wholesale reevaluation of existing gender norms and the institutions that supported them. At its core, the GI Bill was a hedge against the prospect of rampant unemployment. Accordingly, its benefits were directed at those who were expected to staff the postwar workforce, namely, men.

The Gendered Effects of Veterans' Benefits and Preferences

For years, our understanding of veterans' benefits and preferences has been predicated on the notion that military service is an extraordinary sacrifice worthy of extraordinary reward. Soldiers lay their lives on the line in the service of the United States, and when they return, sometimes hobbled by physical injury or the emotional weight of what they have experienced, they require our assistance and generosity in reorienting themselves to civilian life. Clearly the need to facilitate the reintroduction of the veteran to civilian life is a worthy endeavor. But it is not one that should be undertaken without greater reflection of the institutions at the heart of these policies, and the consequences of affording one group extraordinary privileges at the expense of others. Indeed, the notion that military service creates an *entitlement* to certain government benefits has shielded these policies and the institutions that they undergird from scrutiny and has silenced those who have been put aside so that we might reward veterans. By failing to interrogate veterans' benefits and preferences more vigorously, we have overlooked the degree to which they are framed around a deeply gendered ideology of work and dependency.

Our efforts to reintegrate veterans into the fabric of civilian life have largely focused on reintegrating them into their traditional roles within the polity. For most veterans, who, by virtue of custom and military policy, were men, this meant transitioning back to their roles as breadwinners and workers. When we shift our understanding of veterans' benefits and preferences from entitlements for military service to entitlements that are intended to facilitate reentry to work, the effect of these privileges on those who are not socially constructed as workers—women—becomes more focused and clear.

In this new frame, the GI Bill's inherited narrative seems somewhat incomplete. Although the Bill expanded the cadre of Americans who attended college and graduate school, it did so at the expense of women. Indeed, it likely impeded women's educational opportunities in the postwar era. Of the small group of women veterans who were eligible for GI Bill benefits, few availed themselves of its unprecedented educational opportunities. Part of this was because of the social understanding of women as wives and mothers, rather than as students and prospective workers.

However, the structure of the Bill's benefits also contributed to women's difficulties in realizing its educational opportunities. The Bill's education and training provisions had to be used within seven years of the veteran's discharge. For women veterans, many of whom married and started families upon returning to civilian life, the time frame in which they had to use their entitlement coincided with the time in their lives when most were occupied with family responsibilities. Conceived and structured with "men in mind," the Bill overlooked the needs of the minority of women veterans who would be eligible for its benefits.

But the difficulties experienced by the small coterie of women veterans are only one part of the Bill's impact on women in the postwar era. For civilian women, the impact of the GI Bill and the slew of attendant state and federal veterans' preference policies would be even more extreme. Most men were veterans, and most women were not. The effects of this empirical reality were evident in college graduation rates in the postwar era. Between 1940 and 1950 the number of female college graduates increased by 25 percent—a rate comparable to previous years when colleges and universities, desperate to remain solvent during the war, admitted women to fill the seats left unoccupied by enlisting men. This modest increase in women graduates, however, was dwarfed by the explosion of male graduates. Between 1940 and 1950 the number of male college graduates increased by 66 percent, considerably more than in prior years. Following the war male enrollment and graduation rates outpaced that of women by nearly three to one, widening the gender gap in higher education.

Further, by expanding the pool of prospective college applicants, the GI Bill increased the demand for available spaces at colleges and universities throughout the United States.[25] Although many schools responded to the increased demand by expanding enrollment, many other schools also employed veterans' preference policies which ensured that returning veterans, most of whom were men, received priority in allocating available slots. Indeed, some colleges went so far as to place limits on female enrollment in order to accommodate the increased matriculation of veterans, raising the bar for female college applicants to almost unattainable heights. As one male veteran observed "The only women students who got in [to college] were straight-A students."[26]

Our uncritical acceptance of veterans' benefits and preferences has come with considerable costs. By privileging military service so generously, we inadvertently have favored a constituency that is largely male to the detriment of non-veterans, most of whom have been women. However, recognizing the degree to which military service is, in and of itself, skewed in terms of gender is only one aspect of the way in which these policies have overwhelmingly favored men. Indeed, in failing to interrogate veterans' benefits and preferences more vigorously, we have overlooked the degree to which they are framed around a deeply gendered ideology of work and dependency, and, in so doing, have reinforced the understanding of men as workers and women as domestic dependents. Understanding this relationship between military service, work, and gender is critical to excavating the role that entitlements for military service have played in producing gender inequality and hindering gender progress in contemporary society.

Legal Entrenchment of Veterans' Benefits

The gendered impact of the GI Bill was finally challenged in the courts in the 1970s, reaching the U.S. Supreme Court in 1979. In the case of *Personnel Administrator of Massachusetts v. Feeney*,[27] civil service worker Helen Feeney claimed that the preference given veterans in the civil service employment system impermissibly disadvantaged women in violation of the Equal Protection Clause of the U.S. Constitution. As Feeney had learned in her various attempts to move up through the civil service system, regardless of how well one performed on the civil service examination, there was little chance of obtaining the desired position if one was a non-veteran competing against veterans.

During her twelve years as a Massachusetts state employee, Feeney had applied for a number of available civil service positions. Each time her application was evaluated using her score on the civil service examination, and in almost every case she was ranked below male applicants who had earned lower examination scores, costing her the job. A prominent figure in local politics, Feeney had grit and moxie to spare. In 1975 she sued Massachusetts, claiming that the state's veterans' preference unfairly limited her employment opportunities.

Feeney's experience was not exceptional. Most women applicants were disadvantaged by the preference given veterans.[28] At the time, in Massachusetts, more than 98 percent of veterans were men and nearly 47 percent of Massachusetts men over eighteen were veterans. By contrast, only 1.8 percent of Massachusetts veterans were women, and only .8 of one percent of Massachusetts women over eighteen were veterans. Accordingly veteran status occurred *sixty* times more frequently among working-age men than among working-age women. The consequence of this was that women were at a significant disadvantage when seeking entry into, and advancement within, the civil service system, the largest employer in Massachusetts. Whenever they competed for positions with men, Massachusetts women were almost always doomed to failure because so many of their competitors were veterans, entitled to the significant advantage afforded by the veterans' preference scheme. If women wanted civil service employment, they had to apply for the positions that men did not want. As a result, the Massachusetts civil service system was incredibly segregated by sex. Men occupied the most desirable positions, and women were consigned to clerical and administrative work—the less desirable, less lucrative supporting roles that women historically performed and men did not want.

The district court ruled in favor of Feeney. The court found that the laudable goal of providing benefits to veterans had a severe, negative impact on female applicants.[29] The court concluded that, despite the law's gender-neutral language, the veterans' preference scheme was non-neutral and was intended to favor men over women. Because women historically had been excluded from military service (or had served in relatively low numbers), the class of veterans to whom the preference was directed was overwhelmingly male, and those who drafted and implemented the veterans' preference scheme were aware of this fact. Accordingly, the court reasoned, the policy was "anything but an impartial, neutral policy of selection." It was a conscious decision to favor a predominantly male beneficiary class, and its disproportionate impact on women's employment opportunities could not be considered unintentional.

In rejecting this argument, the Supreme Court looked to the statute's text and its understanding of the legislature's intentions in promulgating the veterans' preference scheme. That scheme, it noted, was gender-neutral in its terms and applied to *all* veterans regardless of sex. The preference, the Court observed, did not distinguish on the basis of gender but on the basis of veteran status—it afforded benefits to veterans (whether male or female) while disadvantaging those who were non-veterans (whether male or female). Further, even though the preference operated in a manner that disproportionately put women at a disadvantage, according to the Court, the law evinced no underlying discriminatory intent. Although the Massachusetts legislature was no doubt aware of the preference's impact on women, there was nothing to suggest that its decision to enact the preference was "'because of,' not merely 'in spite of' its adverse effects on [women]."[30]

By focusing narrowly on the statute's text and the absence of explicit discriminatory intent, the Court failed to recognize the subtle—and not so subtle—ways in which the policy reinforced the gendered work-dependency ideology. First, as with the GI Bill, the veterans' preference statute was created with the twin goals of rewarding veterans for their service *and* facilitating their transition from soldiers to workers in the civilian sphere. In doing so, the policy was framed by, and reinforced, the gendered understanding of men as workers.

The force of the worker-dependent ideology in the Massachusetts preference scheme was made clear by those included in its beneficiary class. The Massachusetts statute, like other veterans' preference schemes, extended the veterans' preference to certain non-veteran women. Specifically the scheme required that "widows and the widowed mothers of veterans" be ranked third in the veteran hierarchy, after disabled veterans and veterans but ahead of non-veteran women. Unlike other women, who were presumed to have a working man (whether a husband or son) upon whom they could depend for their sustenance, widows and widowed mothers of veterans had no husband or son to provide for them. As such, the veterans' preference scheme attempted to compensate for the absent breadwinner by conveying to these women the employment advantage that their deceased husbands and sons would have enjoyed, enabling the women to support themselves in the absence of a breadwinning man. In terms that mirrored the Social Security Act's understanding of women's entitlement to benefits, the preference accrued to these women derivatively through their attachment to a deceased veteran, and was available only because the male veteran was no longer available to support the woman as a dependent. Critically the Court made no mention of the fact that the Massachusetts law did not offer a similar benefit to widowers or fathers of deceased veterans—a legislative choice that underscored the normative intuition that men, rather than women, were responsible for providing for the family.

Other aspects of the veterans' preference scheme also reflected the worker-dependent dichotomy in particular ways. As Justices Marshall and Brennan acknowledged in a vigorous dissent, the preference scheme permitted the civil service administration to make sex-specific requisitions on available civil service positions.[31] If a position was denominated as one suitable for women, it was exempted from the operation of the veterans' preference statute.[32] As such, women could compete for these exempted positions unimpeded by the considerable advantage that the preference afforded to veterans. According to the dissent, the requisitions language, which was incorporated into the statute in 1954, surely reflected the notion that certain positions in the workforce *were* suitable for women, and others were not. This by itself, they argued, suggested a retreat to sex stereotypes about women as workers—stereotypes that consigned women to civil service clerical and administrative positions that were used to support the better-paid, more challenging positions for which men typically were selected.

Feeney remains the definitive decision on the legality of the veterans' preference scheme, despite its gendered impact. Since *Feeney*, preference for veterans has been largely unchallenged as a vehicle of government largesse. On a broader scale, the decision in *Feeney* has come to represent the high bar to challenging the constitutionality of facially neutral statutes that evince no discriminatory intent, even in the face of discriminatory effects.

The Future of Veterans' Benefits

In many ways the Court's failure to see the subtleties of Feeney's claim can be explained by the entrenchment of the gendered assumptions that Feeney's claim challenged. In short, the Court may have viewed *awareness* of the differential effects on women as decisively different from *discriminatory intent*, specifically because what it was being asked to take notice of—and long had been—was the status quo that was entrenched in the military, the labor market, and the public/private divide. That veterans' preferences benefited men in access to employment and education at the expense of women did not register with the *Feeney* majority—it was simply the way of the world. Men were workers and providers (and in exigent circumstances, soldiers), and women were their home-bound dependents. A statute whose operation manifested this inevitability could not be considered a constitutional violation absent a clear showing of intent to discriminate against women.

In the thirty years since Helen Feeney fought her case in the U.S. Supreme Court, veterans' benefits and preferences remain largely unchanged in the United States. In June 2008, amid fond recollections of the original GI Bill, Congress authorized more generous educational and training benefits for enlisted personnel and veterans. In addition to the GI Bill, the federal government and all fifty states continue to provide veterans with preferences in public employment—and most continue to include widows and widowed mothers of veterans within the beneficiary class. And in Massachusetts, as in four other states, the absolute preference challenged in *Feeney* persists.

What has changed, however, are the institutions in which the worker-dependent ideology is shaped and replicated. Consider the military, once a paradigmatically male institution. Today women comprise roughly 14 percent of military personnel, and regulations capping women's enlistment at 2 percent have been eliminated. Similarly the workforce has changed dramatically, with the majority of American women employed full-time outside the home. Of course, these personnel changes have not necessarily dimmed the understanding of military service and work as essentially masculine enterprises. Women continue to be underrepresented in the upper echelons of the military and the workplace.

Recognizing the way in which the military and work have functioned historically as institutions that both reflect and reproduce gender norms is imperative to rebuilding these institutions—and society more generally—along more egalitarian lines. It is not enough to look at policies and institutions in a vacuum. As the facts of *Feeney* make clear, the combined force of custom and the social and legal construction of institutions like the military and work can create conditions under which gender neutrality (and equality) is elusive, if not impossible.

Instead, we must view these policies—and the institutions from which they flow—in context. Our understanding of veterans' benefits and preferences is more nuanced and rich if we go beyond law's understanding of gender-neutrality and discriminatory intent to investigate the ways in which benefits have been structured around, and in service of, deeply gendered norms that posit men as protectors and providers, and women as dependent helpmates. Understanding this context provides a more complex and exacting account of the way in which outmoded gender norms may nonetheless pervade gender-neutral policies.

NOTES

Many thanks to Kathy Abrams, Sarah Song, Solangel Maldonado, and Leti Volpp for helpful comments and conversations.
1. Servicemen's Readjustment Act of 1944, Pub. L. No. 346, § 700, 58 Stat. 284, 295–96.
2. Linda K. Kerber, No Constitutional Right to Be Ladies: Women and the Obligations of Citizenship 221–302 (1998).
3. Julie Husband & Jim O'Loughlin, Daily Life in the Industrial United States 1870–1900, 99–119 (2004); Barbara Welter, *The Cult of True Womanhood: 1820–1860*, 18 Am. Q. 151, 152 (1966); Linda K. Kerber, *Separate Spheres, Female Worlds, Woman's Place: The Rhetoric of Women's History*, 75 J. Am. Hist. 9, 15–16 (1988).
4. Nancy K. Cauthen & Edwin Amenta, *Not for Widows Only: Institutional Politics and the Formative Years of Aid to Dependent Children*, 61 Am. Soc. Rev. 427 (1996); Susan Ware, *Women*

and the New Deal, in Fifty Years Later: The New Deal Evaluated 113, 124 (Harvard Sitkoff ed. 1985). Of course, for many women, working outside the home was a reality. For these women, many of whom were immigrants, minorities, and members of the lower classes, the feminine ideal offered by these programs was not just deeply gendered but was also biased with regard to race and class. See, generally, Sonya Michel, A Tale of Two States: Race, Gender, and Public/Private Welfare Provision in Postwar America, 9 Yale J. L. & Feminism 123, 128 (1997).

5. Scott v. Sandford, 60 U.S. 393, 409–10, 420 (1857).

6. Leisa D. Meyer, Creating GI Jane: Sexuality and Power in the Women's Army Corps during World War II 14–15 (1996).

7. Id. at 55.

8. Id. at 86; 32 G.F.R. § 580.4(b) (1975).

9. Kerber, supra.

10. Suzanne Mettler, Soldiers to Citizens: The GI Bill and the Making of the Greatest Generation 144 (2005).

11. Janann Sherman, "They either need these women or they do not": Margaret Chase Smith and the Fight for Regular Status for Women in the Military, 54 J. Mil. Hist. 47, 76 (1990); Melissa E. Murray, Whatever Happened to GI Jane? Citizenship, Gender, and Social Policy in the Postwar Era, 9 Mich. J. Gender & L. 91, 118 (2002); Mettler, 144.

12. Meyer, supra.

13. Edward Humes, Over Here: How the GI Bill Transformed the American Dream 5 (2006); Michael J. Bennett, When Dreams Came True: The GI Bill and the Making of Modern America (1996).

14. See, generally, Paul Dickson & Thomas B. Allen, The Bonus Army: An American Epic (2004); W. W. Waters, B.E.F.: The Whole Story of the Bonus Army (1933).

15. Keith W. Olson, The GI Bill, the Veterans, and the Colleges 4 (1974); Melissa Murray, When War Is Work: The GI Bill, Citizenship, and the Civic Generation, 96 Calif. L. Rev. 967, 970 (2008); Murray, GI Jane, 103.

16. Murray, When War Is Work, 971.

17. § 700, 58 Stat. 284, 295-96.

18. Humes, supra; Murray, When War Is Work, 972.

19. Robert A. Beauregard, When America Became Suburban 108 (2006).

20. Lizabeth Cohen, A Consumers' Republic: The Politics of Mass Consumption in Postwar America 121–22 (2003); Elaine Tyler May, Homeward Bound: American Families in the Cold War Era 165–66 (1988).

21. § 400, 58 Stat. 284, 288–89.

22. Mettler at 67.

23. Humes, supra; Bennett, supra.

24. Mettler, 149.

25. Keith W. Olson, The GI Bill, the Veterans, and the Colleges 3–4 (1974).

26. Mettler, supra.

27. 442 U.S. 256 (1979).

28. See Brief for the Appellee, Personnel Administrator v. Feeney, No 78-233, at 5.

29. Anthony v. Massachusetts, 415 F. Supp. 485 (D. Mass. 1976).

30. Personnel Administrator v. Feeney, 442 U.S. 256, 279 (1979).

31. Id. at 281.

32. Feeney Brief, supra.

5

Fighting Women

The Military, Sex, and Extrajudicial
Constitutional Change

JILL ELAINE HASDAY

Americans often celebrate military service as a badge of honor and an emblem of full citizenship. Though potentially dangerous and difficult, even brief service in the armed forces offers valuable training, employment benefits, and reputational advantages, opening doors to civilian careers. Yet for generations Congress, the executive branch, the military, and the courts denied women equal access to the benefits and burdens of military service. Laws requiring men to register for possible conscription excluded women. Men could serve in combat, but women could not. Men could rise through the ranks, but the military relegated women to lower-status positions. Men could simultaneously be soldiers and fathers, but military service and motherhood were generally deemed incompatible. Underlying this regime of separate status was a pervasive belief that women's true responsibilities were domestic and precluded full participation in public life, including military service.

Some of the most important historical restrictions on women's military role persist: women are still excluded from military registration, draft eligibility, and some combat positions. These explicitly sex-based distinctions have become increasingly anomalous over time. The rise of the modern women's rights movement in the 1970s led legislatures and courts to repeal or invalidate almost all laws subjecting men and women to explicitly different rules. Yet, despite this wave of reform, Congress in 1980 rejected President Jimmy Carter's proposal to register women with the Selective Service System. A year later the Supreme Court held, in *Rostker v. Goldberg,* that male-only registration was consistent with equal protection, and also endorsed male-only conscription and combat positions.[1] Since *Rostker,* few court cases have challenged restrictions on women's military service, and none has reached the Supreme Court.

Notwithstanding the lack of judicial intervention, however, many aspects of women's legal status in the military have changed in striking respects since *Rostker's* decision to protect the status quo. Congress, the executive branch, the military, and the public have become much more supportive of women's military service, including in combat. The proportion of women in the active U.S. Armed Forces has risen from approximately 8.4 percent just before *Rostker*[2] to 14.6 percent in the most recent statistics.[3] Congress repealed the last statutory prohibition on women holding combat positions in 1993, and the military has opened a wide range of combat roles to women. Today women serve—and die—in combat, as the present war in Iraq has amply demonstrated. Women are barred from an unprecedentedly small and steadily decreasing number of military positions, and only by military regulation rather than statute. Public opinion surveys find markedly increased support for women's military service, including in combat.

This chapter brings long overdue attention to the record of women's legal status in the military in order to make three broad theoretical and historical points. First, the record of women's legal status in the military is important counterevidence to the prevalent assumption that sex equality already exists, at least in formal legal rules. Second, this record helps illuminate how extrajudicial events can shape the Supreme Court's constitutional interpretation and then make that interpretation much less plausible over time. Third, and most striking, this record illustrates how extrajudicial actors can develop and enforce their own evolving understanding of sex equality norms, sometimes becoming a more important source of those norms than courts. The extrajudicial transformation in women's military role has shifted the foundational normative commitments that shape the evolving meaning of constitutional equal protection.

The Persistence of Legalized Sex Inequality

Women's continued exclusion from registration, draft eligibility, and some combat positions contradicts any assumption that legalized sex inequality has faded into history. Indeed, *Rostker* illustrates how the notion that legalized sex inequality has been left in the past can facilitate the perpetuation of unequal regimes. In upholding male-only registration, *Rostker* asserted that Congress rejected President Carter's 1980 proposal to register women for entirely new and modern reasons untainted by invidious sex stereotypes. The clear purpose of this contention—which scholars have uncritically accepted—was to insist that any constitutionally problematic modes of reasoning about women were safely confined to the past, and to establish that women's continued exclusion from registration was not a mark of second-class citizenship. In fact, this chapter demonstrates—contrary to current literature—that the record of Congress's 1980 decision to exclude women from registration is most notable for its consistency with earlier congressional decisions to restrict women's military role that were rooted in the conviction that women's familial responsibilities precluded their full participation in public life. In 1980 political and popular forces—on both sides of the debates over registering women—remained committed to restricting women's military service on the belief that women's real responsibilities were domestic and private rather than political and public.

The Court's Constitutional Interpretation and the World outside the Court

The record of women's legal status in the military also illuminates the influence that extrajudicial forces can have on the Court's constitutional jurisprudence. The *Rostker* Court explicitly grounded its decision to uphold male-only registration on congressional, executive, military, and popular opposition to women in combat. *Rostker*'s interpretation of constitutional equal protection built upon a point of considerable extrajudicial consensus—that women should not be in combat—and staked a position on a point of intense extrajudicial disagreement—whether women's exclusion from combat justified male-only registration and conscription eligibility.

Since *Rostker*, the record of women's military status illustrates how extrajudicial developments can undermine the plausibility of the constitutional interpretation in the Court's precedents. Without any constitutional amendment or reversal in the Court's jurisprudence, *Rostker*'s constitutional interpretation has become much less compelling and convincing over time. *Rostker*'s understanding of equal protection was not timeless and ahistorical; it was inextricably intertwined with the factual premise that opposition to women's combat service was widespread and with the cultural assumption that this opposition was too reasonable to need explanation. As Congress, the executive branch, and the military are well aware, the extrajudicial transformation in women's military role since *Rostker* has seriously undercut the transitory premises and assumptions behind *Rostker*'s interpretation of equal protection. This transformation makes clear that *Rostker* is inconsistent with the rest of the Court's sex discrimination jurisprudence.

Extrajudicial Constitutional Change

Commentators often praise the Court's ability to settle constitutional disputes, but *Rostker*'s judgment that women's rights to equality were not at risk did not stop Congress, the executive, and the military from debating the issue, or enforcing their own evolving judgment that sex equality, along with the personnel needs of the volunteer military, called for granting women an increasingly large military role, including in combat. Women's military role has expanded despite *Rostker* because the Court is not the only institution committed to sex equality, actively considering how to advance that commitment, or willing and able to enforce its judgments.

The record of women's legal status in the military demonstrates how equality norms can change, and find legal enforcement, without any change in Court jurisprudence or any Court involvement. The claim that restrictions on women's military role impinged upon sex equality moved from the Court to other parts of government, and was enforced there. Extrajudicial actors have developed and enforced their own evolving understanding of sex equality norms.

Military Service, Citizenship, and Domesticity: Women and the Military before Rostker

Military service represents a complex mix of benefit and burden. The ratio of benefits and burdens varies depending on whether one is a volunteer or a conscript. But both volunteers and draftees share some obvious burdens, like time away from civilian pursuits and risk to life and limb. The benefits of military service are also striking. They include concrete material advantages, such as vocational training and extensive veterans' benefits and preferences.

Another critical benefit is cultural and political: Americans have long understood military service to be a central avenue for establishing and confirming full citizenship. Ten of the first thirty-three presidents were military generals. Overall twenty-eight presidents served in America's armed forces.

Courts have stressed the connection between military service and full citizenship in cases upholding conscription from World War I to the Vietnam era. They have explained that military service is the citizen's "supreme and noble duty," adding "that the very conception of a just government and its duty to the citizen includes the reciprocal obligation of the citizen to render military service in case of need and the right to compel it." In *Scott v. Sandford*, which held that black people were not American citizens, the Supreme Court cited as important evidence a state law limiting military service to "free white citizens." As the Court reasoned, "Nothing could more strongly mark the entire repudiation of the African race."[4]

Discussions of military service and full citizenship have historically made little, if any, mention of whether women were full citizens. In fact, women's military service was severely restricted historically in order to express and enforce the conviction that women's special domestic responsibilities precluded full participation in public roles. Women did not gain permanent status in the military until 1948, and the operative statute—the misleadingly named Women's Armed Services Integration Act—capped women's participation at a maximum of 2 percent of the military; excluded women from registration, conscription, upper-officer ranks, and combat positions; and permitted involuntary discharge for motherhood or pregnancy. The supporters of the Integration Act insisted that women's ultimate responsibilities were familial. General Dwight D. Eisenhower assured Congress that "few" women would accumulate the thirty years of military service necessary for earning retirement benefits. Instead, women "will come in and I believe after an enlistment or two enlistments they will ordinarily—and thank God—they will get married."[5]

Women's military status remained essentially unchanged for decades, with women constituting approximately 1 percent of the military. A 1957 recruiting pamphlet documented the military's commitment to preserving civilian social and economic patterns. The pamphlet included two drawings side-by-side, each picturing a working woman. The only difference was that the first woman was wearing civilian clothes, and the second was in military uniform. Each was sitting before the same typewriter, with the same expression on her face, apparently doing the same work.

By the early 1970s, however, women's legal status in the military had begun to attract unprecedented attention for two reasons. First, the mod-

Department of Defense, Careers for Women in the Armed Forces 18 (1957).

ern women's rights movement, which challenged the social and legal norms confining women to narrow roles in the family and workplace, had emerged as a powerful social movement and sparked the mobilization of an opposing movement intent on preserving women's existing roles, especially in the family. Second, the end of the draft in 1973 made the military more eager to attract women. The military progressively increased its recruitment of women in the 1970s, citing the demands of the women's movement and the need for more military volunteers given the abolition of the draft.

The first decade of modern political and popular debates about women's military role focused on the Equal Rights Amendment (ERA) and President Carter's 1980 proposal to implement by statute and military regulation what many ERA supporters contended the Amendment would establish: women's inclusion in registration and conscription eligibility, and continued exclusion from combat. These debates were tightly intertwined, although the *Rostker* Court and scholars repeating *Rostker*'s account later sought to separate them.

Throughout these debates, powerful forces in government and popular culture remained determined to limit women's military service in the interest of confirming and enforcing the conviction that women's real responsibilities were domestic and private. There was a strong consensus against including women in combat. There was more dispute over whether women should register and be eligible for conscription. But many people who supported including women in registration and conscription did so on the belief that Congress and the military would organize any draft to preserve women's existing roles in the family and workplace. Even so, efforts to include women in registration and conscription failed.

Governmental and Popular Debates about Women's Legal Status in the Military, 1970–1980

The modern women's movement was intent on amending the Constitution to provide that "equality of rights under the law shall not be denied or abridged by the United States or by any State on account of sex." By 1970 Congress was also focused on the ERA. In the extensive congressional debates and testimony on the Amendment, all ERA opponents, and virtually all ERA supporters, agreed that the Amendment would require sex-neutral rules governing registration, conscription, and combat service.

The charge that the ERA would compel women's inclusion in registration, conscription, and combat was a leading objection, perhaps the foremost objection, to the Amendment. ERA opponents stressed that including women, especially mothers, in registration, conscription, and combat would destroy family life by removing the person obligated to maintain it. Senator Samuel Ervin Jr. stated bluntly that women's responsibilities were domestic and private rather than political and public. He explained that "custom and law" had always held wives and mothers responsible for making "homes" and furnishing "nurture, care, and training to their children during their early years." "It is absolutely ridiculous to talk about taking a mother away from her children so that she may go out to fight the enemy and leave the father at home to nurse the children."[6] Representative Emanuel Celler affirmed that women's real responsibilities were familial. "Women represent motherhood and creation," he declared. "Wars are for destruction."[7]

ERA supporters offered two sorts of responses. Some directly contested the premises of ERA opponents. They challenged women's circumscribed role in the military as part of their larger challenge to women's circumscribed role in the family, workplace, and society as a whole. These ERA supporters rejected the "understanding among people that women are not to serve their country, that women are to serve individuals—that is, husbands and families." They stressed the benefits of military service—leadership opportunities, vocational training, educational scholarships, and job preferences for veterans—that would help women surmount the constraints they typically confronted in the workplace. They insisted that women should assume equal responsibility for national defense to establish and confirm their equal citizenship. Representative Bella Abzug observed that "in the Congress of the United States and in the political life of this Nation, political choices and debate often reflect a belief that men who have fought for their country have a special right to wield political power and make political decisions." Until women had equal rights and responsibilities with respect to military service, they would be "denied the status of full citizenship, and the respect that goes with that status."[8]

However, many ERA supporters offered arguments much more closely aligned with the premises of ERA opponents. These ERA supporters belie standard scholarly accounts stressing the radicalism of Amendment advocates. Instead, these ERA supporters appeared to be significantly attached to preserving women's social roles, within and outside the military. They either felt such commitments themselves, or were convinced that the Amendment would fail unless taken to be consistent with such commitments, or both.

These ERA supporters denied that the Amendment would cause as much change as opponents predicted. For instance, they conceded that the ERA would make women eligible for conscription but explained that Congress and the military would structure any draft to preserve women's domestic roles. Mothers would be exempt, and this would not violate the ERA if fathers with the same family responsibilities were also exempt. The Senate Judiciary Committee promised that "the fear that mothers will be conscripted from their children into military service if the Equal Rights Amendment is ratified is totally and completely unfounded. Congress will retain ample power to create legitimate sex-neutral exemptions from compulsory service."

These ERA supporters also opposed including women in combat. They argued that the Amendment would permit Congress and the military to restrict combat service to people fitted for such service, and assumed this would preclude women from actually assuming combat roles. Senator Edward Gurney stated flatly that "the amendment does not require that women become combatants in the Armed Forces although it will subject them to the draft." Representative Michael Harrington explained that "the principle that members of the Armed Forces are used according to their basic ability alleviates the possibility that women will be sent into combat." Representative Martha Griffiths, the ERA's chief House sponsor, confidently predicted that the Amendment would leave servicewomen in the same low-level clerical and administrative jobs women dominated in civilian life and had long been confined to in the military. "The draft itself is equal," she stated. "But once you are in the Army you are put where the Army tells you where you are going to go. The thing that will happen with women is that they will be the stenographers and telephone operators."[9]

The ERA passed the House on October 12, 1971, and the Senate on March 22, 1972. But the charge that the Amendment would transform women's military status, and so transform women's domestic status, raged in state ratification debates.

By 1978 the ERA's ratification deadline of March 22, 1979, was approaching, and only thirty-five of the required thirty-eight states had ratified. During the intense congressional debates over whether to extend the deadline, ERA opponents reiterated that the Amendment would undermine women's family roles by subjecting women to registration, conscription, and combat, and identified the ERA's implications for women's military service as "probably the most serious" obstacle to ratification. ERA supporters again conceded that the Amendment would require women's inclusion in registration and conscription, but explained that Congress and the military would organize any draft to protect women's existing family roles and would exclude women from combat. On October 6, 1978, Congress extended the ratification deadline until June 30, 1982. But the debate over the ERA's consequences for women's military service continued within and outside Congress.

In the midst of this debate, President Carter, a leading ERA advocate, sought to implement by statute and regulation the changes in women's military role that many ERA supporters contended the Amendment would achieve. On February 8, 1980, Carter announced that he would seek congressional authorization to reinstitute registration and register women along with men, but stressed his opposition to including women in combat positions. Carter explicitly linked his proposal to support for the ERA. He identified registration and conscription eligibility as responsibilities that would confirm women's full citizenship and entitlement to equal rights. "Just as we are asking women to assume additional responsibilities," Carter explained, "it is more urgent than ever that the women in America have full and equal rights under the Constitution. Equal obligations deserve equal rights."[10]

Debate over Carter's proposal dominated Congress for months, until Congress passed, on June 25, 1980, and Carter signed on June 27, a statute funding registration for men only. The *Rostker* Court would claim that Congress developed new reasons for limiting women's military service in these months in 1980. On the Court's account, the debate about Carter's proposal was properly considered in isolation. Any earlier discussion of women's military role was irrelevant and not to be examined because Congress, in 1980, had "thoroughly reconsider[ed] the question of exempting women from [registration], and its basis for doing so."

This assertion was meant to facilitate the Court's decision permitting male-only registration to continue, by insisting that any constitutionally problematic modes of reasoning about women had been left in the past. *Rostker* contended that Congress's 1980 debate represented a complete break from history, in which Congress decided to exclude women from registration for fresh reasons, not grounded in constitutionally illegitimate concerns. The Court declared that Congress's 1980 "decision to exempt women from registration was not the 'accidental by-product of a traditional way of thinking about females.'"

Since *Rostker*, scholars have simply repeated the Court's assertion that Congress, in 1980, carefully reconsidered whether to register women without reflexively relying on traditional ideas about women's appropriate societal role. Even *Rostker*'s critics appear to have accepted its characterization of women's unequal treatment as located in the past, a "traditional," "outmoded" practice.

In fact, the debate about Carter's proposal was not a break with the past, and fit smoothly within over a decade of debate over women's military roles. In 1980 powerful governmental and popular voices—whether for or against Carter's proposal—remained determined to limit women's military service in ways designed to maintain and enforce women's place in the family and civilian employment. Throughout this period the notion that women, but not men, had primary responsibilities that were domestic and private was not, as a descriptive matter, out-of-date or a remnant of history. It shaped ongoing political and popular debates over women's military service.

Many congressional advocates of Carter's proposal were the same people supporting the ERA but contending that the Amendment would cause less change than ERA opponents envisioned. Like Carter, they explicitly linked Carter's proposal to support for the ERA. They explained, moreover, that Carter's proposal would establish by statute and military regulation exactly what they argued the ERA would establish.

Congressional advocates of Carter's proposal stressed that Congress and the military would structure any conscription of women to preserve women's domestic roles and would continue to exclude women from combat. Senator Carl Levin explained that "our society mores" required restricting women "to noncombat roles." And he emphasized that Congress and the military would need to arrange conscription "to avoid" the "absurdity" of (in Senator John Warner's words) drafting "a young mother" and requiring her to go "off to boot camp leaving the baby with the husband."

Leaders of the Defense Department and Selective Service System, in turn, testified before Congress that registering women and making them eligible for conscription would promote military effectiveness and national security. But they anticipated that most servicewomen's work would mirror the jobs women dominated in the sex-stratified civilian workplace, while the military would shield men from such work. Robert Pirie Jr., the Assistant Secretary of Defense for Manpower, Reserve Affairs, and Logistics, and Bernard Rostker, the Selective Service System director who would become the named defendant in *Rostker*, both told Congress that it was "in our national security interest to register women at this time." Pirie testified that "the work women in the Armed Forces do today is essential to the readiness and capability of the forces." In wartime the number of women the military required "would inevitably expand" and "having our young women registered in advance will put us in the position to call women if they do not volunteer in sufficient numbers." Yet Pirie also explained that "women have traditionally held the vast majority of jobs in fields such as administrative/clerical and health care/ medical. An advantage of registration for women," he reported, "is that a pool of trained personnel in these traditionally female jobs would exist in the event that sufficient volunteers were not available. It would make far greater sense to include women in a draft call and thereby gain many of these skills than to draft only males who would not only require training in these fields but would be drafted for employment in jobs traditionally held by females."[11]

Despite such arguments, Carter's proposal sparked substantial and effective opposition within Congress and from many of the popular groups successfully fighting ERA ratification. Like Carter's supporters, opponents of registering women explicitly linked Carter's proposal to the ERA. They identified Carter's proposal as an attempt to impose ERA requirements by statute and military regulation, and contended that registering women—even under Carter's proposal—would disrupt women's social roles, particularly in the family.

Rostker would eventually quote a Senate Armed Services Committee report from June 20, 1980, as evidence of strong congressional, military, and popular opposition to women in combat. But in passages of the Senate report that Rostker did not quote, the committee justified its opposition to registering and conscripting women by explaining that women's ultimate responsibilities were familial and private. The committee recounted that "witnesses representing a variety of groups testified . . . that drafting women would place unprecedented strains on family life, whether in peacetime or in time of emergency." The committee itself made the "specific finding" that "under the administration's proposal there is no proposal for exemption of mothers of young children. The administration has given insufficient attention to necessary changes in Selective Service rules, such as those governing the induction of young mothers, and to the strains on family life that would result from the registration and possible induction of women." The committee concluded that "a decision which would result in a young mother being drafted and a young father remaining home with the family in a time of national emergency cannot be taken lightly, nor its broader implications ignored. The committee is strongly of the view that such a result, which would occur if women were registered and inducted under the administration plan, is unwise and unacceptable to a large majority of our people."[12]

Concern for preserving women's family roles pervaded congressional opposition to registering women. Senator Sam Nunn warned that Carter's proposal would "treat the mothers of young children exactly the same as the fathers of young children," so that in "hundreds, perhaps even thousands of cases" there would be "fathers staying home while mothers are shipped off for military service under a draft." Nunn declared it intolerable to create a system in which women could be drafted "leaving their husbands at home to take care of the children." Senator John Warner similarly stressed that Carter's proposal would "require women to go register and become eligible for a draft irrespective of their family situation," making no provision "for excluding a young mother."[13]

Popular groups also testified before Congress that registration would unacceptably remove women from their place in the family as if women had no more private responsibilities than men. Kathleen Teague testified representing Phyllis Schlafly, who was spearheading the fight against ERA ratification and leading the Coalition Against Drafting Women. Teague explained that registering women was "contrary to the Judeo-Christian culture which honors and respects women in their role as wives and mothers. It is irrational because it treats as fungibles men and women, husbands and wives, and fathers and mothers, which they certainly are not." "There is a different role for males and females and it must start with not registering women." "Our young women," she insisted, "have the right to be feminine, to get married, to build families and to have homes."[14]

In sum, the continued conviction that women could not and should not fully participate in military service because their true responsibilities were private and domestic shaped debate over Carter's proposal as it shaped debate over the ERA itself. Governmental and popular forces—on both sides of the debates about Carter's proposal and the ERA—remained intent on restricting women's military role in order to protect and enforce women's social roles outside the military.

Women's Legal Status in the Military and the Development of Modern Sex Discrimination Jurisprudence

One measure of the strength of Congress's commitment to preserving women's domestic roles is that Congress continued to express this commitment openly despite the development of modern sex discrimination jurisprudence. By 1980, Congress's own efforts on behalf of women's equality outside the military context had encouraged the Supreme Court to develop a much more rigorous sex discrimination jurisprudence. This jurisprudence gave Congress good reason to think that arguments about the primacy of women's domesticity would not help male-only registration survive a constitutional challenge in court, and that the existence of such arguments in the legislative history of Congress's rejection of Carter's proposal might actually make a court less likely to uphold male-only registration. Yet members of Congress continued to find arguments about domesticity so convincing that they repeatedly opposed registering women on the ground it would interfere with women's family roles. They confronted the new sex discrimination jurisprudence, implicitly pressing the Court to narrow the reach of that jurisprudence.

For most of its history Congress had no reason to fear that courts might contest limits on women's military service. The Supreme Court had historically applied rational basis review to state action that explicitly treated men and women differently. This review required only that there be some "basis in reason" for the sex-based distinction. Under rational basis review, the Supreme Court did not find any unconstitutional sex discrimination until 1971. Suits contesting male-only registration and conscription systematically failed in the lower courts.

Some courts hardly felt compelled to identify any rationale for women's exclusion. Courts that did identify a reason invoked *United States v. St. Clair*, a 1968 opinion from the U.S. District Court for the Southern District of New York. *St. Clair* endorsed the norms that had shaped women's legal status in the military. It concluded that male-only registration and conscription were rational because women's responsibilities were domestic and private, rather than political and public. "In providing for involuntary service for men and voluntary service for women," *St. Clair* explained, "Congress followed the teachings of history that if a nation is to survive, men must provide the first line of defense while women keep the home fires burning."[15]

However, state action that explicitly differentiated between men and women, like male-only registration, had become constitutionally vulnerable in court by the mid-1970s. The Supreme Court decided in *Craig v. Boren* (1976) to apply heightened scrutiny to sex-based state action, meaning that sex-based state action would be unconstitutional unless the sex-based distinction was "substantially related to achievement of" "important governmental objectives."[16]

By 1980 the Court had repeatedly found that commitments to preserving women's circumscribed roles in the family and workplace would not justify sex-based state action under heightened scrutiny. Indeed, the Court identified such commitments as sources of women's inequality and part of what its sex discrimination jurisprudence was designed to disrupt.

During the congressional debate over Carter's proposal, the Justice Department warned Congress that it needed to create a legislative history that could survive heightened scrutiny. Deputy Assistant Attorney General Larry Simms appeared before the Military Personnel Subcommittee of the House Armed Services Committee to testify that if Congress decided to exempt women from registration, the Justice Department anticipated litigation contesting the decision. In fact, Simms noted that the case that would become *Rostker v. Goldberg* was already under way in the lower courts. Simms further reported that any constitutional defense of male-only registration could not "call on in any way" the legislative history from earlier congressional decisions about women's military service because the earlier legislative history was "unfortunately replete" with "sexual stereotypes." Instead, Simms explained that if Congress wanted to exclude women from registration and survive a constitutional challenge it needed to create a legislative history free from the commitments to limiting women's roles and status that had characterized earlier debates on women's military service. "Speaking solely for the Department of Justice as litigator," he told Congress, "it should be fairly obvious to this committee that the defensibility of the all-male registration is something on which Congress perhaps should speak out clearly and formulate the kind of record, if indeed, it chooses to reject the administration's proposal, which will be helpful rather than hurtful in the litigation."[17]

Congressional opponents of registering women knew they needed a legislative history that could survive heightened scrutiny. But they were so committed to preserving women's roles outside the military, and so certain this was a convincing argument for maintaining male-only registration, that they repeatedly explained that women's military service needed to be limited to protect and enforce the primacy of women's private obligations. They pushed against the Court's sex discrimination jurisprudence, implicitly challenging the Court to limit its scope.

Ultimately the legislative history of Congress's 1980 decision to reinstate male-only registration was little different from the larger ERA debate, raging since 1970, over women's military role. The continued determination to maintain and enforce women's domestic responsibilities through barriers to women's military service was still evident. And, by 1980, male-only registration had become unprecedentedly vulnerable in court.

Rostker *and the Relationship between the Court and the World outside the Court*

On June 25, 1981, the Supreme Court in *Rostker v. Goldberg* upheld the constitutionality of male-only registration. The Court was so determined to reach this judgment that it claimed that Congress had entirely new reasons for excluding women from registration in 1980, reasons not grounded in modes of thinking about women that might be problematic under modern sex discrimination jurisprudence.

The *Rostker* case began in 1971, with four men suing during the Vietnam War and the ERA debate to challenge the constitutionality of registration and conscription. The plaintiffs started with several arguments, including that conscription constituted involuntary servitude and a taking of property without due process. By 1973, however, the lower courts had dismissed all claims except the contention that exclusively male registration and conscription violated constitutional principles of equal protection.

The Supreme Court's *Rostker* opinion, written by Justice William Rehnquist, is a vivid example of the influence that extrajudicial forces can exert on the Court's constitutional jurisprudence. *Rostker* explicitly took congressional, executive, military, and popular opposition to women in combat as sufficient cause to uphold the constitutionality of male-only registration.

Rostker, moreover, offers a window into how extrajudicial influence on judicial constitutional interpretation can function in a specific case. It suggests that the observation that extrajudicial developments can shape the Court's understanding of constitutional requirements should not be taken to imply that the Court is passive or confronts uniform political and public opinion. The *Rostker* Court did not simply respond to extrajudicial debates about women's appropriate military role. Indeed, the Court did not simply defer to political and professional military expertise. While the Court did discuss such expertise, *Rostker*'s position upholding male-only registration was in considerable tension with the military's stated interests. President Carter—Commander in Chief, Naval Academy graduate, and former naval submarine officer—had supported registering women. Leading Defense Department and Selective Service System officials had testified to Congress that implementing Carter's proposal would promote military effectiveness and national security.

Instead of simply responding to extrajudicial events or deferring to military judgment, *Rostker*'s constitutional interpretation actively intervened and enmeshed itself into contemporary extrajudicial debates over women's military status—debates that contained important divisions. *Rostker* drew on substantial extrajudicial agreement that women should be excluded from combat, and staked a position on an issue of significant extrajudicial disagreement: whether the combat exclusion justified male-only registration and conscription eligibility.

The *Rostker* opinion was not organized around the doctrinal test for heightened scrutiny, although it stated that this standard applied. Instead, *Rostker* defended Congress's 1980 decision to fund male-only registration in three steps.

First, the Court explained that Congress had excluded women from registration because Congress intended to limit any future drafts to men. The link between registration and conscription was clear; the purpose of registration is to prepare for possible future conscription. But the Court's argument still left the question of why a male-only draft would be constitutional.

The Court's second step was to argue that Congress intended to limit any future drafts to men because federal statutes and military regulations limited combat service to men. The link between conscription and combat was significantly less clear than the link between registration and conscription. Even during World War II and the Vietnam War, many drafted men never served in combat; the majority of the military consisted of noncombat personnel. The military, moreover, had historically emphasized that women in noncombat roles could free men to fight.

Indeed, the relationship between conscription and combat was a matter of serious dispute in Congress, the White House, state legislatures, and the streets when the Court decided *Rostker*. Many ERA supporters conceded that ratification would require women to be included in drafts. But, perhaps partially to increase the Amendment's appeal, they contended that women would not serve in combat. However, Rehnquist's opinion for the *Rostker* Court reflected greater affinity for the claims of the political and popular forces opposed to the ERA and to expanding women's military roles. Like ERA opponents, *Rostker* insisted on the direct connection between conscription eligibility and combat eligibility.

Yet even assuming that one accepted the connection between conscription and combat, a question still remained: Why could Congress and the military constitutionally limit combat positions to men? On this, the third and ultimate issue, *Rostker* had only one response. The Court's reasoning was remarkably bare. The Court simply relied on the significant political and popular consensus for excluding women from combat—a position that united many ERA supporters and opponents, joined Carter and his critics, and went unchallenged in the *Rostker* dissents. Here the Court recognized and built upon substantial extrajudicial convergence rather than taking sides on a point of divergence. The Court noted that the president intended "to continue the current military policy precluding women from combat" and that strong congressional, popular, and military sentiment supported excluding women from combat. *Rostker* quoted a passage from the June 20, 1980, report of the Senate Armed Services Committee, stating that:

The principle that women should not intentionally and routinely engage in combat is fundamental, and enjoys wide support among our people. It is universally supported by military leaders who have testified before the Committee. . . . Current law and policy exclude women from being assigned to combat in our military forces, and the Committee reaffirms this policy.

This passage, and the rest of *Rostker*, did not explore the reasons behind the support for excluding women from combat. Nevertheless, the Court took the extrajudicial opposition to women in combat as sufficient cause to uphold male-only registration, stating that "the fact that Congress and the Executive have decided that women should not serve in combat fully justifies Congress in not authorizing their registration, since the purpose of registration is to develop a pool of potential combat troops." On the same logic, presumably, banning women entirely from military service would also be constitutional if the president, Congress, military leaders, and a majority of the public did not want women to serve, even voluntarily and in noncombat roles. *Rostker's* conclusion about the constitutional requirements of equal protection was thus deeply responsive to, and actively engaged with, extrajudicial debates.

Women's Legal Status in the Military since Rostker

Since *Rostker*, few lawsuits have challenged restrictions on women's military service, and no challenges have reached the Supreme Court. Two reasons probably explain the paucity of litigation. First, there have long been close connections between the women's movement and pacifism, and some portion of the women's movement—a natural source of litigation on issues implicating sex equality—is not interested in expanding women's military role. Second, people who are interested in expanding women's military service apparently concluded, after *Rostker*, that litigation was an unpromising route to reform. *Rostker* suggested that the Supreme Court would be unlikely to transform women's military role. Moreover, the judiciary's hierarchical organization strongly discourages lower courts from undermining *Rostker*. The few lower courts to consider challenges to restrictions on women's military service since *Rostker* quickly rejected the claims, relying on the *Rostker* precedent. As recently as 2003 the U.S. District Court for the District of Massachusetts cited *Rostker* to uphold male-only registration. The plaintiffs in *Schwartz v. Brodsky*[18]—four men required to register and one woman excluded from registration—appealed on the ground that the extrajudicial changes in women's military status since *Rostker* had undermined the *Rostker* precedent. But at the urging of leading feminist groups, the *Schwartz* plaintiffs decided to dismiss their appeal because they did not want to risk that the appellate court might also be unwilling to undermine a Supreme Court holding, no matter how extrajudicial changes had weakened it.

Yet despite the virtual absence of litigation—and the resultant decline in academic attention—women's legal status in the military has undergone tremendous change outside the courts. Federal law no longer contains statutory combat exclusions; the military has opened many, although not all, combat positions to women; and the public has become steadily more enthusiastic about women in the military, including in combat.

Rostker concluded that women's exclusion from registration, conscription, and combat was consistent with equal protection, generating no pressure to expand women's military role. Commentators frequently stress and admire the Court's ability to settle constitutional disputes. Yet *Rostker*'s judgment that women's rights to equality were not in jeopardy did not mean the end of discussion and dispute about that question. The claim that restrictions on women's military role threatened sex equality moved to other parts of the government for redress, and has enjoyed notable success there. Congress, the executive, and the military have continued to debate how sex equality should be upheld and to generate evolving answers, while the Court's position has remained unchanged. These extrajudicial actors have been driven by their commitment to sex equality—paired with their recognition of the volunteer military's pragmatic need for female talent—to dramatically, if incrementally, expand women's military role, including in combat.

As this record illustrates, the Court is not the only developer and enforcer of equality norms, or even the most important source of those norms in some situations. Indeed, the extrajudicial changes in women's military role increasingly raise questions about the status of *Rostker* itself. The extrajudicial transformation of women's military status has undercut the factual premises and cultural assumptions behind *Rostker's* interpretation of constitutional equal protection.

NOTES

For a longer version of this essay and complete citations, see Jill Elaine Hasday, *Fighting Women: The Military, Sex, and Extrajudicial Constitutional Change*, 93 Minn. L. Rev. 96 (2008).

1. 453 U.S. 57, 75–77, 83 (1981).

2. *See* Office of the Assistant Sec'y of Def. (Manpower, Reserve Affairs, & Logistics), Background Review: Women in the Military 13 (1981).

3. *See* U.S. Census Bureau, U.S. Dep't of Commerce, Statistical Abstract of the United States: 2008, at 332 tbl. 498 (2007).

4. 60 U.S. (19 How.) 393, 415 (1857).

5. *To Establish the Women's Army Corps in the Regular Army, to Authorize the Enlistment and Appointment of Women in the Regular Navy and Marine Corps and the Naval and Marine Corps Reserve, and for Other Purposes: Hearings on S. 1641 before the Subcomm. on Organization and Mobilization of the H. Comm. on Armed Services*, 80th Cong. 5564 (1948).

6. S. Rep. No. 92-689, at 49; 118 Cong. Rec. 9102 (1972).

7. 117 Cong. Rec. 35,785 (1971).

8. *Id.* at 35,311.

9. *Id.* at 35,323.

10. Jimmy Carter, Selective Service Revitalization: Statement on the Registration of Americans for the Draft, 1 Pub. Papers 289, 289–91 (Feb. 8, 1980).

11. *Registration of Women: Hearings on H.R. 6569 before the Subcomm. on Military Personnel of the H. Comm. on Armed Services*, 96th Cong. 6 (1980).

12. S. Rep. No. 96-826, at 159–61 (1980).

13. 126 Cong. Rec. 13,885 (1980).

14. *Registration of Women* 103, 105 (statement of Kathleen Teague, representing Phyllis Schlafly, Coalition Against Drafting Women).

15. 291 F. Supp. 122, 124–25 (S.D.N.Y. 1968).

16. 429 U.S. 190, 197 (1976).

17. *Registration of Women*, at 14–15.

18. 265 F. Supp. 2d 130, 131–35 (D. Mass. 2003).

6

Irrational Women

Informed Consent and Abortion Regret

MAYA MANIAN

This chapter explores the law's failure in the twenty-first century to treat pregnant women as capable of making their own decisions concerning whether to have an abortion. The Supreme Court's 2007 decision in *Gonzales v. Carhart*, which upheld a federal ban on a type of second-trimester abortion that many physicians believe is safest for their patients, brought the question of women's capacity for abortion decision making to the forefront of public legal consciousness. In *Carhart*, the Court abandoned its previous deference and respect for a woman's right to be her own decision maker with regard to abortion and instead determined that a pregnant woman lacks capacity to make her own decisions and give informed consent to abortion-related medical treatment. According to the Court, the government may make the final decision regarding a pregnant woman's health care to ensure that she realizes her "ultimate" role as a mother.

> Respect for human life finds an ultimate expression in the bond of love the mother has for her child. . . . While we find no reliable data to measure the phenomenon, it seems unexceptionable to conclude some women come to regret their choice to abort the infant life they once created and sustained.[1]

This chapter recounts the contradictory history in the late twentieth and early twenty-first centuries of the abortion law's regard for women's agency as decision makers. It also argues that *Carhart*'s disrespect for women's decision-making abilities unjustifiably diverges from the law's deference to patient health-care decision making more generally. The unequal treatment of women as health-care decision makers bolsters the argument articulated by feminist legal scholars that abortion restrictions manifest sex discrimination.[2]

"Partial-Birth" Abortion and Women's Health

Carhart marks the Supreme Court's first refusal to require a health exception to an abortion restriction since *Roe v. Wade* in 1973 and the Court's first use of the anti-abortion movement's "woman-protective" rationale to uphold an abortion ban.[3] The woman-protective rationale claims that banning abortion promotes women's mental health.[4] *Carhart's* woman-protective anti-abortion reasoning casts so-called partial-birth abortion bans as public health measures that serve to protect women from "regret" and depression. Contrary to this claim, the *Carhart* decision not only endangers women's health, but it also may encourage courts and legislatures to approve other restrictive measures under the guise of "protecting" women.

The abortion regulation at issue in *Gonzales v. Carhart* purports to ban a method of second-trimester abortion known as "intact D&E [Dilation and Evacuation]," labeled "partial-birth" abortion by its opponents. "Partial-birth" abortion is not a medical term but a political one.[5] In a 5–4 decision written by Justice Anthony Kennedy, *Carhart* upheld the federal Partial-Birth Abortion Act of 2003. The Court held that the Act was not unduly burdensome on women's right to choose abortion, nor unconstitutionally vague, and, most striking, that the Act did not require a health exception. Previously, in *Planned Parenthood v. Casey* (1992), the Court had reaffirmed *Roe v. Wade*'s holding that abortion regulations must have an exception to protect women's health, even after viability.[6] In *Stenberg v. Carhart* (2000), the first Supreme Court case addressing a "partial-birth" abortion ban, the Court reaffirmed the requirement that abortion regulations contain a health exception whenever "substantial medical authority" supports the medical necessity of the banned procedure. Thus, even where there is a lack of consensus in the medical community, *Stenberg* mandated that legislatures err on the side of protecting women's health.[7] *Carhart* found exactly the opposite, holding that legislatures could choose to err on the side of risking women's health under a mere rationality standard: "Considerations of marginal safety, including the balance of risks, are within the legislative competence when the regulation is rational and in pursuit of legitimate ends."[8] The physicians challenging the Act had presented substantial evidence, accepted by six different federal courts, that the intact D&E procedure is medically necessary in some cases, especially for women with certain medical conditions. *Carhart* acknowledged that the requirements of the Act may, in fact, endanger women's physical health but nevertheless concluded that legislatures could impose those risks on women, in part to protect women from emotional harm.

In a sharply worded dissent, Justice Ruth Bader Ginsburg condemned the Court's retreat from protecting women's health. She emphasized that the Court's precedents had always mandated exceptions to abortion restrictions for women's health "at any stage of pregnancy." Ginsburg found the Court's claim that the Act can survive in the face of alleged medical uncertainty "bewildering" and repeatedly stressed that the Court "def[ied] [its] long-standing precedent affirming the necessity of a health exception, with no carve-out for circumstances of medical uncertainty."[9]

Moreover, Ginsburg argued that the Court's justifications for upholding the Act were "flimsy and transparent," and that the Act's true purpose, as well as the purpose of the Court's defense of the Act, was to "chip away at [the abortion] right declared again and again by this Court—and with increasing comprehension of its centrality to women's lives." In this regard, Ginsburg remarked on the peculiarities of the Court's rhetoric throughout the opinion: "[T]he opinion refers to obstetrician-gynecologists and surgeons who perform abortions not by the titles of their medical specialties, but by the pejorative label 'abortion doctor.' . . . A fetus is described as an 'unborn child' and as a 'baby'; second-trimester, pre-viability abortions are referred to as 'late-term'; and the reasoned medical judgments of highly trained doctors are dismissed as 'preferences' motivated by 'mere convenience.'"[10] Ultimately Ginsburg concluded that the Act is "irrational" since it does not further any legitimate government interest.

Ginsburg's stinging dissent also stressed that assertions of the right to choose abortion "do not seek to vindicate some generalized notion of privacy" but rather "center on a woman's autonomy to determine her life's course, and thus to enjoy equal citizenship stature."[11] In light of this concern for gender equality, Ginsburg particularly attacked the Court's woman-protective reasoning for upholding "partial-birth" abortion bans. The Court began its explanation of how the federal abortion ban serves to "protect" women with the declaration: "Respect for human life finds an *ultimate* expression in the bond of love the mother has for her child." This language harkens back to the century-old decision of *Bradwell v. Illinois* in 1873, in which women were denied the right to practice law in part because "the *paramount* destiny and mission of woman are to fulfill the noble and benign offices of wife and mother."[12] Ginsburg pointed out that the Court gave no explanation for why the mother-child bond is the ultimate bond, as opposed to father-child or parental bonds, especially for a woman with an unwanted pregnancy.[13] Rather, the Court simply declared that the Act recognizes the supposedly "self-evident" reality of women's nature as mothers. Following its statement about women's "ultimate" role as mothers, the *Carhart* Court claimed that it was "unexceptionable" to conclude that women regret their abortions and suffer "severe depression and loss of esteem" as a result, although the Court admitted it had no data to support this assertion of abortion regret.[14]

Ginsburg assailed the Court's alleged concern over abortion regret, stating that the Court's reasoning was "an anti-abortion shibboleth for which [the Court] concededly has no reliable evidence."[15] In fact, studies on the psychological impact of abortion show that women generally do not regret decisions to terminate a pregnancy.[16] Relying on this unsubstantiated claim of women's regret, the *Carhart* Court asserted that because the decision "[is] so fraught with emotional consequence," doctors "may prefer not to disclose precise details of the means that will be used, confining themselves to the required statement of risks the procedure entails."[17] The Court recognized that the law of informed consent generally does not require disclosure of every detail of a particular medical procedure and that "any number of patients facing imminent surgical procedures would prefer not to hear all the details, lest the usual anxiety preceding invasive medical procedures become the more intense." However, it is "precisely this lack of information concerning the way in which the fetus will be killed that is of legitimate concern to the State." The Court concluded:

> The State has an interest in ensuring so grave a choice is well-informed. It is self-evident that a mother who comes to regret her choice to abort must struggle with grief more anguished and sorrow more profound when she learns, only after the event, what she once did not know: that she allowed a doctor to pierce the skull and vacuum the fast-developing brain of her unborn child, a child assuming the human form.[18]

The Court's language portrays women who are "mothers" as too emotionally unstable to make significant decisions and treats pregnant women as "hysterical" and childlike.[19] *Carhart's* woman-protective reasoning declares all pregnant women incompetent to choose appropriate medical care related to abortion. In the Court's view, a rational pregnant woman would make only one choice—the government's choice. *Carhart* also implies that a woman's role as a mother mandates that she sacrifice herself for her fetus or else become psychologically unstable. As Jack Balkin noted, *Carhart* basically claims that "either a woman is crazy when she undergoes an abortion, or she will become crazy later on."[20]

Relying on archaic stereotypes about women's "emotional" nature, *Carhart* denies women's agency by disrespecting their ability to determine for themselves the choices that will protect their physical and mental health. According to the Court's logic, a mentally competent woman is incapable of deciding how best to protect her own mental health. The state is the final decision-maker, because the state knows better than the woman herself that her ultimate role should be as a mother. In her dissent Justice Ginsberg emphasized that the majority's reasoning "reflects ancient notions about women's place in the family and under the Constitution—ideas that have long since been discredited."[21]

Informed Consent to Abortion and Women's Agency

Carhart's portrayal of women evokes a century-old societal view of femininity.[22] *Carhart* marks the culmination of a growing disrespect for women's decision-making capabilities that has been under way for some time in the abortion context. The Supreme Court's approval of abortion-specific informed consent regulations particularly reveals abortion law's disregard for women's capacity for sound decision making. The so-called informed consent legislation regarding abortions belies a deep suspicion of women as medical (and moral) decision makers. This section traces the conflicting history of the Supreme Court's acceptance of abortion-specific "informed consent" legislation and the corresponding ebb and flow of respect for women's autonomy in abortion decision making.

For a period of time, under the doctrinal framework established in *Roe v. Wade*,[23] the law generally treated women as entitled to autonomy in their abortion decision making, as with other patients. The use of the general law of informed consent in both the Supreme Court and lower courts to guide the analysis of abortion-specific informed consent regulations reflected this equal treatment of women. Informed consent law protects patients' decision-making authority by mandating unbiased disclosure of the material risks and benefits of treatment options. In part because the courts viewed female patients seeking abortion as equally capable decision makers as other patients, courts conformed the requirements of abortion informed consent to informed consent law as applied to all other patients.[24]

Two cases decided under the *Roe* regime illustrate the Court's former regard for women's autonomous decision making. First, in *City of Akron v. Akron Center for Reproductive Health* (1983),[25] the Court struck down an abortion-specific "informed consent" ordinance. The Court emphasized that the validity of an abortion "informed consent" regulation "rest[s] on the State's interest in protecting the health of the pregnant woman." *Akron* stressed that the State's interest in ensuring that consent to abortion is informed does not permit the State to impose regulations "designed to influence the woman's informed choice between abortion and childbirth." In other words, the government could not pressure women to conform to its preferred choice—motherhood—under the banner of "informed consent." Applying this view, the Court struck down Akron's abortion informed consent ordinance, finding that the regulation was "designed not to inform the woman's consent but rather to persuade her to withhold it altogether."

Second, in *Thornburgh v. American College of Obstetricians and Gynecologists* (1986),[26] the Court struck down an informed consent to abortion regulation that mandated delivery of seven specific kinds of information to all abortion patients. The Court found that much of this information would be irrelevant or inappropriate for some patients, such as those with life-threatening pregnancies or pregnancies resulting from rape. *Thornburgh* also reiterated that government may not mandate the conveyance of biased information designed to influence the woman's choice against abortion. The Court opined that the sum of the challenged informed consent regulation "is, or comes close to being, state medicine imposed upon the woman, not the professional medical guidance she seeks, and it officially structures—as it obviously was intended to do—the dialogue between the woman and her physician." *Thornburgh* recognized and rejected the State's attempt, under "the guise of informed consent," to advance a coercive agenda contrary to respect for women's autonomous decision making.

As the composition of the Court shifted to the right, the landscape of abortion law changed dramatically, most significantly in 1992 in *Planned Parenthood v. Casey*. For the first time since *Roe*, *Casey* upheld informed consent legislation biased against abortion that would pressure patients' decisions under the misnomer of an informed consent law. Much of the Court's rationale displayed little deference to women's equal capacity for self-determination. For example, in upholding the constitutionality of an abortion "informed consent" provision, *Casey* stated: "Though the woman has a right to choose to terminate or continue her pregnancy before viability, it does not at all follow that the State is prohibited from taking steps to ensure that this choice is thoughtful and informed."[27] Therefore, "measures aimed at ensuring that a woman's choice contemplates the consequences for the fetus do not necessarily interfere with the right recognized in *Roe*." The *Casey* opinion assumed that women lacked the judgment to make "mature and informed" abortion decisions on their own, without pressure from the State, as other patients do with respect to other important medical decisions. As Justice John Paul Stevens pointed out in his separate opinion in *Casey*, the joint opinion "rests on outmoded and unacceptable assumptions about the decision-making capacity of women."[28] Statutes singling out abortion for state-mandated information enforced by criminal sanction imply that women patients cannot be trusted to elicit information from their physicians and sue in malpractice if necessary, as is the norm.[29] One scholar criticizing *Casey* noted that "enhancing deliberative autonomy would appear to be the joint opinion's goal only to the extent that those [J]ustices accept that women are choosing abortion out of ignorance or without due attention to arguments against abortion."[30] A number of scholars have also argued that abortion-specific "informed consent" statutes inherently reflect sex discrimination, because they "fundamentally perpetuate the stereotypical notion of the indecisiveness of women, questioning a woman's ability to make decisions about the course of her life . . . [and reflect] stereotypical assumptions that women choose to obtain abortions carelessly, without thinking through the implications of their decisions."[31]

Casey marks a turning point when abortion law explicitly began treating women as decision makers less capable than other competent adults. It permitted the State to impose biased information when women are choosing to reject the traditional role of motherhood.[32] *Casey* opened the door to so-called informed consent laws in the abortion context that have deviated far from the core principle of respect for patient autonomy protected by the tort law doctrine of informed consent. In fact, although *Casey* emphasized that only "truthful, nonmisleading" information should be constitutionally permissible, post-*Casey* decisions have permitted "informed consent" statutes that are neither truthful nor factually non-misleading.[33]

Some have reasoned that although the general law of informed consent would not permit physicians to impart distorted information designed to manipulate a patient's decision, there are different considerations at play as a constitutional matter that could justify *Casey*'s holding. *Casey* specifically claimed that, under its new "undue burden" test, the government need not be bound by informed consent doctrine (which regulates physicians) with respect to governmental regulation of abortion: "We also see no reason why the State may not require doctors to inform a woman seeking an abortion of the availability of materials relating to the consequences to the fetus, even when those consequences have no direct relation to her health. . . . [I]nformed choice need not be defined in such narrow terms that all considerations of the effect on the fetus are made irrelevant."[34] Yet *Casey* largely failed to explain why the government can impose information *biased* toward childbirth and against abortion if its goal is truly informed choice.

It is noteworthy that *Casey* relied upon the same woman-protective reasoning later used by *Carhart* as one of the primary justifications for upholding biased "informed consent" legislation. The *Casey* opinion characterized women as unable to make decisions and thus in need of the State's "protection" through "informed consent" legislation:

> It cannot be questioned that psychological well-being is a facet of health. Nor can it be doubted that most women considering an abortion would deem the impact on the fetus relevant, if not dispositive, to the decision. In attempting to ensure that a woman apprehend the full consequences of her decision, the State furthers the legitimate purpose of reducing the risk that a woman may elect an abortion, only to discover later, with devastating psychological consequences, that her decision was not fully informed.[35]

As in *Carhart*, the Court lacked any evidence to support its mental health claim but, nevertheless, invoked women's need for special psychological "protection" to justify allowing biased information. The seeds of the woman-protective argument were planted in *Casey* and came to fruition in *Carhart*, which completely disregarded pregnant women's agency by denying their capabilities for sound health-care decision making.

Informed Consent and Patient Agency in Health Care Law

The *Carhart* Court's cabined view of women's decision-making capacity reflects a gender-stereotyped view of women's nature. *Carhart* also exposed abortion law's discriminatory view of women as decision makers by articulating a new paradigm of "informed consent" in the abortion context that controverts well-established rules of a patient's right to informed consent in health care law more generally. An examination of the law on health-care decision making yields the conclusion that compared to how the law treats all other competent adult patient decision making, abortion law treats pregnant women unequally. The denial of pregnant women's agency in abortion decision making unjustifiably diverges from the law's treatment of patient decision making in both the private law doctrine of informed consent and in public law constitutional cases governing medical decision making. This inconsistency between abortion law's approach to women's decision making and the general law on health-care decision making exposes the sex discrimination inherent in the woman-protective anti-abortion claim. This section first reviews the tort law doctrine of informed consent in comparison with abortion law's treatment of informed consent and then contrasts constitutional law precedents on medical treatment decisions.

Informed consent law establishes the legal rules regarding patient medical decision making and therefore provides a useful lens through which to critique abortion law's treatment of women as health care decision makers. It is also important to disentangle informed consent terminology as used in abortion law from informed consent law generally, as the term is often misused in the abortion context. The tort law doctrine of informed consent serves primarily to respect a patient's self-determination and autonomy. In contrast, abortion law invokes "informed consent" as a reason for abortion restrictions that undermine women's autonomous decision making.

By now a well-established principle in health care law, the common law rule of informed consent rejects a paternalistic model of patient decision making in which the physician makes treatment decisions for the patient and instead embodies a model recognizing that competent adult patients have the capacity to make their own medical treatment decisions. Therefore the law requires that physicians obtain their patients' consent prior to treatment by disclosing unbiased information on all the material risks and benefits of the treatment. By mandating disclosure and patient consent, informed consent law protects the twin values of bodily integrity and self-determination. These values reinforce the core principle animating informed consent doctrine: respect for patient autonomy.[36]

Informed consent law disavows the notion that the physician should "protect" the patient by withholding information or usurping the patient's decision making, because "that attitude presumes instability or perversity for even the normal patient, and runs counter to the foundation principle that the patient should and ordinarily can make the choice for himself."[37] *Canterbury v. Spence*, one of the leading cases on informed consent, notably declared: "To the physician, whose training enables a self-satisfying evaluation, the answer may seem clear, but it is the prerogative of the patient, not the physician, to determine for himself the direction in which his interests seem to lie." Numerous scholars have noted that the doctrine operates primarily to respect the capacity of competent adults to make autonomous decisions and "the notion that each mature individual has a right to make the basic choices that affect her life prospects."[38]

The twin values of bodily integrity and self-determination protected by informed consent also underlie the "right to privacy" line of cases that support the constitutional right to abortion.[39] Yet comparing the law of informed consent to abortion law reveals a striking difference in how the law views pregnant women as decision makers.[40] *Carhart,* in particular, ignores the long history of protection for patient decision-making capacity that has been well established in informed consent doctrine and instead incapacitates women as decision makers. *Carhart's* woman-protective rationale invokes "informed consent" as a justification for a ruling that is antithetical to informed consent law. Informed consent law dismisses the belief that patients cannot balance the risks and benefits of medical treatments and determine for themselves how best to protect their overall health. In stark contrast to this notion, *Carhart* asserts that female patients (particularly pregnant women) lack equal capacity to make judgments about their own well-being and therefore need "protection" from their own allegedly unsound decisions. The *Carhart* Court claimed to be worried that women will be denied an informed choice about abortion because doctors may not fully disclose all information it deemed relevant to the banned intact D&E procedure. However, the Court's concern for informed decision making hardly seems genuine when its solution denies decision making altogether. As Ginsburg's dissent noted, "the Court deprives women of the right to make an autonomous choice, even at the expense of their safety."[41]

In addition, the Court's "regret" rationale proves too much. Any medical treatment decision can lead to regret in some percentage of patients. If protection from regret were sufficient to permit government regulation, government could override patient decision making for any medical procedure, eviscerating the legal and ethical norm of informed consent in health care. Adults make important emotional medical decisions that may lead to regret in many situations, but the law does not interfere with those decisions on the ground that someone other than the patient knows better which life choices will lead to mentally healthy consequences. For example, a recent study concluded that as many as one in five men who undergo prostate surgery (which may not always be necessary to preserve life or health) regret their decision, typically because of reduced sexual function.[42] Taking *Carhart's* reasoning to its logical extreme, why should the government not be allowed to restrict access to prostate cancer treatment to "protect" men from the regret that may result from their reduced virility, which may lead to depression and other psychological harms?[43] Treatment for prostate cancer can also be an emotionally fraught decision for men, particularly because of the possible sexual side effects. Yet lawmakers do not respond to this proven risk of regret by limiting men's treatment options; rather, lawmakers and physicians work to ensure the provision of appropriate and accurate information to improve men's decision making. Only in the case of the gender-specific abortion decision does the law react to the possibility of patient regret—present to some degree with any medical treatment—by permitting the government to ban the treatment entirely and endanger the patient's health. Constitutional scholar Reva Siegel has extensively demonstrated that the woman-protective rationale's twisted "informed consent" paradigm—that abortion should be banned to protect women from their own poor decisions—relies not on concern for autonomous decision making but on gender-stereotyped notions of women's capacity and women's roles long rejected under equal protection jurisprudence.[44]

Furthermore, contrary to the Court's assertion that no woman would knowingly choose "partial-birth" abortion, there are in fact sound reasons why a woman might choose the now banned intact D&E procedure. Foremost, there are safety advantages to the intact version of the D&E procedure that are absent in other available methods of second-trimester abortion. Three separate trial courts and three appellate courts accepted the expert testimony of physicians who explained why an intact D&E procedure would be the safest method of abortion for some women. If the State can require a woman to undergo a riskier abortion procedure in order to "protect" her from regret, why not allow the State to ban all the safest methods of abortion? Under the Court's reasoning, the State could argue that if women knew the details of the non-intact D&E procedure (the most common method of second-trimester abortion), which the Court acknowledged could be characterized as equally "brutal" as intact D&E,[45] women would similarly regret such a decision. If all the State must do to satisfy the Constitution is allow some alternative but less safe method of abortion, why not permit the State to ban D&E entirely and force women to undergo induction abortions? Induction abortion involves inducing labor, which entails more health risks to the patient, is significantly more costly as it requires a hospital stay, and is far more emotionally and physically painful for the woman.[46] Given women's supposed lack of decision-making capacity because of their emotional mental state and their presumed nature as mothers, the State could readily argue that women should only have access to induction abortion since this method appears arguably less gruesome and, perhaps, more "natural" as it simulates the birth process. Yet, contrary to the Court's description of women's "self-evident" nature, studies show that when given the option of either induction abortion or D&E, many women choose D&E.[47] Carhart's justification for denying women agency in decision making is admittedly not evidence-based but rather based solely on sex-role stereotypes. The Court parades, as factual, the "self-evident" description of what is in fact a normative view of the proper role of women.[48] In fact, the Court's "regret" rationale could be used as a justification for banning all abortions, which is the ultimate goal of the proponents of the woman-protective anti-abortion rationale.[49] Of course, some percentage of women may regret having an abortion, but rather than seriously engage with the question of how to ensure better decision making for pregnant women, *Carhart's* approach takes their decision away entirely.[50]

Carhart's use (and misuse) of informed consent rhetoric exposes abortion law's anomalous treatment of women as health-care decision makers. *Carhart's* woman-protective reasoning is not only antithetical to informed consent law's deference to patient decision making but also finds no support in constitutional law precedent on medical treatment decisions. In no other area of health care does the State override a competent adult's right to consent to a medical procedure that falls within the bounds of proven and accepted medical practice, and in fact may be *physically* safer for the patient, based on the State's unsubstantiated view that the treatment will be *psychologically* harmful to the patient. The law only subjects the gender-specific abortion decision to this kind of doubt about patient decision-making capacity, therefore denying that women have the same ability as men to make informed health care decisions. The woman-protective anti-abortion rationale's striking departure from both informed consent law properly understood *and* from public law precedents on medical care further exposes abortion law's sex discriminatory treatment of women as health-care decision makers.

Although under informed consent law—private law—we clearly allocate decision-making power to the patient rather than the physician, under constitutional law—public law—we sometimes allocate decision-making power to the government rather than the patient. The Supreme Court has permitted the government to impose some limits on individuals' health-care decision making for the sake of protecting public health.[51] In particular, the Court has permitted the government to mandate vaccination, ban certain controlled substances, restrict access to experimental medications, and ban physician-assisted suicide.[52] Nevertheless, these public health restrictions on patient choice do not undermine the notion that the law generally should grant patients agency in making health care decisions. *Carhart's* woman-protective reasoning—that it is self-evident that abortion would damage women's psychological health—invokes the public health paradigm for government regulation of patient decision making in order to justify the federal abortion ban. *Carhart* asserts that Congress banned "partial-birth" abortions for the legitimate purpose of protecting maternal health. Justice Kennedy's opinion attempts to frame the federal abortion ban as a public health issue, and suggests that, like the Court's other public health cases, the Court should leave it to the legislature to determine the measures that best serve the public's interests.[53]

Yet a comparison of the public health cases reveals that the woman-protective rationale adopted in *Carhart* is readily distinguishable from these precedents allowing government restrictions on medical treatment. Even under constitutional law precedents that allow government limits on patient choice, the State cannot endanger patient health in order to paternalistically protect patients from unproven risks of psychological harm that may result from their own supposedly poor ability to make medical decisions. In other words, in no other context does the law ban a medically necessary treatment on the ground that the State knows better than a mentally competent adult what will be best for her mental health. That kind of paternalism only applies to women seeking an abortion.

The Supreme Court's public health precedents can be reduced to a few simple principles for when and why the government can restrict patients' medical options or deny patients' capacity for decision making. Restrictions on a competent adult patient's right to informed consent are justified when the State intervenes to protect *third parties* other than the competent adult patient—the justification being that the State may intervene "for the common good." The State can intervene *on the patient's own behalf* only where there is a lack of information about the medical treatment such that the informed consent process cannot be expected to function properly and the treatment presents a risk of physical harm to the patient—the justification being that the State can then intervene "for the patient's own good." Neither of these rationales supports *Carhart's* reasoning that the State can trump a woman's right to consent to a physically safer medical procedure, where full information is available, in order to protect her from unsubstantiated psychological harm resulting from her supposedly incompetent decision making.

For example, the Supreme Court has held that the government can mandate vaccinations and ban controlled substances in order to protect third parties from communicable diseases and from recreational drug abuse. In other words, the government may deny patient choice in order to protect third parties from collateral harm—the paradigmatic public health case.[54] The Court has relied upon the rationale "for the common good" to justify compulsory vaccination laws and regulations of controlled substances such as alcohol during Prohibition and medical marijuana today.[55] Of course, one could argue that fetuses are "third parties" that the State may protect by restricting access to abortion. Although the Court's medical treatment cases suggest that government can impose health risks on individual patients for the protection of other persons and thus the public health at large, never before has the Court suggested that government can impose health risks on women in order to preserve the potential life of the fetus. *Carhart*'s reliance on these precedents in support of its decision represents a move toward establishing the fetus as a third-party "person" with interests sufficient to trump the woman's right to preserve her own health. If fetuses are third parties that the legislature can choose to protect over women's right to protect their health, then that would logically lead to a justification for denying the abortion right altogether—a goal that is implicit throughout the *Carhart* opinion.[56]

In addition, the government can paternalistically protect patients from their own poor decision making only in cases where there exists such a lack of information that the informed consent process cannot be expected to function appropriately *and* there is a risk of serious physical harm to the patient—the primary justification given by the federal courts for permitting government regulation of experimental drugs.[57] In contrast, *Carhart* permits the government to second-guess women's medical decision making on the ground of "protecting" them from an uncorroborated risk of emotional injury, while imposing proven risks of physical injury in the process.

Finally, the Supreme Court's justifications for permitting state bans on physician-assisted suicide (PAS) also paternalistically protect patients "for the patient's own good," but the rationales for bans on PAS meaningfully differ from *Carhart*'s woman-protective rationale in several ways.[58] First, bans on PAS serve to protect patients who are not mentally competent or not making voluntary decisions, unlike bans on "partial-birth" abortion. Second, bans on PAS protect patients from the gravest of physical harms, as opposed to the purely speculative risk of psychological harm that purportedly concerned the *Carhart* Court. In contrast to the PAS cases, *Carhart* holds that the government can endanger the health of competent women patients making voluntary choices in order to protect them from a speculative risk of regret. Third, bans on PAS apply to all terminally ill persons regardless of gender, whereas *Carhart*'s gender-specific paternalism raises special equal protection concerns. With regard to bans on PAS, "the rights of a politically vulnerable group are not at stake. . . . [I]n the same, sure way as are black people subject to race discrimination laws [or] women subject to abortion restrictions."[59] There are no sound reasons (other than the sex-based stereotypes articulated in *Carhart*) to treat competent pregnant women as being unable to choose medical treatment for abortion if given appropriate information.

Carhart's brand of paternalism—imposing a ban on the physically safest medical procedure on the ground that someone other than the patient knows what is best for the patient's mental health—is particularly disturbing since it only applies to women patients seeking abortion. *Carhart's* woman-protective rationale for restricting abortion stands in stark contrast to health care law's respect for patient autonomy and rests solely on gender stereotypes long repudiated in our constitutional jurisprudence.

Conclusion

By denying women's decision-making agency, *Carhart* justifies the government's denial of women's autonomy, excusing the imposition of the state's substitute judgment on pregnant women. The Court's adoption of the woman-protective anti-abortion claim has already had an impact on abortion law and policy, particularly with respect to abortion-specific informed consent legislation. For example, relying on *Carhart's* woman-protective rationale, the Eighth Circuit upheld an extremely biased South Dakota "informed consent" to abortion statute, which among other requirements mandates that physicians inform their patients that abortion will terminate the life of a "whole, separate, unique living human being; that the pregnant woman has an existing relationship with that unborn human being . . . [and] that by having an abortion, her existing relationship and her existing constitutional rights with regards to that relationship will be terminated."[60] Efforts to mandate clinically unnecessary ultrasounds under the guise of "informed consent" to abortion have also been spurred on by *Carhart's* woman-protective rationale, even though mandatory ultrasounds impose a medical procedure on a patient in violation of the right to refuse treatment protected by informed consent law.[61] Each of these legal measures claims to act on behalf of women and to care about ensuring their well-informed decision making, but on closer analysis they operate as "harassment masquerading as knowledge." *Carhart* revives the archaic notion that women's supposedly irrational and emotional nature requires that women be subject to special "protection" not imposed on men. Justice Ginsburg's dissent in *Carhart* criticized this claim best: "Eliminating or reducing women's reproductive choices is manifestly *not* a means of protecting them."[62]

This chapter is adapted from *The Irrational Woman: Informed Consent and Abortion Decision-Making*, 16 Duke J. Gender Law & Policy 223 (2009).

1. Gonzales v. Carhart, 550 U.S. 124, 128 (2007).

2. *See, e.g.*, Susan Frelich Appleton, *Unraveling the "Seamless Garment": Loose Threads in Pro-Life Progressivism*, 2 U. St. Thomas L.J. 294, 296–300 (2005).

3. Roe v. Wade, 410 U.S. 113 (1973).

4. *See* Reva B. Siegel, *The New Politics of Abortion: An Equality Analysis of "Woman-Protective" Abortion Restrictions*, U. Ill. L. Rev. 991, 991–94 (2007).

5. Cynthia Gorney, *Gambling with Abortion: Why Both Sides Think They Have Everything to Lose*, Harper's Mag., Nov. 2004, at 33–34.

6. Planned Parenthood of Southeastern Pa. v. Casey, 505 U.S. 833, 879 (1992).

7. Stenberg v. Carhart, 530 U.S. 914, 937–38 (2000).

8. *Carhart*, 550 U.S. at 166.

9. *Id.* at 172, 179.

10. *Id.* at 181, 186–87, 191.

11. *Id.* at 185.

12. 83 U.S. 130, 141 (1873) (Bradley, J., concurring).

13. *See Carhart*, 550 U.S. at 184 n. 8.

14. *Id.*

15. *Id.*

16. *See id.* at 184 n. 7; Brenda Major et al., Report of the APA Task Force on Mental Health and Abortion (2008).

17. *Carhart*, 550 U.S. at 159.

18. *Id.*

19. *See* Siegel, *The New Politics of Abortion* at 1032–33; *Carhart*, 550 U.S. at 184 (Ginsburg, J., dissenting) (challenging the Court's reliance on gender stereotypes, such as emphasizing "women's fragile emotional state" and the "bond of love the mother has for her child").

20. Linda Greenhouse, *Adjudging a Moral Harm to Women from Abortions*, N.Y. Times, Apr. 20, 2007, at A18.

21. *Id.* at 185.

22. *See, e.g.*, Bradwell v. Illinois, 83 U.S. 130 (1873).

23. 410 U.S. 130 (1973).

24. *See* Note, *Abortion Regulation: The Circumscription of State Intervention by the Doctrine of Informed Consent*, 15 Ga. L. Rev. 681, 694 (1980–1981).

25. 462 U.S. 416 (1983).

26. 476 U.S. 747 (1986).

27. 505 U.S. at 872.

28. *Id.* at 918.

29. *See* Susan Frelich Appleton, *Physicians, Patients, and the Constitution: A Theoretical Analysis of the Physician's Role in "Private" Reproductive Decisions*, 63 Wash. U.L.Q. 183, 233 (1985).

30. Linda C. McClain, *The Poverty of Privacy?* 3 Colum. J. Gender & L. 119, 142 (1992).

31. *See, e.g.*, David H. Gans, *Stereotyping and Difference: Planned Parenthood v. Casey and the Future of Sex Discrimination Law*, 104 Yale L.J. 1875, 1902 (1995).

32. *See id.; see also* Erin Daly, *Reconsidering Abortion Law: Liberty, Equality, and the New Rhetoric of Planned Parenthood v. Casey*, 45 Am. U. L. Rev. 77, 78 (1995).

33. *See* Planned Parenthood of Minn. v. Rounds, 530 F.3d 724 (8th Cir. 2008); Jeremy A. Blumenthal, *Abortion, Persuasion, and Emotion: Implications of Social Science Research on Emotion for Reading Casey*, 83 Wash. L. Rev. 1 (2008).

34. *Casey*, 505 U.S. at 882–83.

35. *Id.* at 882.

36. *See* Dayna Bowen Matthew, *Race, Religion, and Informed Consent—Lessons from Social Science*, 36 J.L. Med. & Ethics 150, 154 (spring 2008); Tom L. Beauchamp & James F. Childress, Principles of Biomedical Ethics 120–181 (4th ed. 1994).

37. Canterbury v. Spence, 464 F.2d 772, 789 (D.C. Cir. 1972).

38. Peter H. Schuck, *Rethinking Informed Consent*, 103 Yale L.J. 899, 924 (1994). *See also* Robert Post, *Informed Consent to Abortion: A First Amendment Analysis of Compelled Physician Speech*, 2007 U. Ill. L. Rev. 939, 969–70 (2007).

39. *See* Alan Meisel, *The "Exceptions" to the Informed Consent Doctrine: Striking a Balance between Competing Values in Medical Decisionmaking*, 1979 Wis. L. Rev. 413, 431 n.70.

40. *See* Rebecca Dresser, *From Double Standard to Double Bind: Informed Choice in Abortion Law*, 76 Geo. Wash. L. Rev. 1599, 1620–21 (2008); Rachel Benson Gold & Elizabeth Nash, *State Abortion Counseling Policies and the Fundamental Principles of Informed Consent*, Guttmacher Pol'y Rev. 6–13 (fall 2007).

41. *Carhart*, 550 U.S. at 184.

42. Tara Parker-Pope, Well Blog, *Regrets after Prostate Surgery*, N.Y. Times, Aug. 27, 2008.

43. Prostate surgery for cancer treatment may not always be necessary to protect the patient's life or health—the benefits of treatment are, in fact, not certain for all patients. *See* Gerald L. Andriole, Robert L. Grubb, Saundra S. Buys, David Chia, et al., *Mortality Results from a Randomized Prostate-Cancer Screening Trial*, 360 (13) New England J. of Med. 1310 (Mar. 26, 2009); Gina Kolata, *Prostate Test Found to Save Few Lives*, N.Y. Times, Mar. 18, 2009, at A1; Fritz H. Schröder, Jonas Hugosson, Monique J. Roobol, Teuvo L. Tammela, et al., *Screening and Prostate-Cancer Mortality in a Randomized European Study*, 360 (13); New England J. of Med. 1320 (Mar. 26, 2009).

44. *See* Siegel, *The New Politics of Abortion*, 991–93, 1034; Reva B. Siegel, *The Right's Reasons: Constitutional Conflict and the Spread of Woman-Protective Antiabortion Argument*, 57 Duke L.J. 1641, 1688 (2008).

45. *Carhart*, 550 U.S. at 159.

46. *See* Stephen T. Chasen et al., *Dilation and Evacuation at > 20 Weeks: Comparison of Operative Techniques*, 190 Am. J. of Ob.& Gyn. 1180 (2004); Amy M. Autry et al., *A Comparison of Medical Induction and Dilation and Evacuation for Second-Trimester Abortion*, 187 Am. J. Ob. & Gyn. 393, 393–97 (2002).

47. Chasen, 1163.

48. *Carhart*, 550 U.S. at 159.

49. Siegel, *The New Politics of Abortion*, 991–94.

50. *See* Tracy A. Weitz et al., *You Say "Regret" and I Say "Relief": A Need to Break the Polemic about Abortion*, 78 Contraception 87, 88 (2008).

51. *See* Jessie B. Hill, *The Constitutional Right to Make Medical Treatment Decisions: A Tale of Two Doctrines*, 86 Tex. L. Rev. 277, 281–83 (2007).

52. *See* Gonzales v. Raich, 545 U.S. 1 (2005) (upholding federal ban on medical marijuana); United States v. Oakland Cannabis Buyers' Coop., 532 U.S. 483 (2001) (addressing federal regulation of medical marijuana); Washington v. Glucksberg, 521 U.S. 702 (1997) (upholding bans on physician-assisted suicide); United States v. Rutherford, 442 U.S. 544 (1979) (addressing regulation of experimental drugs); Lambert v. Yellowley, 272 U.S. 581 (1926) (upholding ban on alcohol even for medical uses); Jacobson v. Massachusetts, 197 U.S. 11 (1905) (upholding compulsory vaccination law).

53. *See Carhart*, 550 U.S. at 164.

54. *See, generally,* Lawrence O. Gostin, Public Health Law 20 (2000).

55. *See* Raich, 545 U.S. 1; Oakland Cannabis Buyers' Coop., 532 U.S. 483; Lambert, 272 U.S. 581; Jacobson, 197 U.S. 11.

56. *See Carhart*, 505 U.S. at 181 (Ginsburg, J., dissenting).

57. *See* United States v. Rutherford, 442 U.S. 544, 558 (1979); Abigail Alliance for Better Access to Developmental Drugs v. Von Eschenbach, 495 F.3d 695, 700 (2007) (en banc).

58. *See* Washington v. Glucksberg, 521 U.S. 702 (1997).

59. Yale Kamisar, *On the Meaning and Impact of the Physician-Assisted Suicide Cases,* 82 Minn. L. Rev. 895, (1998).

60. Planned Parenthood of Minn. v. Rounds, 530 F.3d 724, 726 (8th Cir. 2008).

61. *See* Carol Sanger, *Seeing and Believing: Mandatory Ultrasound and the Path to a Protected Choice,* 56 UCLA L. Rev. 351, 360 (2008).

62. *Carhart,* 550 U.S. at 184 n. 9.

Part II

Women's Transformation of the Law

Law should
be applied equally
to women regaurdless
of social standing
or economic standing
(domestic)

7

Elizabeth Cady Stanton and the Notion of a Legal Class of Gender

TRACY A. THOMAS

In the mid-nineteenth century Elizabeth Cady Stanton used narratives of women and their involvement with the law of domestic relations to collectivize women. This recognition of a gender class was the first step toward women's transformation of the law. Stanton's stories of working-class women, immigrants, Mormon polygamist wives, and privileged white women revealed common realities among women in an effort to form a collective conscious. The parable-like stories were designed to inspire a collective consciousness among women, one capable of arousing them to social and political action. For to Stanton's consternation, women showed a lack of appreciation of their own oppression. To shift the status quo, Stanton used stories of real women from different walks of life to develop women's own sense of outrage. In Stanton's stories the law of domestic relations operated the same regardless of class or power, exemplifying the law's treatment of women as a class based on gender. Stanton's writings and public lectures drew upon the law of marriage, divorce, and parenting to demonstrate the gendered implications of coverture on all women. The goal was, first, to facilitate women's own empowerment and, second, to garner that collective power to challenge the law itself.

Stanton, as "the chief philosopher of feminism and women's rights in the nineteenth century," was the main theorist and orator leading the national awareness of "the woman question." She provided the substantive and theoretical basis upon which the specific claims for political and social rights were based, advocating for equal political rights, employment, education, marital rights of property, custody and divorce, and religious reform. Widely read in all fields, including religion, law, social science, and politics, Stanton took emerging theories of the day and used them to formulate feminist theory. Her de facto training in the law under the tutelage of her father, Judge Daniel Cady, and the legal apprentices he trained in his home provided her with more legal education than most men of the day received. This understanding of the nuances and machinations of the law inspired Stanton to action and gave her the foundation to formulate a transformation of the law.[1]

By creating a collective consciousness among women, Stanton identified the operative component important to the law of discrimination—the existence of a class. The recognition of this collective group was important to identity-based politics of both the first- and second-wave feminist movements and was fundamental to modern notions of legal equality. Sex equality law today is premised on the existence of a group of "women" and individual association with the stereotypes and biases of that group. Stanton's work to arouse women to their own subordination and to unite women as a group to reform the laws was the first step to women identifying collectively, and thus providing the social foundation for legal transformation.

The Legal Relevance of a Gender Class

Stanton's insight that the law could be challenged by women as a class has become the foundation of modern sex discrimination law. The Supreme Court has extended heightened scrutiny to gender-based laws because it has identified women as a quasi "suspect class."[2] "A suspect class is a group of individuals whom the Court recognizes as deserving special protection from our majoritarian, political process because the group has a history of having been subjected to purposeful, unjustified discrimination, and a history of political powerlessness." The general principle of equality in the Fourteenth Amendment's guarantee of "equal protection" is that of equal treatment—similar people should be treated similarly. The triggering mechanism and the object of legal inquiry is classification. The plaintiff's association with a class is the key to scrutinizing legal regulations with any stringency, under either competing theory of equal protection. Earlier constitutional cases theorized equal protection as an anti-subordination principle preventing discrimination against certain disfavored social groups. Later cases articulated a more individualist theory of equal protection, prohibiting regulation on the basis of immutable traits associated with a suspect classification, on the principle that one should be judged as an individual rather than as a member of a group.[3]

Both these strands of thought appear in the Supreme Court's only detailed account of why sex is a type of suspect class. In the 1973 case of *Frontiero v. Richardson* a plurality of the Court found sex to be a suspect class.[4] It talked about group-based protections for women as a social group with little political power and systemic subordination. The Court noted the way in which sex-specific laws invidiously relegate the "entire class of females to inferior legal status."

This history of group-based prejudice against women was due in part the Court said to stereotypes of women's inferior status. It noted, "Traditionally, such discrimination was rationalized by an attitude of 'romantic paternalism' which, in practical effect, put women, not on a pedestal, but in a cage." The plurality cited the one-hundred-year-old case of *Bradwell v. Illinois*, denying women admission to legal practice, as evidence of the tradition of discrimination.[5] In *Bradwell*, the concurring Justice Joseph P. Bradley concluded that the "paramount destiny and mission of woman are to fulfill the noble and benign offices of wife and mother." He continued, stating: "The natural and proper timidity and delicacy which belongs to the female sex evidently unfits it for many of the occupations of civil life." Certainly long after *Bradwell*, women were denied the right to vote, serve on juries, and work as bartenders.[6]

The *Frontiero* Court also reasoned that sex is a suspect classification because it is an immutable trait. Immutable traits, like sex and race, are characteristics "determined solely by accident of birth" that cannot be changed and so are improper bases for regulation. Blending the ideas of group- and individual-based protection, the Court identified as the crux of the problem that such discriminatory laws are made without regard to the actual capabilities of the individual members of the class. With respect to women, the Court noted that the "sex characteristic frequently bears no relation to ability to perform or contribute to society."[7]

In recognizing sex as an identifiable and suspect class, the Court drew on its precedent regarding race. Feminist lawyers had hoped that the Court would embrace the analogy between race and sex to extend its precedent under the Fourteenth Amendment to reach women. Following this lead, the Court found that sex, like race, is a characteristic that has "high visibility."

Indeed, throughout much of the 19th century the position of women in our society was, in many respects, comparable to that of blacks under the pre–Civil War slave codes. Neither slaves nor women could hold office, serve on juries, or bring suit in their own names, and married women traditionally were denied the legal capacity to hold or convey property or to serve as legal guardians of their own children. . . . And although blacks were guaranteed the right to vote in 1870, women were denied even that right— which is itself "preservative of other basic civil and political rights"—until adoption of the Nineteenth Amendment half a century later.[8]

Stanton also drew comparisons between women and slaves. She described the condition of married women as slavery, analogizing that a woman is in bondage to her master, the husband, and denied her freedom and the interests of her labors.[9] "It is just as impossible for men to understand the slavery of the women in their own households as it was for slaveholders to understand that of the African race on their plantations."[10] Stanton expounded on this analogy in her public outcries to the decision in *Richardson v. McFarland*. This case of an ex-husband for the murder of his wife's lover dominated the national headlines in 1870. Abbey Sage Richardson, an aspiring actress, divorced her husband because of his alcoholism and abuse, and began a relationship with the prominent journalist, McFarland. Richardson walked into McFarland's office and shot him point-blank. A jury acquitted Richardson on grounds of temporary insanity. He went free and obtained custody of one of his children. Abbey had not been allowed to testify at trial on grounds of marital privilege. Stanton denounced his acquittal, calling the case the "Dred Scott decision for women," comparing the treatment of the wife to that of the freed slave, Dred Scott, in the Supreme Court case that returned him, as property, to his owner. Stanton declared, "I rejoice over every slave that escapes from a discordant marriage. . . . One would really suppose that a man owned his wife as the master the slave, and that this was simply an affair between Richardson and McFarland, fighting like two dogs over one bone."[11]

Stanton was not the first feminist to draw this analogy: the slavery metaphor for women's condition was used by Mary Wollstonecraft in 1799 in *Vindication of the Rights of Woman*.[12] Stanton was familiar with Wollstonecraft and reprinted excerpts of *Vindication* in her newspaper, *Revolution*. Nor was Stanton the last feminist to make the sex-race analogy. Pauli Murray, the African American activist lawyer and co-founder of the National Organization for Women (NOW), made the analogies clear in her article, "Jane Crow and the Law: Sex Discrimination in Employment."[13] Other feminist lawyers of the 1970s also intentionally chose this analogy of sex to race as a strategy to convince judges and other legal decision makers that sex discriminatory laws, long seen as benign and protective, perpetuated inequality and were worthy of redress under existing laws of equal protection.[14]

Many commentators, both modern and past, have challenged the race analogy, vehemently resisting the attempt to equate women's experience with that of slavery.[15] Frederick Douglass, initially a strong supporter of the "woman's movement" and a signatory to Stanton's *Declaration of Sentiments* in 1848, decried his friend's attempts to compare the situation of women to that of slaves.

I must say I do not see how any one can pretend that there is the same urgency in giving the ballot to woman as to the negro. With us, the matter is a question of life and death, at least, in fifteen States of the Union. When women, because they are women, are hunted down through the cities of New York and New Orleans; when they are dragged from their houses and hung upon lamp-posts; when their children are torn from their arms, and their brains dashed out upon the pavement; when they are objects of outrage and insult at every turn; . . . then they will have an urgency to obtain the ballot equal to our own.[16]

Stanton understood the reluctance to equate the discrimination of slaves and white women:

When we contrast the condition of the most fortunate women at the North with the living death colored men endure everywhere, there seems to be a selfishness in our present position. But remember we speak not for ourselves alone, but for all womankind, in poverty, ignorance and hopeless dependence, for the women of this oppressed race too, who in slavery, have known a depth of misery and degradation that no man can ever appreciate.[17]

She found the analogy apt: "In comparing the woman with the negro we but assert ourselves subjects of law. . . . The difference in the slavery of the negro and woman is that of the mouse in the cat's paw, and the bird in a cage, equally hopeless for happiness. One perishes by violence, the other through repression."[18]

The *Frontiero* Court acknowledged a difference between race and sex, but did not find that it negated the extension of equal protection guarantees to women. The Court stated that while "the prejudicial attitudes toward women in this country have not been identical to those held toward racial minorities," it need not determine "whether women or racial minorities have suffered more." Instead, the Court found it necessary only to acknowledge that "our Nation has had a long and unfortunate history of sex discrimination, a history which warrants the heightened scrutiny we afford all gender-based classifications today."[19] However, in the very next case of sex discrimination, *Craig v. Boren*, the Court retreated from this suggestion of strict scrutiny for gender classifications, finding that a lesser "intermediate" scrutiny would suffice. This ruling concluded that gender was a "quasi-suspect" class, meaning that some gender-based regulation might be permissible.[20]

The Court in *Frontiero* concluded with the acknowledgment, that, as a result of paternalistic notions of women, "our statute books gradually became laden with gross, stereotyped distinctions between the sexes." This prevalence of sex-based laws was the starting point for Stanton. She began her collectivization with the reality that laws classified solely on the basis of sex, and that legal reality was a commonality that should draw women together in support of their own cause. Her first hurdle was to awaken women to the reality of their own subordination.

Challenging Women's Indifference

Stanton was shocked by women's lack of interest in their own emancipation. She found that "the apathy and indifference of the women of this nation is as surprising as appalling."[21] Stanton was one of the "strong-minded women" trying to "rouse them from the lethargy of death."[22] In trying to arouse women to action, she mostly heard this response: "I have all the rights I want." They did not align themselves with other women nor appreciate the systemic control over their lives by virtue of their gender. Simone de Beauvoir made this same observation one hundred years later writing in *The Second Sex*, in 1949, that "women do not say we." In her view, the "proletarians" and the "Negroes" did, but women did not display the common consciousness of saying *we*. The lack of collective support from all women plagued Stanton throughout her fifty-four years of advocacy, and it was an issue to which she returned during her later years, finding that "the cowardice and treachery of this class [women] has been the most pitiful phase of our movement."[23]

Women's indifference was a sticking point in feminist reform efforts. The standard response from men and politicians presented with demands was that women themselves did not want the reforms that Stanton and other feminist leaders proposed. In a written address submitted to the New York State Legislature in 1854, Stanton challenged this claim that only a few rogue women were demanding change: "You may say that the mass of the women of this state do not make the demand; it comes from a few sour, disappointed old maids and childless women. You are mistaken; the mass speak through us." Stanton described the plight of teachers, widows, and women of the state who supported themselves and their children, and asked, "Who are they that we do not now represent?" She dismissed the indifference of a few women of luxury who had not embraced the call for reform: "But a small class of fashionable butterflies, who through the short summer days, seek the sunshine and the flowers; but the cool breeze of autumn and the hoary frosts of winter will soon chase all these away; then, they too will need and seek protection, and through other lips demand, in their turn, justice and equity at your hands."[24]

Stanton took on the women of luxury many times, trying to goad them into awakening to the cause. She challenged privileged women in speeches and editorials in newspapers in an appeal called, "I Have All the Rights I Want." Stanton attacked the "utter vacuity" of the lives of these women of wealth "clothed in purple and fine linen" living objectless lives with no fixed purpose. She did not understand how these women could not see the injustices of society, and concluded that such a woman "must be selfish, ignorant and unthinking, who can wrap the mantle of complacency about her and say 'I have all the rights I want.'" Stanton cringed at this phrase that she heard over and over again as a defense of the status quo. "We have allowed this saying from the mouth of women to pass quite long enough unrebuked, seeing that it is utterly and entirely false, and every woman who utters it knows in her own soul that it is so."[25]

Stanton also searched for explanations for the cause of the indifference of so many women. She found the church largely responsible for the prevalent views in society of women's subordinate status. "We must remember the tremendous pressure brought to bear to hold women in bondage. Not only all powers of the earth—laws and constitutions—but the decrees of Heaven, the Scriptures, and religious superstitions."[26] Fifteen years earlier she had reached the same conclusion: "I have traveled from Maine to Texas, trying by public lectures and private conversations 'to teach women to think,' but the chief obstacle in the way of success has everywhere been their false theology, their religious superstitions, their low estimate of themselves as factors in human progress."[27] Stanton attacked the views of the organized church in her work, *The Woman's Bible* (1896), in which Stanton used her training in Greek to translate selected passages of the Bible and comment upon the most sexist passages.

> I have discovered that the large majority know very little of the Book, by whose authority they suppose all men are divinely ordained to rule over all women. They never ask who wrote that Book, how it was compiled, whether its parables and allegories are to be taken literally or figuratively. Whether our English translation is fair at all points, whether advice suited to women, centuries ago, has any significance in our day. . . . As the majority of women will not think and read for themselves, they believe in a masculine God, a masculine Bible, and masculine religion. . . . Having presumed to do some reading and thinking for myself I present another picture drawn from the Bible for our women to consider.[28]

She thought her religious reform work important to attacking the underlying foundation of women's subordination, finding it strange that women would

Everything is an enemy for a woman when is an ally?

"still be so oblivious to the machinations of her worst enemy"—the church. Stanton's alleged heresy in interpreting the Bible resulted in her being ostracized from the women's movement in her final years, destroying her influence and historical legacy.[29] Yet it was Stanton's firm belief that changing the prevailing norms by going to the source of those beliefs was crucial to the ultimate success of legal reforms and the full emancipation for women.

Stanton also appreciated the practical limitations of women's lives that contributed to their apathy.

> The indifference of educated women to their political disabilities may be traced in large measure to their comfortable environments, and their fear of assuming new responsibilities. The indifference of the working classes is due to their imperative necessities which fully occupy their hands and thoughts. Thus as a class we are sacrificed to plenty on the one side and poverty on the other, the few only being roused to action by the vindication of a principle.[30]

She understood that women have been "trained for centuries to obedience to the powers that be, submission to established usages."[31] She knew that radical change was needed to shock them out of their indifference. One strategy Stanton used to draw women together was the sharing of women's experiences to inspire a commonality of gendered realities as a basis for legal reform. She concentrated her stories around women's experiences in the family and the legal limitations and control of the husband. It was this collective power that drew women out of their isolation into the political realm.

First-Wave Consciousness Raising

Stanton drew on the law of domestic relations as the best way to illustrate the gender binary of the law. Stanton first realized that she needed to address women's own lack of understanding of their own subordination by highlighting their collective experiences. Such consciousness raising, which was popular in the 1970s second-wave feminist movement, aimed for women to share personal and lived experiences in order to appreciate the connections and similarities that might otherwise remain invisible. In the second-wave the mantra was "the personal is political" as women told their stories and found shared realities and concerns that became the basis for political action. Feminist legal theory, emerging later, picked up on these personal accounts, using experiential narratives as vehicles for using women's experiences to critique and shape legal doctrine.[32] These narratives of rape, childbirth, and harassment often had an element of emotion, departing from the detached, seemingly objective tone of traditional legal scholarship. The purpose was to incorporate women's experiences into legal analysis and to connect women by these shared experiences.

Stanton focused much of her collectivizing efforts on the law of domestic relations, where the law governed the lives of many women in their roles as wives and mothers. The law of marriage and coverture affected the daily lives of women and had a practical connection with women's lives. As recounted in Stanton's edited work, *The History of Woman Suffrage*, women who attended grass-roots organizing efforts across the nation initially took interest in the women's movement because of the limitations they suffered in marriage, property, and parenting. The law of the family, unlike the claim for political rights, was close to the women.

Stanton told parable-like stories of women's experiences. In classic parable fashion, the stories often had fictitious elements and were intended to convey a moral or universal truth. In Stanton's case, this was a truth about women's subordination. Stanton's narratives were derived from real women she met but took on an element of hyperbole and symbolism. The stories emphasized the binary nature of the law based on gender. Stanton also used the stories to make connections among women, reaching out to include women of varying classes, races, and ethnicities in the rhetoric of the women's movement.

Working-class women were the focus of several of Stanton's stories. Some derived from her experiences with her Irish neighbors in Seneca Falls, New York, where she lived after her marriage, with her seven children. Stanton served as a counselor to the families, mediating domestic violence and offering homeopathic medical care. She described how the arrangement began: "There was quite an Irish settlement at a short distance, and continual complaints were coming to me that my boys threw stones at their pigs, cows, and the roofs of their houses. This involved constant diplomatic relations in the settlement of various difficulties, in which I was so successful that, at length, they constituted me a kind of umpire in all their own quarrels." She consulted with women regarding their marital problems and domestic violence, and these stories fueled her interest in liberal divorce laws. "Who can measure the mountains of sorry and suffering endured in unwelcome motherhood in the abodes of ignorance, poverty, and vice, where terror-stricken women and children are the victims of strong men frenzied with passion and intoxicating drink?"[33]

Stanton also recalled stories of working-class neighbors of her childhood home in Johnstown, New York. In her autobiography, *Eighty Years and More: Reminiscences,* she portrayed the injustice of Flora Campbell, the wife of a Scottish farmer and a former Cady servant. Flora sought the legal advice of Stanton's father when Elizabeth was ten years old. The young Elizabeth spent hours in her father's office, attached to the family house, where she listened to clients stating their cases and talking with the law students Judge Cady apprenticed. Flora wanted to recover a farm her father had left her that had been mortgaged by her husband. There was also another story of an "old Mrs. Brown" whose husband had willed her farm to her stepson, leaving her with no home. Judge Cady patiently explained to these women that the law gave ownership of a woman's property to her husband upon marriage, and thus there was nothing the lawyer could do. It was these stories that Elizabeth attributed as her first awakening to the injustices of women. As a child, she threatened to cut all the odious laws from the books; as an adult Stanton worked on behalf of the injustices of women across class.[34]

Stanton also took up the cause of Hester Vaughan, an English immigrant and domestic servant who, in 1868, in Philadelphia was sentenced to death for infanticide. In court, the prosecutor told a story of an unmarried woman giving birth in a boardinghouse, found by neighbors with her dead infant, with the baby's skull crushed and bludgeoned by a blunt instrument, as the coroner testified. Stanton's version of the sensational story, which she advanced in the press, was one of a poor, young girl abandoned by a supposed fiancé who was already married, raped by her employer, and then thrown into the streets when she became pregnant. Living in a tenement house in a garret room with no heat and a blizzard wailing outside, Hester, malnourished and alone, gave birth to an infant. Dr. Clemence Lozier, a women's rights supporter, gave her medical opinion that Vaughan had puerperal mania causing her to be oblivious to the circumstances and likely lay on the baby, causing the injuries. In Stanton's hands, Hester's story elucidated the violent oppression of working-class women and made it an issue for all women. "This case," Stanton stated, "carries with it a lesson for the serious thought of every woman. . . . In the name of womanhood, we implore the mothers of that state to rescue that defenceless girl from her impending fate. Oh! make her case your own, suppose your young and beautiful daughter had been thus betrayed."[35] Stanton used Vaughan's story as a morality play to illustrate the role of law in the perpetuation of injustice based on gender. Stanton emphasized the double standards of women's sole social responsibility for pregnancies out of wedlock, referring to Hawthorne's novel, *The Scarlet Letter,* as an example of men's condemnation of women and failure to assume their own responsibility. Stanton continued to retell her parable to unite and inspire women to action, despite Vaughan's own affidavits and actions that seemed to contradict Stanton's account of the facts. The case had assumed parable-like stature, operating as an illustrative fiction, disconnected from reality. Hester Vaughan was eventually pardoned and returned home to England.[36]

Elizabeth Cady Stanton also developed narratives of Mormon women to portray the hypocrisy of marriage. Her point was that Mormon women were no different from other women, subjugated in marriage because of gender. "Though the Mormon, like all other women, stoutly defend their own religion, yet they are not more satisfied than any other sect. All women are dissatisfied with their position as inferiors, and their dissatisfaction increases in exact ration with their intelligence and development." By this time antipolygamist advocacy had become a "women's issue," taken up by social purity and Protestant activists who sought to end the enslavement of women. For Stanton, the patronizing views of political men and moralistic women seeking to "protect women" from the evils of polygamy failed to see the hypocrisy of women's subordination within their own, traditional monogamous marriages. In what Stanton called "man-marriage," monogamous marriage was created by and for men in patriarchal relationships that made men the head of women, as the master to the slave.[37] Stanton emphasized that patriarchy existed in all current forms of marriage and that all women, including Mormon women, were unhappy in marriage. Stanton visited the Mormons in 1871 giving her standard lecture on marriage and maternity. Stanton's stories of Mormon women touted their practice of powerful motherhood and their status as independent women, educated and entitled to vote. Mormons were the pariahs of the time, castigated and targeted nationally on social, religious, and political fronts. Stanton reached out to incorporate these women into the collective of "women," trumpeting the virtues of Mormon motherhood and inviting the Mormon women to share the organizational stage in the national fight for suffrage.[38]

Finally, Stanton also created several fictional heroines from the experiences of wealthy friends and other "heiresses." Stanton's message in these stories of privileged women was that women, regardless of class or economic status, were still subordinated under the law because of gender. She intentionally used examples of wealthy women to emphasize the powerful nature of the law to show that even the most powerful, those armed with money, education, and influential friends, cannot avoid the subordination of the law based solely on sex. A repeated story concerned one of Stanton's "dear" friends who served as a bridesmaid in her wedding. This character may be an elaboration of Stanton's cousin, Cornelia Barclay, and her situation with an abusive and alcoholic husband.[39] Stanton recounted the tale of a woman who was victimized by a patriarchal system that gave all property rights to the husband.

> Think of a husband telling a young and trusting girl, but one short month his wife, that he married her for her money; that those letters, so precious to her, . . . were written by another; that their splendid home, of which on their wedding day, her father gave to him by deed, was already in the hands of his creditors; that she must give up the elegance and luxury that now surrounded her unless she can draw fresh supplies of money to meet their wants.[40]

In another story, intended to teach through humor, Stanton tells the story of a Seneca Falls neighbor and her cook-stove. The neighbor, "pretty Louise," a "refined, cultivated, beautiful woman," desperately needed a new cook-stove. She would not buy the stove without her husband's consent and approval, but her husband was a member of Congress and away from home much of the time. Stanton talked Louise into getting the stove as a "personal declaration of independence." The husband, Stanton recalled, who was rich enough to afford a stove, ranted and raved, but eventually the couple moved on, with Louise "taking up the reins of government in her own sphere." Later recounting the story at a dinner party, Louise's husband said he liked her better that way. Stanton's goal here was to challenge the "generally accepted theory that 'woman's sphere' is home," by illustrating the continued ramifications of coverture.[41]

These stories provide a unified vision of "woman's" identity. Stanton presents these experiences as shared values rather than essentialist truths. The stories worked to incorporate multiple experiences and perspectives into the debate over women's rights through sharing experiences and appreciating commonalities. The narratives, in what has become a hallmark of feminist legal theory, personalized the experience of women and shared it, making it relevant and actionable in the ongoing debate. Towards the end of Stanton's fifty-year advocacy, she stated her vision of a "woman's" movement: "My idea of that platform is that every woman shall have a perfect right there; that she and her wrongs shall be represented in our conventions. . . . We want all types and classes to come. We want all races as well as all creeds and no creeds—including the Mormon, the Indian, and the black woman."[42]

Essentialism as an Avenue to Change

Feminists in the later twentieth century challenged this notion of women as a uniform group. They objected to the feminist attempts to essentialize all women and to assume that the experience of white, middle-class women represented them all. The classic "anti-essentialist" theory critiques feminists for reflecting white privilege when they describe gender problems from their own perspective. These critics argue that it is important to take into account differences of race, religion, class, and sexual orientation in order to fully appreciate women's experiences. Anti-essentialist feminists have pushed away the notion of a commonality among women, insisting upon the inclusion of multiple identities in feminist theory.[43]

These stories, however, show that Stanton did not essentialize her experience as an educated, middle-class, married, mother of seven as that of all women. Her work on women's behalf incorporated the experiences of women of different classes and religion. Her disavowing of the social butterflies eschews an elitism on her part. She strove to expose the binary and subordinate nature of gender that transcended class and privilege.[44] She tried desperately to expose the inferior precept of the Fifteenth Amendment, "making all men sovereigns, all women slaves."[45]

The universalizing of women's experience is not based on a homogenous view of women. Instead, it has been the foundation that formed the power base for tangible legal and political reform. Universality allowed Stanton to speak on behalf of women—working women, Mormon women, and divorced women. She advocated for the rights of black women, invisible in the debate over suffrage for black men in the Fifteenth Amendment. She worked in the abolition movement and was involved in the Equal Rights Association seeking universal suffrage for all. Stanton was one of the few voices highlighting the exclusion of black women from the Fifteenth Amendment, asking "What about the slave woman? Is she not also in bondage? Not also entitled to the vote?" "May I ask just one question based upon the apparent opposition in which you place the negro and the woman? Do you believe the African race is composed entirely of males?"[46] Sojourner Truth shared these views and at a meeting of the American Equal Rights Association in 1867, joined Stanton's opposition to the Fifteenth Amendment. Truth said she was fearful of putting more power into the hands of men that would add to the oppression of black women. "There is a great stir about colored men getting their rights, but not a word about the colored women . . . , and if colored men get their rights, but not colored women theirs, you see the colored men will be masters over the women, and it will be just as bad as before."

Some contemporary legal scholars have embraced the universality of women's experiences as a foundation for gendered reform. Joan Williams and Catharine MacKinnon resist the anti-essentialist pull because it immobilizes continued legal action for change. MacKinnon rejects the abstraction of the anti-essentialist theory that ignores the social realities of women's lives and impedes further legal and political action by weakening the universality among women. Williams moves away from anti-essentialism, recognizing that "today we find ourselves bumping up against its limitations." Williams argues for a new type of "reconstructive feminism" that instead of focusing on women and women's identities, focuses on the masculine norms and the gender dynamics that frame those identifies. She explains: "The news that feminism is not responsible for describing women's identities should alleviate feminist angst about how to accomplish the task of taking into account all of the differences among women (antiessentialism)." The power in feminist legal change, in Williams' view, is located in the underlying gendered norms and the alteration of those norms." As Nancy Cott stated, "As much as feminism asserts the female individual—by challenging delimitation by sex and by opposing the self-abnegation on behalf of others historically expected of women—pure individualism negates feminism because it removes the basis for women's collective self-understanding or action."[47]

Stanton worked in this vein, seeking to establish a basis for women's collective action against the gendered norms. Her outreach to different identities and perspectives was not intended to explore all experiences, but rather was intended to harness the collective power of women by illustrating the existence of overlapping commonalities of gender. Stanton, working at the birth of a movement, faced strong denial of gendered commonalities that threatened to leave existing gendered dynamics in place. Stanton's work brings feminism back to a focus on the norms that impact the group of women based on gender. The existing law of gender discrimination is based upon this core insight of some commonality among women due to gender. Focusing on the individualization of experience and the absence of commonality harkens back to Stanton's time when women were not politicized and failed to see the connections among their shared experiences. Stanton's recognition of the need for a collective group to politically and legally challenge women's subordinate status provides an example of the importance of feminist strategies of collectivization that are critical to continued legal change for women.

1. *Meetings in Washington Hall,* Chi. Daily Trib., May 17, 1893 (statement of Susan B. Anthony). All Stanton papers can be found in The Papers of Elizabeth Cady Stanton and Susan B. Anthony (Patricia G. Holland and Ann Gordon, eds. 1991) (microfilm); *see also* Elisabeth Griffith, In Her Own Right (1983); Lori D. Ginsburg, Elizabeth Cady Stanton: An American Life (2009). For Stanton's work on family law, see Tracy A. Thomas, The Feminist Foundations of Family Law (forthcoming NYU Press); and Tracy A. Thomas, *Elizabeth Cady Stanton on the Federal Marriage Amendment,* 22 Const. Comment. 137 (2005); on religious reform, see Kathi Kern, Mrs. Stanton's Bible (2001); and on political advocacy, see Sue Davis, The Political Thought of Elizabeth Cady Stanton (2008).

2. Mississippi Univ. for Women v. Hogan, 458 U.S. 718 (1982); Reed v. Reed, 404 U.S. 71 (1971).

3. *See* Mark Strasser, *Suspect Classes and Suspect Classifications: On Discriminating, Unwittingly or Otherwise,* 64 Temple L. Rev. 937, 938–40 (1991); Suzanna Sherry, *Selective Judicial Activism in the Equal Protection Context: Democracy, Distrust, and Deconstruction,* 73 Geo. L.J. 89, 97 (1984); Owen M. Fiss, *Groups and the Equal Protection Clause,* 5 Phil. & Pub. Aff. 107, 108, 128 (1976).

4. Frontiero v. Richardson, 411 U.S. 677, 687–92 (1973) (Brennan, J., plurality). Eight Justices in *Frontiero* agreed that the law denying dependent spousal benefits to female military officers was discriminatory, but only four Justices agreed that sex was a suspect classification, and three wanted to defer the question pending consideration of the Equal Rights Amendment. For more on the back story of *Frontiero,* see Fred Strebeigh, Equal: Women Reshape American Law 48–61 (2009).

5. 83 U.S. (16 Wall.) 130, 141 (1873).

6. Minor v. Happersett, 88 U.S. (21 Wall.) 162 (1874); Hoyt v. Florida, 368 U.S. 57 (1961); Goesaert v. Cleary, 335 U.S. 464 (1948).

7. *Frontiero,* 411 U.S. at 687-92.

8. *Id.* at 685.

9. Elizabeth Cady Stanton (ECS), *The Degradation of Woman,* Revolution, Jan. 15, 1868; Elizabeth Cady Stanton, Susan B. Anthony, and Matilda Joslyn Gage, v. 1 History of Woman Suffrage 27 (1870).

10. ECS, *A Private Letter,* Revolution, Nov. 10, 1870.

11. ECS, *Editorial Correspondence,* Revolution, Dec. 23, 1869; *see also* ECS to Victoria Woodhall, Woodhall & Clafflin's Weekly, Mar. 11, 1871; ECS, *Side Issues,* Revolution, Oct. 6, 1870; ECS, Speech to the McFarland-Richardson Protest Meeting, May 1869; George Cooper, Lost Love: A True Story of Passion, Murder, and Justice in Old New York (2003).

12. Nancy Cott, Public Vows: A History of Marriage and the Nation 65 (2002); Marilyn Yalom, A History of the Wife 194 (2002).

13. 34 Geo. Wash. L. Rev. 232 (1964).

14. Serena Mayeri, *Reconstructing the Race-Sex Analogy,* 49 Wm. & Mary L. Rev. 1789, 1796 (2008); *see* Brief for Petitioner-Appellant at 15–16, Reed v. Reed, 404 U.S. 71 (1971).

15. *See, e.g.,* Paula J. Giddings, When and Where I Enter: The Impact of Black Women on Race and Sex in America 64–65 (1996); bell hooks, Ain't I a Woman 141 (1981); William Chafe, Women and Equality: Changing Patterns in American Culture, 51–78 (1977).

16. *Debates of the American Equal Rights Association Meeting,* May 12–14, 1869, *in* The Concise History of Woman Suffrage: Selections from the Classic Work of Stanton, Anthony, Gage, and Harper 258 (Mari Jo Buhle & Paul Buhle, eds. 1978).

17. ECS, *Editorial Correspondence,* Revolution, Jan. 22, 1869.

18. ECS, *Man the Usurper,* Revolution, Mar. 12, 1868.

19. JEB v. Alabama, 511 U.S. 127, 136 (1994) (citing *Frontiero*).

20. 429 U.S. 190 (1976).

21. ECS, *Letter to Editor of the Golden Age,* Washington Convention, Jan. 10, 1874.

22. *Degradation,* 25.

23. ECS, *Women do not Wish to Vote,* The Nat'l Bull., Apr. 1894.

24. ECS, *Address to the Legislature of New-York,* Feb. 14–15, 1854.

25. ECS, *I Have All the Rights I Want,* Rev., Apr. 1, 1869; ECS, *I Have All the Rights I Want,* 1859.

26. ECS, *Women Their Own Emancipators,* Woman's J., Aug. 25, 1894.

27. ECS, *Teach Women to Think,* Nat'l Citizen & Ballot Box, Sept. 1880.

28. *Id.*

29. Kern, *supra; see also* Kathi Kern, *"Free Woman Is a Divine Being, the Savior of Mankind": Stanton's Exploration of Religion and Gender,* in Elizabeth Cady Stanton: Feminist as Thinker (Ellen Carol DuBois & Richard Candida Smith eds. 2007).

30. ECS, *The Indifference of Women Themselves: The Greatest Block in the Way of Emancipation,* Boston Investigator, Aug. 25, 1900; *accord* ECS, *The Cause of Their Indifference,* Commonwealth, Feb. 18, 1899.

31. *Women do not Wish to Vote, supra.*

32. Kathryn Abrams, *Legal Feminism and the Emotions: Three Movements in an Evolving Relationship,* 28 Harv. J. Gender & L. 325, 327 (2005).

33. ECS, Eighty Years and More 146–50 (1898); Lois Banner, Elizabeth Cady Stanton 50 (1972).

34. Eighty Years, ch.2; Banner, 7–8; Alma Lutz, Created Equal: A Biography of Elizabeth Cady Stanton 3–4 (1940).

35. ECS, *Hester Vaughan,* Revolution, Nov. 19, 1868.

36. *Id.*; ECS, *Governor Geary and Hester Vaughan,* Revolution, Dec. 10, 1868; *The Case of Hester Vaughan,* Revolution, Dec. 10, 1868; ECS, *Hester Vaughan,* Revolution, Dec. 10, 1868; *see* Sarah Barringer Gordon, *Law and Everyday Death: Infanticide and the Backlash against Women's Rights after the Civil War,* in Lives in the Law 55 (Austin Sarat et. al., eds. 2002).

37. ECS, *The Man Marriage,* Revolution, Apr. 8, 1869; ECS, *Anniversary of the National Woman Suffrage Association,* Revolution, May 19, 1870, at 305.

38. ECS, *Reminiscences,* Woman's Trib., Sept. 13, 1890; ECS, *The Central Idea of Woman's Degradation,* Woman's Trib., Dec. 3, 1884; Lutz, 271; *Mrs. Elizabeth Cady Stanton Discourses on Marriage and Maternity,* S.F. Chronicle, July 14, 1871.

39. Editor's Note, v. 1 The Selected Papers of Elizabeth Cady Stanton and Susan B. Anthony 429 (Ann D. Gordon, ed. 1997).

40. Eighty Years, 215–26; HWS v.1, *supra*; ECS, *Marriage and Divorce,* Rev., Oct. 22, 1868; Address of Mrs. Elizabeth Cady Stanton, Proceedings of the Tenth National Woman's Rights Convention, May 10 & 11, 1860.

41. ECS, *A Story for Wives,* Revolution, Apr. 6, 1871.

42. *Mrs. Stanton's Remarks,* Woman's Trib., Mar. 8, 1890.

43. Martha Chammallas, Introduction to Feminist Legal Theory (2d ed. 2003).

44. Scholars have revealed the racist and nativist rhetoric Stanton used in opposing the Fifteenth Amendment granting black men the right to vote. *See* Angela Davis, Women, Race & Class 70–72 (1981); Michele Mitchell, *"Lower Orders," Racial Hierarchies, and Rights Rhetoric: Evolutionary Echoes in Elizabeth Cady Stanton's Thought during the Late 1860s, in* Feminist as Thinker, 128. A frustrated Stanton resorted to such political rhetoric in order to expose the depths of gender prejudice by shocking people into appreciating women's subordinate status below other disenfranchised men like blacks and immigrants. Davis, 2. For more on the historic juxtaposition of race and sex, see Tracy A. Thomas, *Sex v. Race, Again, in* Who Should be First? Feminists Speak Out on the 2008 Presidential Campaign (Beverly Guy-Sheftall & Johnnetta Betsch Cole, eds.) (State University of New York Press 2010).

45. Letter to Woodhall, *supra.*

46. ECS to Wendell Phillips, May 25, 1865.

47. Catharine A. MacKinnon, *Points against Postmodernism,* 75 Chic.-Kent L. Rev. 687, 689, 692 (2000); Joan C. Williams, *Reconstructive Feminism: Changing the Way We Talk about Gender and Work Thirty Years after the PDA,* 21 Yale J. Law & Fem. 79, 81 (2009); Nancy Cott, The Grounding of Modern Feminism 6 (1987).

8

"Them Law Wimmin"

The Protective Agency for Women and Children and the Gendered Origins of Legal Aid

GWEN HOERR JORDAN

In 1888 a woman seeking protection for her stepdaughter arrived at the Protective Agency for Women and Children (PAWC), a new organization in Chicago offering free legal services to women and children. Several nights earlier she witnessed her husband sexually assault his daughter. The stepmother had him arrested, but the justice of the peace released him. Once freed, the father tried to abduct his daughter. The PAWC's agent, Charlotte Holt, persuaded the justice to re-arrest the father, but the father secured his release by bribing the constable. Holt then persuaded the State Attorney to have the father arrested once more. He was finally tried, convicted, and sentenced to the penitentiary.[1]

This incident was one of countless crimes against women and children that occurred regularly in the late nineteenth century.[2] It was only the intervention of the PAWC and the outcome that were unusual. Women professionals and activists, who had begun to perceive a pattern in these crimes of physical violence and sexual abuse, determined to use the legal system to protect women's bodies and advance their rights. They persuaded various women's associations in Chicago to support their mission and, in 1886, founded the PAWC. Within months the agency began offering free legal assistance to women and children who had been the victims of every type of financial, physical, and sexual crime.[3]

The agency activists were a distinct faction within the labyrinth of women's reform organizations during the long Progressive Era. The PAWC was a product of the clubwomen's network; it depended upon the financial and social support of various women's associations for its operations, and its officers were clubwomen. Women's clubs were a means for middle-class women to advance their education, secure their autonomy, and assert influence in the public sphere without threatening the domestic ideal.[4] But as the PAWC began its work, its activists began to reject the strict, Victorian code of sexual conduct advanced by many middle-class reformers and their efforts to instill white, American, middle-class values on poor and immigrant women.[5] The daily interactions that PAWC activists had with workingwomen, many of whom had a sexual history that violated Victorian standards of chastity, led them to develop less restrictive definitions of womanhood and justice.[6] Rather than attempt to reform their clients, they worked to reform laws and legal procedures "to obtain justice."[7]

The agency activists were also part of a distinct faction within the women's rights movement. They were among those that used the law and law reform as their main strategy to secure women's substantive equality.[8] These women employed a pragmatic search for justice that was separate from the debate that animated the suffrage and temperance movements over women's sameness or difference to men.[9] They focused instead on women's humanity, as the women's rights movement had in its formative years, and attempted to use the legal system to both advance women's rights and redress the harms acted upon them.

Through conventional and unconventional means, the agency activists infiltrated the legal system and began to change the way society responded to the social and legal injustices workingwomen and children suffered. First, they provided direct services to workingwomen to address their legal harms. Second, they undertook law reform and public education campaigns to meet their clients' immediate needs and secure broader social change. Finally, they entered into courtrooms to hold judges accountable for their actions and to influence the way they applied the law. These activities amounted to a kind of grass-roots lawyering that operated on the periphery of the legal system and served to transform the relationship between workingwomen and the law.[10]

The PAWC activists complemented the efforts of the small cadre of women lawyers that fought for women's rights as official members of the legal profession. Although women had won the right to be lawyers in Illinois in 1872, only nineteen women had secured their law licenses in that state in the succeeding fourteen years.[11] Because the bar maintained its masculine character and fought against most egalitarian reform efforts, the agency activists created new ways to access the legal system.[12] Their work represented the blurred lines between legal activism and state-sanctioned lawyering, as they contributed to the development of both legal aid lawyering to indigent clients and cause lawyering that took on "controversial and politically charged activities" with "a sense of commitment to particular ideals."[13]

The PAWC's role in the development of legal aid as one of the country's first two legal aid societies is well documented.[14] But its role in the development of cause lawyering has been overlooked. Scholars have been wary to define cause lawyering, but most agree that it includes attempts by lawyers to "reconnect law and morality . . . using their professional work as a vehicle to build the good society."[15] The grass-roots model of cause lawyering includes strategies of litigation, public education campaigns, political organization, legislation, and lobbying—all activities of the PAWC.[16]

The origins of cause lawyering are most often tied to the twentieth-century activism of the National Association for the Advancement of Colored People (NAACP)[17] and the American Civil Liberties Union (ACLU).[18] The canons of cause lawyering scholarship do not include nineteenth-century accounts of such activity, but a few scholars suggest that cause lawyering was practiced before the twentieth century. Justice Thurgood Marshall, a former cause lawyer for the NAACP, acknowledged that many nineteenth-century African American lawyers "used their legal training . . . [to fight for] 'equal justice under the law.'" Marshall credits their efforts as "lay[ing] the foundation for social change" that manifested in the twentieth century.[19] Felice Batlan, in chapter 9 of this volume, also contends that cause lawyering occurred in the nineteenth century but ties its genesis to the work of women reformers rather than that of state sanctioned lawyers. The activities of the PAWC support Batlan's contention.

This chapter argues that the PAWC's development of legal aid and cause lawyering strategies shaped the twentieth-century evolution of these practices but faced constant and often overwhelming opposition to its efforts to secure justice for the gendered crimes women suffered. The activists engaged in legal aid lawyering by giving their clients legal advice, conducting investigations of their legal claims, accompanying them to court, and arguing on their behalf with state prosecutors, private attorneys, and judges. They engaged in cause lawyering by conducting public education campaigns, organizing women to support their efforts, advocating for changes in legal procedure, drafting legislation, lobbying legislatures, and instigating litigation. Their work contributed directly to the development of legal aid in Chicago and created the model for twentieth-century cause lawyering. Their efforts were also integral to a transformation in the way the legal system and society treated workingwomen and the way workingwomen used and understood the legal system.

The Origins and Radicalization of the PAWC

In Chicago in 1886 few women ventured into courtrooms. Although there were a handful of women attorneys practicing in the state, women were neither judges nor jurors.[20] Workingwomen, who were especially vulnerable to abuse, had few opportunities to secure redress or protections from the legal system.

As the population of workingwomen in Chicago increased during the 1880s, the injustices they suffered became more visible.[21] Newspapers published stories of violent, sexual, and financial crimes against women in a self-proclaimed effort to "arouse the public to take action."[22] Workingwomen organized to fight for better treatment.[23] In 1886 a number of middle-class women activists joined the effort and persuaded the Chicago Woman's Club (CWC) to undertake a cooperative effort with several other Chicago women's associations to establish the PAWC.[24]

The coalescence of several factors in the last decades of the nineteenth century created an opportunity for the PAWC. Foremost among these was the precarious living and working conditions laboring classes endured in industrialized cities like Chicago.[25] Workingwomen, susceptible to economic, physical, and sexual abuse by their employers and husbands needed legal assistance to protect themselves and their children.[26] Numerous women's associations designed to help workingwomen and their children formed in Chicago and throughout the country, but none of these provided legal services.[27] The cultural bias against publicly discussing acts of rape and domestic violence exacerbated the problem and increased the need for the agency.[28]

A second factor that created an opportunity for the PAWC was the transformation of the American legal system. After the Civil War all facets of the legal system were reconstituting. The new view was that law was a science and should be administered only by experts.[29] Elite lawyers secured new standards for state bar admissions requiring law school degrees, rather than apprenticeship training, in an effort to limit the profession to educated, white men. Against their intentions, however, these reforms spurred the growth of commercial law schools that provided non-elites new opportunities to become lawyers.[30] Simultaneously, women began to challenge their exclusion from the legal profession and persuaded states, one by one, to allow women to earn law licenses.[31] It was during this transition, when the courts and the profession were in flux, women activists were able to gain access to the legal system and engage in lawyering activities.

Legal thought also was transforming in these decades. After the Civil War elite lawyers and judges argued against the early-nineteenth-century practice of using law as "an instrument of economic policy."[32] They advocated an objective, formal conception of the law, insisting that it be strictly applied without regard to politics.[33] Alternatively, women's rights activists, populists, Oliver Wendell Holmes, and settlement workers advanced a third ideology that insisted the law was subjective and urged judges to apply the law in light of the changing social and economic circumstances.[34] The PAWC activists seized this moment to advocate their vision that the law be used to secure social justice.[35]

Another factor that contributed to the rise of the PAWC was the development of new theories regarding crime causation. Within the emerging field of sociology, a few scholars challenged the notion that criminals were biologically determined. They developed new conflict theories, based on the work of Emile Durkheim and Karl Marx, positing that inequitable social and economic conditions were the root causes of crime. Progressive reformers increasingly adopted these ideas.[36] These theories supported the PAWC's social justice strategies.

A final factor enabling the work of the PAWC was the rise of a diverse women's rights movement and its focus on crimes against women. Various crusades by suffragists, temperance workers, and professional women began to publicly expose the harms women suffered. Some launched "social purity" campaigns calling for an end to the sexual double standard that condoned marital rape and incest, and punished women who engaged in prostitution without consequences for male clients. A number of activists advocated abstention of alcohol as a means to protect wives who were beaten by drunken husbands. These efforts provided the PAWC activists the social capital necessary for its work providing legal services to those who had been victims of such abuse.[37]

The activists developed a multifaceted approach to secure justice for their clients. One of their first strategies was a collaborative effort with working-women and middle-class labor activists to redress the economic abuses workingwomen suffered. The PAWC joined with the Ladies Federal Labor Union and the Illinois Woman's Alliance to insist that employers provide safe working conditions and better pay. They also lobbied for compulsory education legislation, campaigned for additional public schools and bath houses, and organized clothing drives.[38]

A second PAWC strategy was to directly confront employers who had financially wronged their clients. Many of their clients sewed clothes at home or in sweatshops. One common industry practice was to require "sewing girls" to work for two weeks before being paid. If they left their employment during this time, they forfeited all earned wages. Employers often created negative workplace conditions to encourage the girls to leave just before this period ended to avoid paying the girls for their work. PAWC activists went directly to the employers and demanded payment. When an employer refused, they used their social capital as influence.[39]

Through a reverse practice of moral suasion, called "whitemailing," the activists employed moral arguments to persuade unscrupulous businessmen to make restitution.[40] The PAWC also used whitemailing to persuade creditors to deal fairly with their clients. Creditors, especially, were a problem for working-women who sewed at home and relied on their sewing machines to provide for their families. Salesmen sold sewing machines on credit through installment contracts with exorbitant rates and then repossessed the machines at the first late payment.[41] The PAWC used whitemailing to secure the return of the machines.[42]

The PAWC's advocacy on behalf of workingwomen regarding these installment contracts illustrates a fundamental difference between the agency activists and many of the women settlement workers in Chicago and the Northeast. Settlement workers' objectives in such cases were "to reform and control immigrant practices." They focused on installment contracts that immigrant women signed for "luxury goods," characterized the women as ignorant, and advocated legislation that would prohibit the sale of such items "to 'socially undeveloped people.'" In contrast, the PAWC represented women who contracted for sewing machines, characterized them as the working poor, and attempted to alter the practices of businessmen to allow the women to maintain the items.[43] The agency's social control efforts were directed to the salesmen and creditors, not their clients.

The PAWC also developed strategies to assist women who had been the victims of violence by their husbands.[44] The activists were particularly disturbed by these cases because of the severity of the violence they observed.[45] The agency provided social services to wives who wanted separations and divorces from their husbands. They undertook this work despite the strong opposition to divorce expressed by many clubwomen. Anti-divorce sentiment had intensified during the late nineteenth century as incidents of divorce increased throughout the country.[46] Opponents considered the institution of marriage to be the foundation of social order. Divorce, therefore, was a threat to the core structure of society. Although women had secured the right to divorce their husbands on the grounds of cruelty in all but six states by 1886, many opponents did not allow for any exceptions.[47]

The PAWC membership was divided on whether the agency should assist in divorce cases. Initially the agency determined not to take divorce cases, but it reversed this decision in its first year. The cases involved such "great cruelty and violence to wife and children," the chairman explained, that the agency activists felt justified in their efforts. As a compromise with members who opposed divorce, the PAWC restricted its assistance to the most extreme cases of cruelty.[48]

The PAWC also assisted women who had suffered sexual assault, providing legal counsel, social services, and moral support. It explained that these women suffered a second victimization by the way they were treated in the legal system and in society. Courts rarely prosecuted such offenses, victims endured public attacks on their character, and most were blamed for their victimization. Initially the PAWC only represented virtuous women who had been sexually victimized. But similar to their position on divorce, they quickly and publicly came to support all sexual assault victims, virtuous or not.[49]

The PAWC suffered public attacks for its support of unchaste women. It acknowledged that this practice might be a disappointment to some PAWC supporters who did not have an "intimate knowledge of [its] daily work." It argued, however, that the social and economic circumstances of the victims made them more, not less, deserving of assistance. Despite their "sinful" appearance, it explained that those "who were victims of an environment of poverty and its attendant exposures to evil influences" especially deserved protection and redress "for the injuries perpetrated upon them."[50]

Their daily experiences with the harms workingwomen suffered, the inadequacies of the legal system, and the social opposition they faced radicalized the activists and altered workingwomen's relationship to the legal system. The agency provided workingwomen access to the courts and served as their advocate in the business community. Women who knew of the agency advised friends in need to "hunt up 'them law wimmin.'"[51]

Law Reform and Public Education Campaigns

PAWC activists also attempted to advance the rights and protections of workingwomen and children through law reform campaigns. These measures often evolved from cases they handled where their "work [was] handicapped by defects in the laws or their execution."[52] They initiated legislative campaigns to help their clients and to secure a broader social justice. Their efforts included drafting legislation, lobbying for its passage, and generating public support to ensure its enforcement.

One of the first legislative endeavors the PAWC undertook was to reform the chattel mortgage laws. It initiated this campaign as a complement to its whitemailing efforts in direct response to the numerous cases of women left destitute when their sewing machines were repossessed. The activists persuaded a judge to draft a bill ending the existing "confiscation" practice that permitted a creditor to "tak[e] the goods when and how he pleases and render such surplus to the mortgagor as he chooses." PAWC members lobbied for the bill and secured its enactment in 1889.[53]

The PAWC also championed legislation intended to protect women and young girls from sexual assault and exploitation. One of these campaigns was an effort to criminalize acts of nonconsensual sexual intercourse that fell outside the existing narrow definition of rape. In 1887 the crime of rape required proof of force and non-consent. Incidents of nonconsensual sex that did not involve the use of physical force were commonly called acts of seduction.[54] These acts typically involved emotional and psychological coercion and included the use of incapacitating drugs, incest, and promise to marry.[55]

The legal recourse available to victims of seduction was severely limited. The primary remedy was a civil tort action, filed by the victim's father, demanding damages for his loss of services, reputation, and honor. If the seduction produced a child, a woman could also bring the criminal charge of bastardy (paternity support cases). This action was critical because of the social costs to women who had a child out of wedlock, including public humiliation and diminished opportunities for marriage.[56] For working-class women the additional financial burden of a child forced some to turn to prostitution in order to survive.[57] The PAWC therefore drafted a law that would make seduction a crime.[58]

It took thirteen years for the PAWC to secure the law. The agency launched its campaign during its first year of operation. Despite persistently lobbying legislators in Chicago and the state capital at Springfield, the bill failed.[59] In 1899 the PAWC renewed its efforts after it was forced to charge a forty-year-old man, who had fathered a baby with a fourteen year old girl, with bastardy for want of any other available charge. The PAWC drafted another bill and lobbied women's clubs and the Chicago bar to help secure its passage. The bill passed, but only after the state senate reduced its force. It amended the bill to limit the crime of seduction to unmarried females under the age of eighteen "of previous chaste character" and reduced the category of the offense from a felony to a misdemeanor.[60]

Another legislative effort intended to protect girls from sexual assault involved amending the age of consent laws. The Woman's Christian Temperance Union began a legislative campaign in 1886 to raise the age of consent.[61] The PAWC joined this effort, sending "hundreds of letters" to Illinois legislators asking that the age a girl be deemed legally capable of consenting to sexual intercourse be raised from ten to eighteen.[62] In a similar fate to many of its law reform efforts, the legislature passed a lesser version of the bill. In this case the age of consent was raised to fourteen.[63]

In a related effort, the PAWC advocated laws that made conspiring to seduce a female into prostitution a crime.[64] It asserted that these cases were commonplace and explained that they involved both instances of kidnapping and using false promises to lure girls into their control. Once abducted, the girls were taken to a house of prostitution where they were forced to work.[65] The agency initiated these legislative campaigns amid a growing international movement to end forced prostitution, commonly referred to as "white slavery."[66] Over the ensuing decades numerous crusaders used white slavery to support a vast range of reforms.[67] PAWC activists drew on some of the rhetoric surrounding these efforts but stayed outside those campaigns.

The PAWC maintained that it would represent any woman who had been abducted and forced into prostitution. But the Illinois law criminalizing abduction only applied to "unmarried female[s] of a chaste life and conversation."[68] The PAWC secured a new law criminalizing conspiracy to seduce females into a house of prostitution in the hope that it would provide broader redress and protection for women and girls than the existing statute.[69] Immediately after its enactment, the agency sought to enforce the new law. It assisted in the prosecution of four separate cases of conspiracy, but was only successful in securing a conviction in one of the cases.[70]

The activists believed that society's sexual mores remained at the heart of the system's failure. These social prejudices were able to thwart every strategy the agency employed. Even when the agency finally secured a new abduction law that did not require the victim to be chaste, social prejudices diminished its effect.[71] The PAWC therefore initiated a campaign to educate society women on the negative consequences of their prejudices. The activists publicly asked them to support all women who were victims of sexual crimes rather than add to their victimization by discrediting their character and casting them out from the ranks of respectability.[72]

The experiences of the agency activists trying to secure justice for working-women taught them that changing laws and providing representation alone could not protect women from abuse and exploitation. They believed that it was also necessary to change the attitudes and actions of those in power. "While the law aims to do justice," Charlotte Holt explained, "the actions of the servants of the law often do injustice."[73] The PAWC therefore worked to reform the way that the law was administered and applied in the courts.

Inside the Courthouse

The PAWC viewed the courts as its last resort in securing justice for its clients. It attempted to resolve disputes and seek retribution through alternative means whenever possible. When these efforts failed, however, the agency invaded the halls of justice.[74] It organized its members to sit vigil in Chicago courtrooms to offer support to its clients and to ensure that judges followed the law. Additionally the activists assisted in prosecuting those who committed crimes against its clients.

The PAWC concentrated much of its reform efforts on the vastly corrupt police and justice courts. These tribunals heard cases involving minor civil and criminal claims. They were overseen by either a police magistrate or a justice of the peace, both commonly referred to as justices. The governor filled the positions based on political considerations rather than merit, resulting in many unqualified and dishonest justices.[75]

The PAWC experienced this corruption firsthand as it represented clients subject to these courts. In 1890, for example, the PAWC was presented with a series of cases involving a scheme undertaken between a "crook," a corrupt police officer, and a corrupt justice of the peace.[76] The PAWC attorney, S. B. Minshall, explained that in these cases the dishonest man would file false charges of disorderly conduct against honest men and women with whom he owed some debt. Each time the person was arrested for disorderly conduct he or she would have to pay a sum to the constable or the justice of the peace as a bond even if the charges were never pursued or substantiated. The PAWC intervened on behalf of those falsely accused. It was able to secure the dismissal of the charges, costs, and fees in its cases, by threatening appeals to the Superior Courts, but was frustrated that the practice continued for those who did not have representation.

The PAWC instituted a campaign to replace the corrupt justices. Its chairman, Caroline Brown, had spent a year observing in the justice courts and had documented a vast array of corruption. Of particular concern was the systematic dismissal of criminal assault cases involving husbands who beat their wives, because the justices did not believe that wifebeating was a crime. The PAWC wrote to the Cook County judges urging them to replace the current justices with qualified men of high character. Judge Kirk Hawes, who had a reputation for fighting corruption, responded to the petition and requested that the PAWC provide specific evidence. PAWC officers met with Judge Hawes, provided a year's worth of evidence of corruption, and named names. They reported that only one of the justices against whom they made complaints was reappointed.[77]

During its second year the PAWC extended its strategy of attending court sessions, persuading society women to join them. Arguing against those women who believed it was "a matter of pride to say, 'we were never in a court-room,'" the activists described the courtroom as the locus where individuals could assert their rights. They reasoned that "the presence of a delegation of reputable women . . . change[d] the moral tone of a Police court." The activists hoped that their presence would limit defense attorney attacks against the character of women victims and that they "impart[ed] courage" to agency clients who were otherwise the only female in a room with "so many strange men." It further hoped that women who witnessed court proceedings would be moved to abandon their own prejudices against "unchaste" women.[78]

The PAWC also entered the courtrooms to assist in the prosecution of men charged with sexually assaulting its clients. The agency railed against the ways that men were able to manipulate the system by using social and legal tactics to limit the rights of victims and dissuade them from taking action. The agency described how the perpetrator would threaten and harass the victim, while the defense attorney engaged in stall tactics, such as repeatedly rescheduling court dates requiring the woman to lose a day's work with each rescheduling. When the trial finally commenced, the woman who was assaulted was forced to answer "whatever dreadful and insulting question the lawyers chose to ask her" and was subjected to the testimony of witnesses who would falsely accuse her of promiscuous sexual activity.[79] The activists tried to limit these abuses and bring the offenders to justice.

Only a small percentage of the PAWC caseload involved defending women charged with a crime. It took on this work when women sought its assistance or intervened on its own initiative when it believed that a woman was in desperate need. In these cases, similar to its other work, the PAWC came to represent women regardless of their reputation, ethnicity, or race. It was most proud of its work in support of Nancy Harris, an African American woman from Atlanta, who had been sentenced to the Illinois state prison.[80]

Harris had been the victim of a confidence ring. When she and her sister arrived at the train station in Chicago in 1889, a man who claimed to know her relatives offered her an opportunity to work for a woman friend of his. After just two days of work, Harris was accused of stealing thirty-five dollars from her employers. When an officer investigated and discovered that Harris's sister had 140 dollars in cash, he arrested Harris. Although she pleaded not guilty, on the advice of her court-appointed attorney, Harris did not demand a jury trial and instead "threw herself upon the mercy of the court." She was found guilty and sentenced to one year in the state prison. Less than two weeks after she had arrived in Chicago, Harris was imprisoned at Joliet Stateville Correctional Center for a crime she did not commit.[81]

An acquaintance of Harris informed the PAWC about the case after Harris was sentenced. The agency conducted an investigation and verified that Harris's sister had received the money in a court judgment in Atlanta. It filed a writ of error with the Supreme Court. Three months later the court overturned the conviction, and all charges were ultimately dismissed. Though PAWC activists did not publicly discuss their attitudes of race, Charlotte Holt described Harris's case as the most "notable" one brought to the agency, and S. B. Minshall expressed it as his most "gratifying."[82]

The Gendered Origins of the Legal Aid Society of Chicago

The PAWC played an important role in the transformation of society's response to the social and legal injustices working people suffered. Because it served women and children exclusively, it made visible legal harms that were specific to women as it worked to redefine them. Its work also inspired other women activists to replicate its efforts at the local and national level.[83] It inspired PAWC attorney Joseph Errant to found a similar agency for workingmen, the Bureau of Justice (BOJ). The BOJ shared the social justice approach of the PAWC. It believed that poverty was the result of economic forces rather than a flaw in the individual character of the poor. Its aim was not to reform the poor but to give them equal access to the systems of justice. It also employed the PAWC's multidimensional cause lawyering approach, which included providing direct legal services, public education, and legislative law reforms.[84]

Despite their similar missions, the work of the two agencies differed significantly. Unlike the PAWC women who stood at the periphery of the justice system, the men of the BOJ began their work as official members inside the system they were seeking to change. Additionally, because the BOJ was established primarily to handle the cases of men, its efforts did not include a fight for political or social equality. Men had full citizenship rights and were accepted in the public sphere.

The BOJ was immediately inundated with clients. It received more than eleven hundred requests for assistance its first year, most of which centered on financial matters. The BOJ did handle a small number of cases involving crimes against women, but these comprised only a fraction of 1 percent of its total cases.[85] By its second year the BOJ doubled its caseload.[86]

The work of the BOJ soon came to the attention of progressive-minded men throughout the country who were similarly interested in providing legal assistance to the poor. Although it was the PAWC that established the model and provided the inspiration for the BOJ, it was the Bureau that brought this new strategy for addressing the criminal victimization suffered by the poor into the popular public discourse. In 1891 the *New York Herald* devoted an editorial to the BOJ, calling for New York to follow Chicago's example. The following year Indianapolis established a bureau modeled after Chicago's BOJ.[87]

In 1905 the PAWC consolidated with the BOJ. For fifteen years it had rejected invitations to merge, because the BOJ refused to agree to share equal power in governing the new agency and to allow the PAWC activists authority over all cases involving crimes against women.[88] When the BOJ finally conceded to both conditions, they formed the Legal Aid Society (LAS) of Chicago in 1905.[89] The LAS adopted the PAWC's dual approach of legal aid and cause lawyering and maintained a Women's Committee that handled all cases involving crimes against women. A decade later the United Charities of Chicago (now the Metropolitan Family Services) took over the LAS and renamed it the Legal Aid Bureau, which continues to operate today.

Conclusion

The PAWC merger with the BOJ was part of a larger trend of professionalization that diminished the agency's independence and influence.[90] State laws governing the practice of law and court procedures grew more stringent during the twentieth century. State and national bar associations also became more protective of their expertise. These transformations limited the opportunities for non-licensed law activists to participate in the legal system, extinguishing the conditions that had allowed for much of the PAWC's work. A few of the activists, including Charlotte Holt, responded by becoming licensed members of the legal profession.[91]

The PAWC left two legacies. The first is its cause lawyering paradigm. Cause lawyers have been an integral part of the movements for African American civil rights and women's rights since the mid-twentieth century. Their work, engaged in struggles for social change, employed the model established by the PAWC.[92] The PAWC's second legacy is its campaigns to redress acts of sexual and physical violence against women and the legal and social prejudices that served as a barrier to social justice. Although agency activists failed in most cases to transform social attitudes, legal procedures, or outcomes, their campaigns continued through the twentieth century.[93]

At the turn of the twenty-first century the consensus among many feminist scholars is that "legal reform as currently constituted cannot by itself eliminate violence against women. The cultural, economic, and social roots of gender and race inequality are too deep." But the quest endures. Feminist scholars, activists, and cause lawyers continue to "chart the social forces at work in and around the law as it attempts to address the concerns of those women [who are subject to violence]" and legal aid attorneys continue to represent them.[94]

NOTES

The author thanks Eric Arnesen, Arthur McEvoy, Susan Levine, Katrin Schultheiss, Felice Batlan, David Tanenhaus, Jane Larson, Rima Schultz, J. Gordan Hylton, Perry Duis, Julie Globokar, and the comments of anonymous reviewers on earlier versions of this essay.

1. PAWC, Second Annual Report, 20 (1888).

2. See Reva Siegel, "The Rule of Love": Wife Beating as Prerogative and Privacy, 105 Yale L.J. 2117–2207 (1996); Jane Larson, "Even a Worm Will Turn at Last": Rape Reform in Late Nineteenth-Century America, 1 Yale J.L. & Human. 9 (1997); Elizabeth Pleck, Feminist Responses to Crimes Against Women, 1868–1896, 451–52 Signs 8, no. 3 (1983).

3. Marguerite Raeder Gariepy, The Legal Aid Bureau of the United Charities of Chicago, 124 Annals Am. Acad. Pol. & Soc Science 33 (1926).

4. Karen J. Blair, The Clubwoman as Feminist: True Womanhood Redefined, 1868–1914, 4 (1980).

5. See Felice Batlan, Law and the Fabric of the Everyday: The Settlement Houses, Sociological Jurisprudence, and the Gendering of Urban Legal Culture, 15 S. Cal. Interdisc. L.J. 236, 258–61, 266, 271–72 (2005–2006); Mary E. Odem, Delinquent Daughters: Protecting and Policing Adolescent Female Sexuality in the United States, 1885–1920, 1–2 (1995).

6. In and About Chicago, Christian Union, Jan. 26, 1888, at 4; see also Linda Gordon, The Moral Property of Women: A History of Birth Control Politics in America 9–11 (1974) (2007 ed.).

7. Chicago Woman's Club, Board Minutes, Jan. 19, 1887, Box 1, Chicago History Museum.

8. See Gwen Hoerr Jordan, Agents of (Incremental) Change: From Myra Bradwell to Hillary Clinton, 9 Nev. L.J. 580, 583 (2009).

9. See Linda K. Kerber, Separate Spheres, Female Worlds, Woman's Place: The Rhetoric of Women's History, 75 J. Am. Hist. 9–13 (1988).

10. Thomas Hilbink, You know the Type . . .: Categories of Cause Lawyering, 29 Law & Soc Inq. 11–12, 657, 681–90 (2004).

11. Senate Bill, No. 275, J. House Rep (Mar. 21, 1872) 1024–26; Bar None:125 Years of Women Lawyers in Illinois, Chicago Bar Ass'n 32–33 (Gwen Hoerr McNamee ed. 1998).

12. Karen Berger Morello, The Invisible Bar 173–74, 179 (1986); Virginia G. Drachman, Sisters in Law: Women Lawyers in Modern American History, 78–80 (2001).

13. Austin Sarat and Stuart Scheingold, Introduction, in Cause Lawyering and the State in a Global Era 7 (Austin Sarat and Stuart Scheingold, eds. 2001).

14. Reginald Heber Smith, Justice and the Poor 185–86 (1919); Gariepy, The Legal Aid Bureau, 33; Marguerite Raeder Gariepy, Legal Aid as Part of a Community Program, 205

Annals Am. Academy Pol. & Soc. Sci. 72 (Sept. 1939); Jack Katz, Poor People's Lawyers in Transition 34–35 (1982).

15. Sarat and Scheingold, 3.

16. Hilbink, 681. See also Michael McCann and Helena Silverstein, Rethinking Law's "Allurements": A Relational Analysis of Social Movement Lawyers in the United States," in Sarat and Scheingold, 266–269.

17. Jack Greenberg, Crusaders in the Courts (1994); Richard Kluger, Simple Justice: The History of Brown v. Board of Education and Black America's Struggle for Equality (1975, 2004); Mark V. Tushnet, The NAACP's Legal Strategy against Segregated Education 1925–1950 (1987, 2005).

18. Samuel Walker, In Defense of American Liberties: A History of the ACLU (1990); Robert L. Rabin, Lawyers for Social Change: Perspectives on Public Interest Law, 28 Stanford L. Rev. 207, 210–14 (1976); Ruth B. Cowan, Women's Rights Through Litigation: An Examination of the American Civil Liberties Union's Women's Rights Project, 1971–1976, 8 Colum. Human Rights L. Rev 373 (1976).

19. Justice Thurgood Marshall, Foreword, in J. Clay Smith Jr., Emancipation: The Making of the Black Lawyer, 1844–1944, 148 (1993), xi.

20. See Gwen Hoerr McNamee, Mary Margaret Bartelme, in Women Building Chicago 666, 668 (Rima Lunin Schultz and Adele Haste, eds. 2001); Grace H. Harte, A Momentous Victory, 25 Women Lawyers J. 54 (1938–1939).

21. U. S., Bureau of the Census, A Compendium of the Ninth Census of the United States 8, 444–45 (1870); see Robyn Muncy, Creating a Female Dominion in American Reform, 1890–1935, 11–12 (1991); Joanne J. Meyerowitz, Women Adrift: Independent Wage Earners in Chicago, 1880–1930, 13(1988).

22. Protection for the Weak, Chic. Trib., Mar. 27, 1886, at 9.

23. Meredith Tax, The Rising of Women: Feminist Solidarity and Class Conflict, 1880–1917 (1980), 65–89; Allan H. Spear, Black Chicago: The Making of a Negro Ghetto, 1890–1920 (1967) 101–3.

24. Henriette Greenebaum Frank and Amalie Hofer Jerome, Annals of the Chicago Woman's Club for the First Forty Years of Its Organization 1876–1916, 371–373, 375–378 (1916).

25. Donald Miller, City of the Century: The Epic of Chicago and the Making of America 456–58 (1996); Victoria Bissel Brown, Introduction, in Jane Addams, Twenty Years at Hull House 1, 15–16 (1999); Michael Willrich, City of Courts: Socializing Justice in Progressive Era Chicago xxi–xxii (2003).

26. Larson, 15– 18; Lawrence M. Friedman, Crime and Punishment in American History 215, 222–23 (1993); PAWC, First Annual Report, 16.

27. Hull House was one of the most active of these Chicago institutions. Muncy, Creating a Female Dominion, 13; see also Blair, The Clubwoman as Feminist, 73: Felicia Hillel, Working-Girls, 10 The Chautauquan 331 (Dec. 1889).

28. Friedman, 217, 223; Pleck, 453–55; Larson, 14–15; Babcock, 4–5.

29. Lawrence M. Friedman, A History of American Law 638–39 (2d ed. 1973, 1985); Robert S. Gordon, Critical Legal Histories, 36 Stan. L. Rev. 57, 89 (1984).

30. Jerald Auerbach, Unequal Justice: Lawyers and Social Change in Modern America 108–13 (1976).

31. Bradwell v. Illinois, 83 U.S. (16 Wall.) 130 (1873); Drachman, Sisters in Law, 26; Jordan, Agents of (Incremental) Change, 620–21.

32. William Wiecek, The Lost World of Classical Legal Thought: Law and Ideology in America 1886–1937, 44 (1998).

33. Wiecek, 175, 177–80.

34. See Adam Winkler, A Revolution Too Soon: Woman Suffragists and the "Living Constitution," 76 NYU L. Rev. 1456, 1458 (2001); Jordan, Agents of (Incremental) Change, 603–8, 618–21; Wiecek, 177–82; Horowitz, 109–42; Hall, 223–24; Batlan, Fabric of the Everyday, 235, 248–50; see also Roscoe Pound, The Need of a Sociological Jurisprudence, 19 Green Bag 607 (1907).

35. First Annual Report, 31; Katz, 7.

36. C. Ronald Huff, Historical Explanations of Crime: From Demons to Politics, in Crime Reading (2d ed. 2009) 13–24, 17–18 (Robert Crutchfield et. al., eds. 1996, 2000); Willrich, City of Courts, xxii–xxiii.

37. Pleck, 451–65; Siegel, 27–29.

38. Mari Jo Buhle, Women and American Socialism 1870–1920 71–73, 91–92 (1981).

39. Second Annual Report, 21; Willrich, 11.

40. Second Annual Report, 20.

41. See Batlan, Fabric of the Everyday, 267.

42. First Annual Report, 26–27.

43. Batlan, Fabric of the Everyday, 267, 271; First Annual Report, 26.

44. First Annual Report, 12, 23; Third Annual Report, 13; Fourth Annual Report, 15; Fifth Annual Report, 11; see also Siegel.

45. Third Annual Report, 10.

46. First Annual Report, 8, 10; Fourth Annual Report, 13. Carroll D. Wright, A Report on Marriage and Divorce in the United States, 1867–1886 (1889); Norma Basch, Framing American Divorce: From the Revolutionary Generation to the Victorians 2 (1999); Robert Griswold, Law, Sex, Cruelty, and Divorce in Victorian America, 1840–1900, 38 Am. Q. 721, 722 (1986).

47. See Basch, Divorce, 2–3; Griswold, 722–24; Pleck, 468.

48. First Annual Report, 10; Fourth Annual Report, 21.

49. Third Annual Report, 9; Fourth Annual Report, 10.

50. Fourth Annual Report, 10.

51. First Annual Report, 19.

52. Second Annual Report, 11.

53. First Annual Report, 7, 19; Third Annual Report, 10, 19.

54. See Lori D. Ginzberg, Women and the Work of Benevolence: Morality, Politics, and Class in the Nineteenth-Century United States 77–78 (1992).

55. Larson, Even a Worm, 14 –15, 18; First Annual Report, 20.

56. Jane E. Larson, "Women Understand So Little, They Call My Good Nature 'Deceit'": A Feminist Rethinking of Seduction, 93 Colum. L. Rev. 374, 383–86 (1993).

57. Linda R. Hirshman and Jane E. Larson, Hard Bargains: The Politics of Sex 92 (1998).

58. First Annual Report, 20.

59. Id.

60. Thirteenth Annual Report; Laws of Illinois 1899, 148; 38 Ill. Rev. Stat. 3936.

61. Ruth Bordin, Woman and Temperance: The Quest for Power and Liberty, 1873–1900, 110 (1990); Larson, Even a Worm, 24.

62. First Annual Report, 20.

63. Laws of Illinois 1887, 171.

64. *Id.* at 168.

65. First Annual Report, 24.

66. Larson, Even a Worm, 25.

67. See Brian Donovan, White Slave Crusades: Race, Gender, and Anti-vice Activism, 1887–1917 (2006); David Pivar, Purity and Hygiene: Women, Prostitution, and the "American Plan," 1900–1930 (2001); J. R. Walkowitz, Prostitution and Victorian Society: Women, Class, and the State (1980).

68. 38 Ill. Rev. Stat. par. 5, sec. 1 (1874); *Accused of Abduction*, Chic. Trib., Oct. 30, 1887, at 9.

69. Laws of Illinois 1887, 170; 38 Ill. Rev. Stat. 3436 (1874).

70. Annie Herman et al. v. Illinois, 131 IL 594 (1890); Second Annual Report, 18, 23–25.

71. Fourth Annual Report, 11; Laws of Illinois 1889, 112; 38 Ill. Rev. Stat. par. 7b (3).

72. Second Annual Report, 11; Fourth Annual Report, 11.

73. First Annual Report, 31.

74. *Id.* at 8.

75. Willrich, 11.

76. Third Annual Report, 20.

77. First Annual Report, 9–10; *Bettering the Justice Courts*, Chic. Trib., Mar. 1, 1877, at 1; *Judge Hawes Wants Specific Proof*, Chic. Trib., Mar. 2, 1877, at 1.

78. Second Annual Report, 13; Seventh Annual Report, 8; First Annual Report, 13; Fourth Annual Report, 11–12.

79. First Annual Report, 1180; Third Annual Report, 14.

81. *Id.* at 14.

82. *Id.* at 14–15, 21.

83. Second Annual Report, 14; Third Annual Report, 12.

84. First Annual Report, 1, 20.

85. *Id.* at 8–9.

86. BOJ, Sixth Annual Report, 12.

87. BOJ, Fourth Annual Report, 14.

88. Ninth Annual Report, 4–5; Twelfth Annual Report, 8.

89. Seventeenth Annual Report, 5, 8; BOJ, Seventeenth Annual Report, 25.

90. See Muncy, Creating a Female Dominion, 124–25.

91. James Bradwell, *Women Lawyers of Illinois*, Chi. Legal News, June 2, 1900 at 340; Fifth Annual Report, 3.

92. Sarat and Schneigold, Introduction, 4.

93. Nancy Matthews, Confronting Rape: The Feminist Anti-Rape Movement and the State (1994); R. Emerson Dobash and Russell P. Dobash, Women, Violence, and Social Change (1992).

94. Lisa Frohmann and Elizabeth Mertz, *Legal Reform and Social Construction: Violence, Gender, and the Law*, Law & Soc. Inq. 850–51 (1995).

9

Legal Aid, Women Lay Lawyers, and the Rewriting of History, 1863-1930

FELICE BATLAN

This chapter demonstrates that the origins of free legal aid for the poor was deeply gendered and grew out of women's work. In fact, the provision of legal aid in New York City, Chicago, and Philadelphia first involved the creation of legal aid organizations for poor women, and this aid was provided primarily by other women functioning as lay lawyers.[1] By the late 1890s, as women in small numbers began graduating from law schools, some joined the newly developing legal aid societies as full-fledged attorneys. Likewise, women as clients and their claims against employers and husbands saturate the records of these new legal aid societies. Thus, from the 1860s through the first decade of the twentieth century, the sphere of legal aid was deeply feminized. This, however, would not remain the case.

Quite remarkable is that this history of women's monumental involvement in legal aid is virtually unknown. Such silence can be traced to the second generation of male legal aid leaders, who began writing the first histories of legal aid and creating an expansive future agenda for it. How such leaders constructed these histories and erased women's participation was not unintentional. Rather, it served a variety of purposes, including locating legal aid as the brainchild of male attorneys, and envisioning the substantive work of legal aid as being conducted and controlled by male lawyers. The work of this generation served to masculinize legal aid, enhance its status, and align it with the bar association. This had significant ramifications not only for who provided legal aid but also the services that legal aid provided, especially to poor women. This model of declension is a counterintuitive story, for it argues that, in the post-bellum period and gilded age, women had more power in legal aid organizations than they would have in the late progressive period.

The origins of legal aid date back to the Civil War and the very dramatic creation of the Working Women's Protective Union (WWPU) in New York

City.[2] In 1863 New York City, like much of the country, was suffering from significant wartime inflation. Prices had risen dramatically, but workers' wages had not. Male skilled workers, led by machinists, called for a citywide strike. Women workers, who were primarily concentrated in the sewing and notions trades, soon began engaging in their own labor agitation and contemplating strikes.[3] Workingwomen, along with a number of male allies who supported workers' collective action, formed the Working Women's Union, which was open to all workingwomen.[4] The establishment of such a union was radical, as it was composed of and led by women at a time when many believed that women were incapable of collective labor action.[5]

Emphasizing the perceived radical nature of the new Union, newspapers reported, probably incorrectly, that Susan B. Anthony, in the company of a "colored woman," attended one of the meetings. The report of her presence tarred the Union as being associated with suffrage and abolition.[6] Furthermore, the new Union was deeply democratic and, instead of electing delegates, held open meetings in which all women could participate.[7] In quick succession, however, this nascent union of women was taken over by a group of male labor leaders and their professional allies, a number of them attorneys. The name of the Union was changed to the Working Women's Protective Union, and its mission was redefined as providing legal aid to working women whose employers had failed to pay their wages.[8] The addition of "Protective" to the Union's name signaled that the women were to be protected by others rather than engaging in self-help through collective action such as strikes. Although the formation of the WWPU represented a coup by a group of men over working women's self-directed and collective action, over the years the WWPU provided legal services to tens of thousands of women who claimed that their employers had withheld their wages.[9]

The mission of the Union was now quite narrow, yet it was the first organization devoted to providing free legal aid to the poor. Why legal aid was first provided to women perhaps can be found in a combination of the material reality of working women's lives and the ideological operation of gender and capitalism. In the 1860s workers, politicians, and reformers widely acknowledged that women's wages in the sewing trades were barely enough to survive on and employers often refused to pay them altogether. Furthermore journalists, along with the WWPU and others, acknowledged that women, especially soldiers' widows and those displaced by war, often did not have a male breadwinner to rely on. Hovering over all of this was the fear that sewing women faced with starvation would turn to prostitution.[10] Although poor and impoverished women with children and without male breadwinners had always existed, the war made such women particularly visible. Moreover, as the WWPU highlighted, these women were impoverished not because they did not work but rather because they were not paid for their work. If what separated slave labor and wage labor was the payment of wages, white women's supposed chastity, and the non-commodification of white women's sexuality, here women whose employers failed to pay them, and who stood on the cusp of starvation and prostitution, too closely resembled slaves and thus challenged the very concept of free labor.[11]

In addition, working women were widely understood and constructed to be weak contractual actors, with little bargaining power and in need of male protection. Wage claims were also a particularly opportune site where law and lawyers could intervene, for they were upholding the contractual regime on behalf of women whom the WWPU always portrayed as helpless without the power of a male attorney. Thus the two constructs of gender and wage labor functioned in tandem by upholding the contractual paradigm of wage labor while tapping into the belief that women were helpless and worthy of aid when a male breadwinner was absent. In other words, women needed male support to be full contractual actors.

The WWPU was a widely popular charity that elicited the support of many of New York's most elite lawyers and judges. At Union benefits, such men grandly praised the legal work of the Union and the immense number of cases that it handled.[12] Reading on the surface of the Union's extant documents, it appears that male attorneys ran the organization and provided legal aid to those women who sought help. Yet this was not the case. Rather, it was the Union's superintendent, who was always a woman, and her all female staff who carried out the day-to-day work of the Union, including much of the legal work. Through the many decades that the Union existed, a working-woman who sought legal aid would go to the Union's offices. There she would meet with the superintendent who would advise her about her claim. If the superintendent believed she had a legal claim, the woman would be asked to return to meet with a male attorney. Before a court case would be filed, however, the superintendent would send a demand letter to the employer and would attempt to negotiate a settlement. What must be recognized is that the Union had a very high volume of cases but actually filed few suits. Rather, creating a pattern which almost all legal aid societies would follow in the future, the great majority of claims were settled, and it was the supervisor who would negotiate such settlements. The primary activity performed by the Union's part-time male lawyer was appearing in court. All other office work from intake on was the domain of the supervisor.[13] Thus, at a time before women in New York could become members of the bar, the WWPU's supervisor and her assistants were essentially practicing law.

Likewise, in Philadelphia legal aid first grew out of women's philanthropic work. In the 1870s Rebecca Cole, one of the first African American women to become a physician, created the Woman's Directory, which provided medical services to women and probably some form of legal services as well.[14] More concretely, in 1879, women who were members of Philadelphia's New Century Club created the Committee for the Legal Protection of Working Women (CLPW). Like the WWPU, women staffed the office and provided legal advice to poor women on a wide range of issues. It also attempted to settle claims without going to court. Only in the event that an actual suit had to be filed would the CLPW involve a male attorney.[15] Thus again we see women, who were not formally trained in the law, providing legal advice to poor women. Eventually it was this committee, along with a group of male lawyers, who created the Philadelphia Legal Aid Society.[16]

In connection with the development of legal aid in Chicago, Gwen Jordan, in chapter 8 of this volume, examines how the Chicago Woman's Club, in 1886, created the first free law office in Chicago, known as the Protective Agency for Women and Children (PAWC). The PAWC was fully aware of the existence of the WWPU and its success in collecting wages for women. Yet the PAWC defined its mission more broadly than the WWPU.[17] As Jordan has demonstrated, the types of cases that the PAWC handled were quite varied, and the organization had a keen and perhaps unique awareness of and sensitivity to poor women's legal problems. Although the agency specialized in abuse and domestic relations cases, many of its more mundane cases, like the WWPU and CLPW, involved wage claims for women.[18] Significantly, the bulk of the PAWC's work, like the WWPU's and the CLPW's, was handled by a woman and her female assistants.[19] In all three organizations, a male attorney became involved only when a case went to court. The PAWC statistics indicate that for the years 1898, 1899, and 1900, cases that were filed in court constituted approximately 5 to 10 percent of cases the PAWC accepted. Thus the female staff of the PAWC, functioning as lay lawyers, controlled 90–95 percent of cases. Although the WWPU did not keep similar statistics, it is likely that the superintendent and her female staff handled a similar percentage of cases.[20]

The WWPU, the PAWC, and the CLPW demonstrate that, in the postbellum era through the gilded age, women were deeply involved in legal philanthropic work, functioning as lay lawyers and ministering to the legal needs of the poor. In part, it was through such women's very exclusion from traditional legal institutions, such as law schools and bar associations, and the acceptance that charity work, especially on behalf of other women, was appropriate for elite and middle-class women that these organizations were able to carve out a space for women lay lawyers. As such, the growing field of the provision of legal aid to poor people was deeply feminized, filled with women clients and women workers. By the 1890s legal philanthropic work even provided a justification for women entering law schools or at least receiving more formal legal training.

The history of New York's Arbitration Society and Women's Legal Education Society provides perfect examples of the transition from women lay lawyers engaged in providing legal services to poor women to formally trained women attorneys providing such services. In 1888 Emily Kempin-Spyri, a Swiss woman who received a doctorate in jurisprudence from the University of Zurich, arrived in New York City hoping to practice law. Within a year, Kempin became acquainted with Fanny Weber, a socially prominent woman.[21] Weber already had considerable experience as a reformer. In 1887 she founded an organization that offered cooking and hygiene classes to poor immigrant women. Through such work she concluded that working women required legal services more than anything else.[22]

Weber and Kempin formed the Arbitration Society whose purpose was to offer arbitration services and legal advice to the poor. The Arbitration Society's directors and founders were, with one exception, women.[23] Its focus upon arbitration was undoubtedly a tactical decision. Few women were admitted to practice law in New York City, which was necessary to appear in court; arbitration, of course, occurred outside the courts. As soon as the Society's office opened, people flocked there, overwhelming the small staff. As Weber stated, "We could not find a sufficient number of charitable women to help—such women as could give the necessary assistance with that authority that comes from legal knowledge."[24] Weber and Kempin determined that an institution was needed that could educate women in the law. The two formed the Women's Legal Education Society. The Society immediately attracted the support of some of New York's most prominent women and was born out of the idea that women needed legal training to engage in philanthropic legal work. In 1890 New York University (NYU) allowed the Society to function under its auspices.

That first year Kempin delivered law lectures to approximately twelve women. Although some of the women enrolled were socially prominent, others were not and attended the lectures on scholarship.[25] Elite legal luminaries of the New York bar such as Chauncey Depew, David Dudley Field, and Judge Noah Davis, all supporters of the WWPU, now also supported the Society.[26] Further, as NYU Law School began admitting women, the Society inaugurated full scholarships so that women could attend the Society's course of study, and then seek admission to NYU. As a number of these students graduated from law school, they formed the Women's Law League, and defined its mission to include providing counsel to poor women and bringing their legal skills to philanthropic efforts.[27] Other women lawyers (who had graduated from a handful of law schools that admitted women), with few law firms or clients willing to hire them, also began to specialize in "poor people's law."[28] Thus the provision of legal aid by women was becoming professionalized. Indeed, it was, in part, women who graduated from NYU Law School who would go on to staff the New York Legal Aid Society (NYLAS).

By the turn of the century the NYLAS, first established in 1876 to provide legal services to German immigrants, became the largest provider of legal aid services in New York City. This occurred as the Society dropped its requirement that clients be German, anglicized its name, and sought to establish offices throughout the city.[29] Although the Society was controlled by male lawyers, it also reached out to women lawyers, clients, and benefactors. NYLAS was one of the first legal aid locations where formally trained women lawyers provided legal advice to men and women.[30] The legal staff of NYLAS was always small, but between 1897 and 1910 numerous women lawyers worked for it, including Rosalie Loew, who had been with NYLAS since 1897 and, in 1901, was appointed as its chief attorney. At various times at the turn of the century Mary Quakenbos, Annette Fisk, Josephine Stary, Sadie Frances Rothschild, and Bertha Rembaugh all worked as attorneys for NYLAS. In 1905 Rembaugh became the head attorney of the Society's uptown branch.

With one foot in philanthropy and the other in law, legal aid was a particularly appropriate location for women attorneys, as the work performed was on a continuum with that performed earlier by women lay lawyers. Further, if what differentiated the work of the female lay lawyer and the male attorney was the ability to go into court, legal aid work blurred this distinction. With the volume of cases handled by legal aid societies, most of them never found their way into court. NYLAS also differentiated the practice of a legal aid lawyer from that of a private lawyer, describing NYLAS as a "quasi-public corporation" which did not take cases that were "morally wrong." As one legal aid attorney explained, legal aid's "relation with its clients is not exactly that of attorney or advocate. Frequently the Society mediates between its client and other parties, and sometimes it is even necessary to decide against its client."[31] A practice that was morally upright, which took place primarily in the office, not the courtroom, and bridged philanthropy and law, was precisely the type of work considered appropriate for women lawyers.[32] As demonstrated, women who were not formally trained in law had been doing such work for years at the WWPU, the Arbitration Society, the PAWC, and the CLPW.

By 1901 women as both lawyers and benefactors were so important to NYLAS that Arthur Brieson, the Society's longtime president, ended its twenty-fifth anniversary dinner by acknowledging the important work that women had done on its behalf and announcing the opening of the Society's Women's Branch, which was an office entirely staffed by women attorneys.[33] One early report justifying the establishment of the branch stressed, "Women will always find one of their sex ready to listen to and appreciate their cases."[34] The opening of the branch signified the idea that formally trained women lawyers should provide legal services to poor women. Importantly, part of the rationale for and uniqueness of the branch was its location in the Charities Building. As the Society wrote:

This bureau is in such close touch with the charity organizations in and near the building that it can and does co-operate with them in many important instances. For example, when a poor woman with a number of children applies for bread to one of the charities it is proper after her immediate needs have been met, for investigation to be set on foot to ascertain the precise wrong done her and the means for righting it. Thus it frequently happens that such women are deserted by their husbands, who can then be forced to help support them.[35]

One of the elements that is important to see here, and which would become fully manifest in the next decade, is that women lawyers and women clients were already becoming associated with the emerging field of social work. The establishment of the branch was thus part of a larger understanding that a client's problems, especially in connection with women, were not just legal. Josephine Stary, head attorney for the Branch, wrote, "First and foremost in interest, to our branch at least, are the women who come to unburden themselves of their home life." Thus here her role was to listen to the stories that poor women told of their home life, and often there were no legal solutions. Stary drops a disturbing hint of the problems women brought to her, writing that frequently women who came to the office had suffered "indignities" at the hands of their husbands. One might infer that she was referring to marital rape and other types of domestic abuse that the law, at the time, did not recognize. For reasons not entirely clear, the Women's Branch closed within two years. It was not closed for lack of need, for in 1901 alone it saw 1,622 clients.[36]

As the model for legal aid changed from women lay lawyers, who were not formally trained in law, providing legal aid to poor women, to a model in which formally trained lawyers, both men and women, provided legal advice to male and female clients, women's legal aid organizations such as the PAWC and the CLPW attempted to preserve their power. For example, a group of male lawyers and the women of the CLPW created the Legal Aid Society of Philadelphia in 1903. The CLPW insisted that women be appointed to the new board of directors. Further, Frances Anne Keay, a 1902 graduate of the University of Pennsylvania law school, along with a male attorney functioned as the Society's lawyers.[37] Keay, however, actually managed the office and had the primary day-to-day contact with clients. Moreover, even as male lawyers began working with the Society, its client base remained predominately female. In 1903 it handled 173 cases, of which 130 involved female clients. Much like other legal aid organizations, matrimonial and wage claims filled its docket.[38]

Chicago's PAWC also negotiated an arrangement with the Chicago Bureau of Justice before the two organizations merged. The merger agreement ensured that half the board of the new Chicago Legal Aid Society would be composed of women. For years the PAWC adamantly refused to merge without this explicit agreement.[39] Clearly the PAWC was suspicious of the Bureau's commitment to poor women and feared that women lay leaders of legal aid would be removed from positions of power.

This was precisely what occurred in multiple cities, as male lawyers began to take over the provision of legal aid. In doing so, they masculinized and cleaved it from a feminized sphere of philanthropy, lay women lawyers, female clients, and the developing field of social work. In part, the mechanisms of this takeover involved aligning legal aid with bar associations and law schools while defining women lay lawyers as social workers who had no place within legal aid.[40] For example, a 1928 survey of legal aid organizations co-authored by the New York City Bar Association noted, with some condescension, that all the work of the WWPU was performed by a full-time social worker.[41] The implication was that the WWPU was not a real legal aid organization. Clearly the work that the WWPU superintendent had been performing for decades, which certainly included providing legal advice, was now considered social work, which was seen as distinctly inferior to the practice of law.

By the second decade of the twentieth century social work was firmly associated with women and was under attack. Social work had developed largely from women's earlier reform and charitable activities. Although social work was in the process of professionalizing, with the creation of social work schools and a new emphasis on casework rather than reform activities, it still was primarily concerned with the poor, often used volunteer workers, paid low wages, and was dominated by women.[42] In 1915 Abraham Flexner critiqued social work as lacking a core set of skills, that, instead, it was the social worker's job to call in professionals and experts. Flexner pointedly implied that social work also confused "intelligence" with "vigor."[43] In part, social work was understood as more about traits, often associated with women, such as empathy, sympathy and resourcefulness, than about knowledge.[44]

Legal aid, concerned with the poor, relying upon charitable contributions, often involving female clients, and confronting problems that were not purely legal looked a great deal like social work and the work that had been performed by women lay lawyers. If court appearances were what had separated women lay lawyers from male attorneys, in legal aid societies such a distinction no longer worked, as most cases never reached court. The male leaders of legal aid were thus haunted by the question of what distinguished the legal aid lawyer from the social worker. Reginald Heber Smith's canonical *Justice and the Poor* answered this question, in part, by fiat situating legal aid on the law side of the equation and disassociating it from social work and women. As he wrote, "The societies are engaged in the practice of law and not in social service work. . . . More closely than anything else, the work resembles an attorney engaged in general practice."[45]

The relationship between social work and legal aid was more than a matter of semantics. It determined who would provide such services and the status of legal aid lawyers. Three years before the publication of *Justice and the Poor*, Smith, an attorney at the Boston Legal Aid Society (BLAS), had already narrowly defined BLAS as a thoroughly legal and masculine organization. For Smith, demonstrating the pedigree of BLAS was crucial. He titled a 1917 article on BLAS "A Lawyers Legal Aid Society," and stated that the "distinguishing characteristic of [BLAS] is that it is pre-eminently a lawyers' institution."[46] A "lawyers' institution" was sufficiently manly in contrast to those legal aid organizations that had been managed by women lay lawyers. Thus what differentiated BLAS was that its origins, unlike New York, Philadelphia, and Chicago, were unconnected to women lay lawyers and, by implication, social work. It was this very connection of women to legal aid that Smith systemically erased in *Justice and the Poor*.

Contextualized as such, we can understand why *Justice and the Poor* failed to mention the WWPU, contending that the NYLAS was the first legal aid organization in the country. Although Smith mentions the PAWC, he defined its work narrowly as preventing the "great number of seductions and debaucheries of young girls under the guise of proffered employment."[47] Certainly that was part, but not all, of the PAWC's work. To have described the full scope of its work, including taking matrimonial and wage claims, would have made it look too much like a legal aid society. In contrast, Smith wrote of the Chicago Bureau of Justice, formed after the creation of the PAWC, but run by and employing male lawyers, "This was in fact the first true legal aid organization."[48] Smith's interpretation of the role of the PAWC differed significantly from an earlier article written by Maud Boyes, who had formerly worked for the PAWC and was now superintendent of the Chicago Legal Aid Society. Boyes understood that the PAWC was a full-blown legal aid society which had handled a wide variety of cases.[49]

Smith's writings were undoubtedly influenced by his own experiences at BLAS, and legal aid in Boston had developed differently than in other cities. BLAS, from its inception in 1900, was primarily associated with the Boston Bar Association and Harvard Law School—institutions that excluded women. Yet even BLAS's history did not comport with Smith's radical distinction between social work and legal aid, between lawyers and lay lawyers, or the claim that legal aid constituted the delivery of pure law by an attorney who had a "legal mind."[50] For example, a 1911 speaker from BLAS complained that it and various charitable organizations duplicated one another's work. His solution was that charitable organizations should handle uncontested and routine legal cases. He thus admitted that legal aid work and social work for charitable organizations significantly overlapped. Moreover, in connection with bastardy cases, the speaker praised the work and effectiveness of women social workers in handling these matters for BLAS.[51] BLAS also relied upon its female "social secretary" to investigate domestic relations cases. A 1913 BLAS report explained, "Domestic-relation cases continue to increase in number, and a thorough examination of the home conditions and causes for the disagreement takes the greater part of the time of our social secretary."[52] In fact, between 1912 and 1915 domestic relations cases, which were primarily brought by poor women, outnumbered any other type of case handled by BLAS.[53]

In addition to distorting the history of legal aid, Smith's opinion of even formally trained women attorneys must have colored his understanding of who provided legal aid. In general, he did not believe that women should be lawyers. In 1924 he moderated his opinion, writing that the "legal aid office is different. It is much easier for [women] to practice in such an office and they seem to get along alright."[54] Smith wrote this passage twenty-three years after Rosalie Loew was appointed chief attorney of the NYLAS. Smith was not alone in his suspicion of both women lay lawyers and formally trained women lawyers. The Pittsburgh Legal Aid Society was so concerned with distancing itself from women and social work that it prohibited women from serving on its board of directors.[55] Part of Smith's and others male lawyers' objection to social work was its supposed challenge to the basic tenets of the rule of law in a democracy. Smith believed that social workers would destroy the confidentiality of the lawyer-client relationship. Furthermore, traditional rules of evidence did not apply in family and juvenile courts where social workers presented information regarding litigants' backgrounds.[56] Other criticisms of social workers (often bordering on the misogynistic) included that they were "too sympathetic to their clients, they were too idealistic, too controlling, and gave too much legal advice."[57]

By the 1920s the question of the relationship between legal aid and social work began to be openly debated. At a 1922 meeting of the National Alliance of Legal Aid Societies a committee on social work, headed by Alice Waldo, delivered its report. The report began, "The relationship between Social Service Work and Legal Aid Work . . . present[s] what is perhaps the most important . . . question . . . . [I]t directly throws us back to first principles—what is Legal Aid Work, what is a Legal Aid case, who is a proper Legal Aid client."[58] Unlike Smith's work, the report acknowledged the wide use of social workers in legal aid organizations, including social workers who were in charge of intake. Furthermore, it called "untenable" the claim that legal aid societies were like any other law office. Rather, the report argued that legal aid lawyers, unlike private lawyers, had a duty to ensure that the client received necessary social services.[59]

The repositioning of legal aid into the masculine field of law was not just a question of recognition and power; it also had substantive repercussions for poor women. As legal aid societies sought to separate themselves from the feminized field of social work, they also sought to narrow the services that they provided to women clients. For example, Smith strenuously argued against legal aid societies taking on divorce cases.[60] Although we can understand legal aid's hesitancy to take such cases as reflecting the view that divorce itself was immoral and as part of an ideology that sought to keep families together, we must also understand that it was primarily women who sought divorces. Although the PAWC often spoke out against divorce, as did the NYLAS, at the turn of the century, in practice, they did accept such cases.[61] By the 1920s, however, numerous legal aid societies no longer accepted either divorce or separation cases. In contrast, the Chicago Legal Aid Society (CLAS), where women lawyers and social workers had substantial power, continued to accept such cases.

In fact, the CLAS was one of the greatest proponents of an integrated social work–legal aid approach. By 1918 social workers dominated CLAS with two social workers for every lawyer.[62] Maude Boyes proudly wrote that the CLAS was "socialized."[63] Marguerite Raeder, the senior attorney at CLAS, explained that to be "socialized" meant that attorneys and social workers worked closely with one another, and that social workers provided basic legal advice, often investigated cases, handled intake, and engaged in settling cases. More broadly, as Raeder stated, "Clients receive not only legal assistance but also assistance in solving their social problems which are often at the root of the legal difficulty."[64] Thus the CLAS, with its board comprised of an equal number of men and women, functioned in a manner that more closely resembled the roots of legal aid. Not coincidentally, the CLAS had little contact with the Chicago Bar Association until the 1920s.

Women social workers and women legal aid lawyers were at times dumbfounded by male leaders' overt hostility to social work, and some began a sustained critique of the narrowness of legal aid. For example, Kate Holladay Claghorn's *The Immigrant's Day in Court* (1923) contended that legal aid was too focused on narrow legal technicalities. She wrote, "The legal mind trained in analyzing technical distinctions in laws . . . tends to regard legal protection as the task of fitting a given law to a set of circumstances . . . without reference to the personality of the client, or to any service rendered him other than that of securing the technical right involved."[65] Thus unlike social work, which analyzed individuals and their problems holistically, legal aid failed to contextualize the full subjective and material reality of their clients' lives. Such constricted understandings resulted in legal aid lawyers failing to communicate with their clients or understand their lives and problems.

Claghorn also was aware of the gender dynamics involved. She remarked that NYLAS had only a small number of women lawyers on staff. When questioned, the chief attorney responded that "the clients prefer to tell their troubles to a man, the Europeans especially feeling greater respect and confidence in a man in regard to legal matters."[66] This, of course, had not proved to be the case in the earlier part of the century, when Loew, Rembaugh, Quakenbos, and other female attorneys worked for the NYLAS. Claghorn also criticized the interactions that she observed between male attorneys and their female clients, commenting that such male attorneys often failed to believe or were uninterested in women's claims.[67]

One of the puzzles regarding legal aid's hostility toward social work is that during this period legal progressivism and sociological jurisprudence had begun to dominate legal reform.[68] Sociological jurisprudence created and embraced by reformers, both male and female, had done much to spread a sociological or social work approach into the courts, including the creation of juvenile courts, domestic relations courts, tenants' courts, and probation departments.[69] These institutions were also often staffed, at least to some extent, by women social workers and lawyers. The conservatism of legal aid societies was thus out of touch with what was occurring around it, and yet it would continue to shape how legal aid societies functioned as well as the services they provided.

This reconstructed history of legal aid establishes that the origins of legal aid reside in women lay lawyers providing legal counsel to poor women. Before either law or social work became entirely professionalized, such women lay lawyers had significant space to engage in legal philanthropic work. As legal aid societies expanded, and as they sought full recognition from the bar, women's role was significantly constricted. Legal aid leaders sought to masculinize legal aid and radically divorce it from social work, which was now closely associated with women. Thus even as women won political rights, including suffrage and the ability to gain admission to law schools and the bar, their visibility, power, and influence within legal aid diminished. Professionalization of law and social work thus had complicated and mixed consequences for those elite and middle-class women who provided legal aid, and for those poor women who depended upon the services that legal aid provided.

NOTES

1. The term "lay lawyers" refers to women who were involved in providing legal advice but who did not have formal legal training in terms of either attending law school or clerking in a lawyer's office.

2. For a full discussion of the WWPU, *see* Felice Batlan, *The Birth of Legal Aid: Gender Ideologies, Women, and the Bar in New York City, 1863–1910*, 28 Law & Hist. Rev. (2010).

3. *See* Alice Kessler-Harris, Out to Work: A History of Wage-Earning Women in the United States 76–77 (2003).

4. *Meeting of the Sewing Girls Last Evening*, N.Y. Herald, Nov. 19, 1863, at 10.

5. *See, e.g.,* Christine Stansell, City of Women: Sex and Class in New York, 1789–1860 (1987).

6. *Meeting of the Sewing Girls Last Evening*, at 10.

7. *Another Great Meeting of Working Women*, N.Y. Sun, Nov. 19, 1863, at 1.

8. *Meeting of Working Women*, N.Y. Daily Tribune, Nov. 25, 1863, at 8.

9. WWPU, Twenty-Five Years' History: 1863–88 (1888).

10. *See, e.g., Sad Story of a Poor Girl—A Communication*, N.Y. Sun, Nov. 17, 1863, at 1; *Another Working Girl's Experience*, N.Y. Sun, Nov. 18, 1863, at 1; *Working Womens'* [sic] *Protective Union*, N.Y. Sun, Mar. 24, 1864.

11. See Amy Dru Stanley, From Bondage to Contract: Wage Labor, Marriage, and the Market in the Age of Slave Emancipation (1998).

12. *See, e.g., Working Women's Protective Union: Third Annual Report*, N.Y. Times, Feb. 28, 1867; *Protection of Working Women*, N.Y. Times, Dec. 9, 1879; Twenty-Five Years' History, *supra*.

13. *See, e.g.,* S. Comm. on Educ. & Labor, 45th Cong., Report on the Relations between Capital and Labor (Comm. Print 1885); WWPU: Fifth Annual Report (1868); WWPU, The Work Done and Doing by the WWPU (1873); Twenty-Five Years' History.

14. *See* Ruth Abram, Send Us a Lady Physician, 1835–1920, at 113 (1986); Brenda Galloway Wright, *Rebecca Cole, in* Black Women in America: An Historical Encyclopedia 261–62 (Darlene Clark Hine & Elsey Barkely Brown, eds. 1993).

15. *See* Civic Club Digest of the Educational and Charitable Institutions and Societies in Philadelphia (1895); J. Thomas Scharf & Thomas Westcott, History of Philadelphia, 1609–1884 (1884).

16. *See* First Annual Report of The Legal Aid Society of Philadelphia (Jan. 1, 1903).

17. Maud Parcells Boyes, *Legal Aid Societies: For the Protection of Home and Family, in* The Woman Citizen and the Home 3135 (Shailer Mathews, ed. 1914).

18. *See, e.g.,* Second Annual Report of the PAWC (1888).

19. *See* Marguerite Raeder Gariepy, *The Legal Aid Bureau of the United Charities of Chicago*, 124 Annals Am. Acad. Pol. & Soc. Sci. 33, 33, 41 (1926).

20. *See* Twelfth Annual Report of the PAWC (1898); Thirteenth Annual Report of the PAWC (1899); Fourteenth Annual Report of the PAWC (1900).

21. *See* Eveline Hasler, Flying with Wings of Wax: The Story of Emily Kempin-Spyri (Edna McCown, trans. 1993); Drachman, at 122–26.

22. Women's Legal Educ. Soc'y, For the Better Protection of Their Rights: A History of the First Fifty Years of the Woman's Legal Education Society and the Woman's Law Class at New York University 10 (1940); Virginia G. Drachman, Sisters in Law: Women Lawyers in Modern American History 122–23 (2001).

23. *The Sohlichtungsverein*, N.Y. Times, Mar. 3, 1889, at 15; Drachman, 123.

24. Women's Legal Education Soc'y, at 10.

25. *Lady Lawyers of New York*, The Woman's Column, Dec. 20, 1890, at 1.

26. *See Articles File*, Women's Legal Education Soc'y (on file at NYU Archive).

27. *The Woman's Law League of New York*, The Bus. Woman's J., April 1893, at 1.

28. *See New Field of Legal Work among the Poor*, N.Y. Times, June 11, 1905, at SM7.

29. *See* John MacArthur Maguire, The Lance of Justice: A Semi-Centennial History of the Legal Aid Society, 1876–1926, 16–17, 58 (1928).

30. *See* Batlan, *supra*.

31. Benjamin M. Price, Esq., *Charging of Fees, in* First Conference of Legal Aid Societies of the United States 59 (1911).

32. On whether trial work was appropriate for women, see Drachman, 181–90; Virginia G. Drachman, Women Lawyers and the Origins of Professional Identity in America: The Letters of the Equity Club, 1887 to 1890 (1993).

33. Report of Speeches and Letters Delivered and Read at the Banquet of the Legal Aid Society, Mar. 23, 1901, at 34.

34. Twenty-fifth Annual Report of the NYLAS for the year 1900, at 13.

35. *Id.*, at 13.

36. *Id.*,

37. *See* First Annual Report of the Legal Aid Society of Philadelphia.

38. Second Annual Report of the Legal Aid Society of Philadelphia 2 (1905).

39. Nineteenth Annual Report of the PAWC 7 (1905).

40. *See* Michael Grossberg, *The Politics of Professionalism: The Creation of Legal Aid and the Strains of Political Liberalism in America, 1900–1930, in* Lawyers and the Rise of Western Political Liberalism: Europe and North American from the Eighteenth to the Twentieth Centuries 305, 306–7 (Terence C. Halliday & Lucien Karpik, eds. 1997).

41. *See* NYC Bar Ass'n & NYC Welfare Counsel, Report of the Joint Committee for the Study of Legal Aid 27 (1928).

42. *See* Linda Gordon, Pitied But Not Entitled: Single Mothers and the History of Welfare 73, 102 (1995).

43. Abraham Flexner, *Is Social Work a Profession?* Proceedings of the National Conference of Charities and Corrections at the Forty-Second Annual Session, May 12–19, 1915, *reprinted in* 11 Res. on Soc. Work Prac. 152 (Mar. 2001).

44. See John H. Ehrenreich, The Altruistic Imagination: A History of Social Work and Social Policy in the United States 57–58 (1985).

45. Reginald Heber Smith, Justice and the Poor: A Study of the Present Denial of Justice to the Poor and the Agencies Making More Equal Their Position before the Law, with Particular Reference to Legal Aid Work in the United States 152 (1919).

46. 23 Case & Comment 1008 (1917); Grossberg, 332.

47. Smith, 135; *see, e.g.,* Esther Lucile Brown, Lawyers and the Promotion of Justice 267 (1938).

48. Smith, 136.

49. Boyes.

50. Smith, 63.

51. William Sabine, *Character of Litigation to Be Undertaken, in* First Conference, at 46.

52. Thirteenth Annual Report of the BLAS 7 (1912–13).

53. Fifteenth Annual Report of the BLAS (1914–15).

54. Grossberg, 343,citing Reginald Heber Smith to Dean Theodore W. Swan, Yale Law School, June 12 1924 (*on file at* Boston Legal Aid Society, 1924 files).

55. A.O. Elzner, *Address of Welcome, in* Third Biennial Convention, at 149.

56. Reginald Heber Smith, *Forward, in* John S. Bradway, Law and Social Work: An Introduction to the Study of the Legal-Social Field for Social Workers vii (1929).

57. *A Lawyer Looks at Social Workers*, Survey, Feb. 15, 1925, at 585.

58. Alice Waldo, *Report of the Committee on the Relationship between Social Service Work and Legal Aid Work, in* Ass'n of the Bar of N.Y., Record of Proceedings at the Meetings of the Central Committee of the National Alliance of Legal Aid Societies 35 (Dec. 15, 1922).

59. *Id.* at 35–36, 43.

60. Smith, 155.

61. *See, e.g,* NYLAS, Legal Aid Rev. 1 (No. 4, 1904).

62. Kate Holladay Claghorn, The Immigrant's Day in Court 487 (1923).

63. Maud P. Boyes, *Should Legal Aid Societies Charge Fees for Services Rendered, in* Third Biennial Convention, 91.

64. Marguerite Raeder, *Relation between Social Service Agencies and Legal Aid Organizations, in* Fifth National Conference, at 34–35, 39.

65. Claghorn, 470.

66. *Id.* at 480–82.

67. *Id.* at 480–82.

68. *See, e.g.,* Morton J. Horwitz, The Transformation of American Law, 1870–1960: The Crisis of Legal Orthodoxy (1994); Roscoe Pound, *Scope and Purpose of Sociological Jurisprudence*, 25 Harv. L. Rev.140 (1911–12).

69. David S. Tanenhaus, Juvenile Justice in the Making (2004); Michael Willrich, City of Courts: Socializing Justice in Progressive Era Chicago (2003); Elizabeth J. Clapp, Mothers of All Children: Women Reformers and the Rise of Juvenile Courts in Progressive Era America (1998).

Sisterhood of Struggle

*Leadership and Strategy in the Campaign
for the Nineteenth Amendment*

——— LYNDA DODD ————————————————————

Alice Paul's campaign for the Nineteenth Amendment is one of the
paradigmatic examples of transformative constitutional reform. From 1913
until the amendment granting women the right to vote was ratified in 1920,
Paul rejected the more conciliatory style of lobbying and state-level campaigning practiced by the leaders of the National American Woman Suffrage
Association (NAWSA) and instead chose more contentious methods to promote the suffrage cause, including spectacular public demonstrations, hard-
fought political campaigns, and courageous wartime picketing.[1] To support
the campaign for a new federal amendment, Paul established the Congressional Union in 1913 and the National Woman's Party in 1916, recruiting
thousands of like-minded suffragists eager to support her more militant
approach. Under Paul's leadership, these suffragists played an essential role
in the enfranchisement of more than 26 million women.[2] Among the ranks
of women seeking legal reforms to bolster their political and civic agency,
they achieved unparalleled success.

This chapter examines the role of Alice Paul's leadership in securing passage of the Nineteenth Amendment. Recent scholarship on popular constitutionalism reminds us that constitutional history encompasses more than
the work of litigators and judges; it also addresses movements for social and
political reforms, including constitutional amendments.[3] To achieve success, reformers must consider opportunities and constraints posed by the
broader social and political context, make use of available resources, and
devise appropriate tactics. All these strategic choices depend upon effective
leaders and organizations. When the twenty-eight-year-old Paul assumed
the leadership of the militant suffrage campaign, she sought to establish her
place among an older generation of remarkable female reformers and activists: Jane Addams, Ida B. Wells-Barnett, Carrie Chapman Catt, Charlotte

Perkins Gilman, Emma Goldman, Florence Kelley, Mary Church Terrell, Lillian Wald, among many others. Historians like Anne Firor Scott have called attention to the "extraordinary efflorescence of female leadership" in this era, and a rich literature in women's history has examined these leaders' lives and legacies.[4] Paul's work in the militant suffrage campaign is one of the most notable examples of successful leadership in the "age of reform," and yet her role has never received similarly sustained appraisals.[5]

This chapter focuses, in particular, on two important features of her strategy: her use of a *passionate politics* relying on emotional appeals for recruitment, mobilization, persuasion, and contention; and her commitment to *unruly defiance*, through the party accountability campaigns and wartime acts of civil disobedience. Rather than simply describe these tactics and their results, this chapter instead draws on recent scholarship examining the role of leadership style and organizational form in social movements—what one scholar has called "strategic capacity"—in order to explore *how* these strategies were chosen and implemented, and to assess the strengths and limitations of Paul's approach.[6]

Passionate Politics

In 1913, when Paul took charge of NAWSA's Congressional Committee, the U.S. suffrage movement was slowly emerging from a period of "doldrums."[7] Many suffragists—especially those impressed by the more militant campaigning introduced by the Pankhursts' Women's Social and Political Union (WSPU) in Britain—began to question NAWSA's "slow and academic methods."[8] Paul was similarly inspired by the tactics introduced by the British suffragettes. She had first encountered the Pankhursts in 1907, during her postgraduate studies in England, and she spent the following two years working as an organizer for the WSPU.[9] After returning home in 1910, Paul hoped to apply their campaign tactics in the U.S. She would soon discover that thousands of like-minded suffragists were eager to begin a new phase of suffrage campaigning.

Emmeline Pankhurst's motto—"deeds, not words"—succinctly describes the WSPU's tactics.[10] Their campaigning was designed less to provoke deliberative debate about the merits of woman suffrage than to inspire support through grand processions and rallies, to irritate through disruptive demonstrations and heckling of political figures, to win sympathy by engaging in hunger strikes in prison, and even to generate fear by engaging in vandalism and other crimes against property.[11] They pursued, in short, a passionate politics. Paul had seen firsthand how these techniques focused the British public's attention, and she was convinced that this style of campaigning could reinvigorate the U.S. suffrage movement.

After successfully pursuing an appointment to become the chair of NAWSA's Congressional Committee, Paul's first goal was to arrange an enormous parade, to be held in Washington, D.C. on the eve of President-elect Woodrow Wilson's inauguration. Her careful planning revealed her skill in attending to the aesthetic dimensions of persuasion—what one suffragist called "a genius for picturesque publicity."[12] From her experience working with the Pankhursts, Paul appreciated how emotional appeals, especially when cultivated through dramatic outdoor events, could both develop and consolidate support for her campaign by inspiring suffragists, impressing bystanders, and generating admiring press coverage. In contrast to other suffragists who held parades primarily in order to "sell suffrage" to the public, she was also determined to send a message to the politicians in Washington, especially President Wilson.[13] A spectacular parade of unprecedented scope could, she believed, offer a demonstration of power.[14]

On March 3 more than half a million people gathered along the Pennsylvania Avenue campaign route. A near riot broke out within an hour of its start, marring the ending of a beautiful parade but also producing even more publicity for Paul. Both the *New York Times* and the *Washington Post* praised its beauty, acknowledged its impressive scope, and rebuked the D.C. police for failing to maintain order.[15] Seeking to take advantage of this spirit of outrage and sympathy, Paul sent out numerous press releases, prepared witness affidavits, and called for action at the highest levels of government. The parade and its aftermath provided the first indication of her talent for responding quickly to events in order to reclaim the tactical advantage. Paul's ultimate goal was for the parade to raise awareness of her call for a federal amendment. Measured by that standard, the suffrage parade, despite its chaotic ending, was a resounding success.[16]

Soon after the parade ended, Paul set out to lobby President Wilson and Congress, joining a delegation to speak with the president and organizing a series of delegations, auto parades, and petition ceremonies to draw the attention of Congress. Her continuous barrage of inventive public demonstrations required funding, so she established the Congressional Union to serve as the fund-raising arm of the Congressional Committee. To keep the Union's supporters informed and involved, Paul enlisted the help of journalist Rheta Childe Dorr to publish a new journal called the *Suffragist*. The journal not only offered supporters official "talking points" regarding tactics; it also helped provide members far from the Washington, D.C., headquarters a sense of identity as part of a vibrant and successful political organization. Paul arranged for professional photographers to attend most of her organizations' suffrage activities, and their images were featured regularly in the journal. The *Suffragist* also included detailed accounts of recent activities—all the meetings, parades, delegations, speaking tours, and pickets—in order to help its far-flung readers feel more intimately familiar with and involved in the work of the organization.[17]

Paul's style of passionate politics also produced a vast increase in the amount of newspaper coverage devoted to the federal amendment. To help shape the coverage of the Union's public demonstrations and events, Paul established a professional press office in 1913, with a full-time paid staff member, and sent out a steady stream of press releases to wire services and newspapers across the country. In her memoir Rheta Childe Dorr emphasized the transforming effect of Paul's leadership, observing that suffrage was rarely mentioned in the D.C. press before Paul arrived on the scene. By the end of 1913 it was a topic of coverage on an almost daily basis.[18]

It was a remarkable showing for one year's work. The NAWSA leadership, however, was evidently threatened by Paul's success. By early 1914 the Congressional Union separated from NAWSA and became an independent suffrage organization.[19] Paul was also confronted with some rumblings of discontent among suffragists associated with the Union. Several members wrote letters to Paul, protesting the hierarchical structure of the organization and requesting more decision-making authority.[20] Paul rejected these complaints and defended her method of organizing. Drawing again from her experience with the WSPU's similarly hierarchical approach, she insisted that the top-down leadership structure was essential for rapid reactions in a fluid political environment.[21] Transforming the Union into an "immense debating society," she argued, would render the organization useless for its political mission.[22] Paul was unmoved by the claim that there was some inconsistency in fighting for democratic equality with an organization structured in such a hierarchical manner.[23]

Paul's insistence on this point is noteworthy in light of the rich social science literature examining various organizational models within social reform movements. Sociologist Elisabeth Clemens's study of woman suffrage organizations, for instance, focuses on the state-level organizations during this era and emphasizes their willingness to experiment with innovative organizational structures.[24] Paul, however, was convinced that her leadership style was essential for success, and indeed it does not appear to have caused irreparable harm to her organizations' ability to achieve their strategic goals during the suffrage campaign.

In exploring the prerequisites for the success of social movement leaders—what he calls "strategic capacity"—sociologist Marshall Ganz identifies three concomitant attributes of effective leadership: the ability to motivate others, access to relevant sources of expertise, and collaborative styles of decision making.[25] Paul's rejection of more democratic and collaborative organizational structures, however, did not undermine her members' motivation. Nor did her refusal to engage in extensive and robust debates keep Paul from choosing and refining consistently effective strategies and tactics.

Perhaps the reason why her leadership during the suffrage campaign proved to be a successful exception is that she had developed unusually deep "salient knowledge" regarding available targets, tactics, and timing, which rendered less important a more collaborative style of decision making.[26] The suffragists who worked so tirelessly to implement Paul's strategies also believed in her abilities and trusted her to develop strategy.[27] Paul's success in crafting and implementing strategies further increased her members' motivation and admiration. Maud Younger, a leading suffrage organizer, wrote of Paul: "She is a genius for organization, both in the mass and in the detail."[28] Lucy Burns endorsed this view: "Her great assets . . . are her power to make plans on a national scale; and a supplementary power to see that it is done down to the last postage stamp."[29] Doris Stevens, a leading suffrage campaigner and author of the memoir *Jailed for Freedom* suggested that Paul's record of success itself converted the "timid" members who questioned her strategy, observing that "most of the doubters" eventually "banished their fears" and came "to believe with something akin to superstition that she could never be wrong, so swiftly and surely did they see her policies and her predictions on every point vindicated before their eyes."[30]

One of Paul's greatest strengths as a leader was her ability to inspire the suffragists who worked for her. Despite her use of a hierarchical organizational structure, she never felt the need to control the implementation of her strategy by leaving only the more insignificant tasks to her members. Instead, Paul delegated a great deal of responsibility to various colleagues within her organizations—the tasks of writing speeches, preparing press releases, delivering speeches, organizing voters, and lobbying Congress—and she sought every opportunity to remind them of the importance of their jobs. Paul always provided the strategic direction, but her "lieutenants" had ample freedom to develop their talents and each knew that their contributions were essential. Paul never shied away from honoring them for their efforts and success. Each issue of the *Suffragist* was filled with praise for suffragists assuming leadership roles as organizers, lobbyists, public speakers, and demonstrators. Even decades later, in her interviews with historian Amelia Fry, Paul constantly veered off into lengthy digressions, changing the topic in order to emphasize the important contributions of various suffragists and their roles.[31]

Similarly, throughout the suffrage campaign, Paul shifted the focus away from herself and to her illustrious forebears. She continually sought to strengthen the collective memory of suffragists in the U.S. by invoking, with reverence, the prior generation of leaders who had fought for suffrage and died before it had been won.[32] These efforts constituted one of the more distinctive features of Paul's brand of passionate politics. Paul's efforts to honor Susan B. Anthony, especially, were truly sincere. Their shared Quaker heritage, uncompromising devotion to woman suffrage, and willingness to defy government authority in pursuit of that cause likely encouraged Paul to identify personally with Anthony. Even in private, her esteem was obvious. Anthony's former rosewood writing desk was one of Paul's first acquisitions when setting up the new Congressional Committee headquarters in 1913, and she kept that desk for decades, even taking it to her retirement cottage in Connecticut.[33] During the campaign, Paul changed the name of the proposed federal amendment to the "Susan B. Anthony Amendment," marking the occasion with a large pageant in Washington, D.C.[34] When campaigning against the Democratic Party in 1914 and 1916, Paul attributed the political strategy to Anthony (rather than the Pankhursts). During the picketing, a number of the suffragists' placards incorporated quotations from Anthony. After the first victory in the House, the *Suffragist* included a story titled "Miss Anthony's Vindication."[35] To celebrate the ratification of the Nineteenth Amendment, Paul organized an elaborate ceremony—on February 15, 1921, the 101st anniversary of Anthony's birth—featuring the installation of a group sculpture of Lucretia Mott, Elizabeth Cady Stanton, and Anthony, the first women so honored, in the Statuary Hall of Congress.[36] Crystal Eastman later observed that Paul's name, during this carefully orchestrated ceremony, was never even mentioned.[37] Just as Paul appreciated the need to share recognition with her colleagues, she also understood the importance of portraying ratification as the vindication of a multigenerational struggle. Her attention to the power of collective memory to inspire and enhance solidarity never wavered in future years. Paul would continue organizing similar events, such as one celebrating the seventy-fifth anniversary of Seneca Falls in July 1923, during which she revealed the final wording of her proposed Equal Rights

Amendment. On this occasion Paul arranged to have a photographer accompany her to Anthony's grave, for an official portrait of Paul kneeling at the gravesite. It is a moving depiction of Paul's wish to pay her respects—and one likely designed to summon Anthony's memory in order to rally others to support the next phase of her work on behalf of the new amendment.[38]

Unruly Defiance

If Paul was a master at forging bonds of allegiance among her followers, she proved to be just as adept when it came to provoking discomfort, anger, and even fear in her opponents. Her preference for a more contentious style of politics was rooted in her deep appreciation for the Pankhursts' style of campaigning, which relied on both party accountability campaigns and civil disobedience in order to transform the suffrage debate. No longer would suffrage be framed as a request to be granted out of politicians' sympathy or enlightened benevolence. Instead Paul, like the Pankhursts, pursued strategies that would make suffrage a matter directly affecting politicians' self-interest. Paul's pursuit of a strategy of unruly defiance eventually earned her the moniker, "the Pankhurst of the Potomac."[39] It also proved to be the most distinctive feature of her campaign's success.

Although today Paul's party accountability campaigns are either forgotten or dismissed as ineffective, they were an essential component of her strategy of unruly defiance. In 1914 and 1916, Paul sent suffrage organizers to the western states where women already held the right to vote, to urge these women to punish Democratic Party candidates for their party's failure to pass a federal suffrage amendment. When introducing her plans for these campaigns, Paul simply presented a fully developed strategy for an up or down vote. No alternatives were offered, and the outcome of these meetings was never in doubt. Paul always took the opportunity to convince as many as possible to support her plans, but those who did not typically resigned their position and left the organization. While most of her supporters accepted her rationale for the 1914 campaign, her plan to create a new organization, the National Woman's Party (NWP), for the 1916 presidential campaign was far more controversial—owing largely to the high stakes of the election for the war question. During his campaign for reelection, Wilson was thought to be the only candidate who would avoid declaring war. For many suffragists, even those who favored Paul's more defiant tactics, their commitment to pacifism clashed with the NWP's plan to punish the Democratic Party. Although the results were mixed—in 1916 Wilson won most of the western states—Paul's determination ultimately forced the Democratic Party to fear the consequences of her continued use of the party accountability strategy. Following the 1916 election Vance McCormick, Chairman of the Democratic Party, described the stakes going forward: "Our weakest spot is the suffrage situation," he concluded. "We must get rid of the suffrage amendment before 1918 if we want to control the next Congress."[40] If Paul failed to hold the Democratic Party accountable in 1916, as she intended, she certainly succeeded in placing Wilson and his party on notice.[41]

Paul's rejection of a collaborative approach incorporating diverse perspectives did not undermine this phase of the suffrage campaign. With her sophisticated appreciation of the president's strategic importance and the dynamics of party competition in this era, she could rely on her own expert judgment regarding the need for the party accountability campaigns.[42] Paul also avoided the negative impact of disgruntled members by encouraging those who disagreed with her choices to leave her organizations. An important sorting dynamic had developed with NAWSA. Suffragists frustrated with NAWSA's more conciliatory approach sought out Paul's leadership and were more likely to find her strategy of unruly defiance appealing. Those suffragists who balked at Paul's choices of contentious tactics were left to find other more amenable venues to support suffrage or to promote other causes, such as the peace movement in 1916. To be sure, it is not as though Paul disrespected the opinions of her staff and rank-and-file members. Indeed, she expended considerable effort defending her most controversial tactics—both the party accountability campaigns and especially the wartime picketing—to her followers and other potential supporters.

Paul's persuasive abilities were never more essential than during what has been called the "endgame" of the suffrage campaign, when the National Woman's Party began picketing the White House during World War I.[43] After his reelection Wilson refused to receive any more suffrage delegations. Paul, however, was determined to keep his attention focused on the suffrage issue. Once it appeared that war was imminent, she sought input from the leaders of her suffrage organizations. Paul emphasized how much the suffrage fight mattered in the current climate: "We must do our part to see that war, which concerns women as seriously as men, shall not be entered upon without the consent of women."[44] She also reminded them that if they wanted to work on behalf of the peace movement, or to help prepare for the war, there were separate organizations devoted to those causes. The NWP leadership met in Washington and voted to support Paul's strategy just in time to organize a picket on March 4, the day of Wilson's second inauguration. Despite the cold and stormy weather, hundreds of suffragists carrying banners circled the White House, hoping to deliver their message to the president, but Wilson refused to acknowledge them.[45]

Once the U.S. officially entered the war, Paul was determined to continue picketing. In her doctoral dissertation, she had assessed the harm resulting from suffragists' suspension of their campaign for the duration of the Civil War. For this reason, she was extremely wary of NAWSA's war stance, to publicly end lobbying and to mobilize in support of the war.[46] Even knowing that the Pankhursts had suspended their activities immediately once war was declared in Britain, she was not dissuaded. Paul's decision may have cost her a sizable portion of the NWP's membership.[47] Some of Paul's senior colleagues, including Harriot Stanton Blatch and Mary Beard, chose to leave the organization at this time.[48]

Although the NWP picketing continued with few disturbances for several weeks, the situation became more adversarial once the picketers began holding banners with quotations from Wilson's speeches, carefully chosen in order to point out the hypocrisy of defending a fight for democracy abroad while ignoring the failure to live up to democratic ideals in the United States. Such confrontational rhetoric caused much distress and alarm throughout the NWP membership. Letters came in from suffragists across the country expressing concern that Paul's tactics would cost the movement much-needed support.[49] Other suffragists worked to counter the negative press coverage, by passing resolutions of support in their state branches, sending copies of the *Suffragist*, or writing editorials for their local newspapers.

This rhetoric also goaded the government into responding with more heavy-handed tactics. The District of Columbia Chief of Police, Raymond Pullman, notified Paul that further picketing would lead to arrests. She immediately informed the NWP picketers of these developments, so they could decide whether they wished to go on and risk arrest.[50] The volunteers agreed to forge ahead despite the threat, and over the next few weeks, beginning on June 22, dozens of NWP picketers were arrested. Mobs attacked the picketers when they unfurled banners proclaiming "Kaiser" Wilson's hypocrisy.[51] Then, on July 17, sixteen picketers were sentenced to sixty days at the Occoquan Workhouse in Virginia.

At this stage the NWP picketing commanded front-page news coverage, an impressive feat during wartime that was largely because of the elite social status of the women receiving the long sentences.[52] As Nancy Cott explains, "The usefulness of suffrage militance was biased toward the elite; the wealthier its proponent was—the more ladylike she was supposed to be—the greater the effect of her subversion of the norm."[53] Paul had always sought to recruit supporters from the working class, but most of her paid staff and leading advisers were socially prominent, highly-educated, and well-connected women. The suffragists who were arrested and imprisoned during the picketing campaign included daughters of senators and congressmen, wealthy socialites, and wives of prominent journalists and party leaders.[54] Paul sought to take advantage of the publicity produced by their arrests, even going so far as to ask the most socially prominent of her members to volunteer for duty when there was a need for more publicity.[55]

As the picketing continued the suffragists' defiance in the face of arrests and longer imprisonments eventually roused public sympathy. The *Boston Journal* observed, "The little band representing the NWP has been abused and bruised by government clerks, soldiers and sailors until its efforts to attract the President's attention has sunk into the conscience of the whole nation."[56] Paul's decision to endure the initial hostility and continue protesting, despite the risks, proved to be a crucial part of her campaign's eventual success. The publicity resulting from these longer sentences and reports of dreadful prison conditions appeared to push members of Congress to offer unprecedented demonstrations of support.[57] On September 15, the day after Senator Andrieus Jones, the Chair of the Senate Committee on Woman Suffrage, visited Occoquan, the suffrage amendment was reported out of the Committee.[58] The House created a standing committee on suffrage just days later on September 24.[59]

In October Paul herself was arrested while picketing the White House, and she received the most severe sentence of all—seven months at Occoquan.[60] From her own prison cell, Lucy Burns had been quietly organizing within Occoquan for several weeks to circulate a petition among the imprisoned suffragists. The petition was smuggled out and sent to government officials, but this only resulted in each of the signers being placed in solitary confinement.[61] In protest, Paul launched a hunger strike on November 5.[62] The publicity generated by the hunger strikes—especially when combined with reports of violence against suffragists sent to jail on November 15—created an untenable situation for Wilson.[63] On November 27 and 28 all the suffrage prisoners were released.[64] A few weeks later, pressured by Wilson's first public endorsement of a federal amendment, the House passed the Susan B. Anthony Amendment.[65] Paul continued to rely on the politics of unruly defiance for the remainder of the campaign, introducing a series of new protest tactics during the long fight to win the Senate's support and the amendment's ratification.[66]

Victory and Beyond

Paul's preferred style of leadership certainly did not satisfy all the prerequisites for optimal strategic capacity. Her rejection of shared decision-making power marginalized diverse views, even to the extent of driving most dissenters away. Her organizations failed even the most minimal test of democratic legitimacy. Paul, however, made up for those deficits predicted to follow from the rejection of collaborative models of deliberation. She was a student of spectacle and politics. Her prior education, protest experiences, and leadership strengths were uniquely suited to the passionate politics and acts of unruly defiance that she chose to pursue. Her instincts during the final years of the suffrage campaign were almost unerring, informed as they were by years of study and experience. Her pursuit of a strategy of unruly defiance through party accountability campaigns, even if they did not defeat many candidates, caused both Wilson and members of Congress to worry about the damage the suffrage issue might cause to their parties' electoral fortunes. The picketing, prison protests, and hunger strikes may have been unpopular with some of her followers, but Paul's strategy attracted a sufficient number eager to participate and sustain a level of unremitting protest that kept the public riveted. These picketers' determination, even in the face of the government's hostility and lengthy prison sentences, pushed Wilson and other party leaders to confront the suffrage issue, despite their preoccupation with the war.

Paul's style of leadership, in those times and for that cause, worked. Most of her followers admired her more contentious approach and supported her choice of tactics. Because Paul's strategy of unruly defiance operated in tandem with the lobbying of the more conciliatory NAWSA, suffragists of different temperaments and political views could choose which tactics to support, creating a division of labor that served to strengthen the movement. This sorting dynamic left Paul with an uncompromisingly determined band of protestors who could more effectively pursue her preferred strategies. She could act as a "commander" of troops eager to achieve a shared goal: suffrage.

Yet once the fight for suffrage ended, so did the common purpose holding together the various constituents of the NWP. As Harriot Stanton Blatch explained, although "all sorts and conditions of women were united for suffrage, that political end has been gained, and they are not at one in their attitude towards other questions in life."[67] The post-suffrage context called for different skills to negotiate a new source of conflict: What should women fight for, now that they had the vote? As they sought to form a new substantive agenda, former suffragists confronted sharp disagreements—and rising stakes. In contrast to the suffrage era, when opposing camps with different strategic philosophies formed a useful division of labor, competing factions now supported irreconcilable goals.

The most prominent of these clashes pitted advocates of equal treatment against those favoring protective labor laws, but there were many additional sources of conflict.[68] Paul had hoped that a campaign for equality of legal rights might form the basis for unified action going forward, but the discord surrounding the 1921 NWP Convention demonstrated that the era of single-issue campaigns for women's rights had ended. When planning the meeting, Paul thwarted her members' efforts to offer a more diverse agenda, leaving advocates of birth control, the peace movement, protective labor legislation for women, and voting rights enforcement for African American women to search for other venues to advance their causes.[69] "The old crowd has scattered never to gather in the old way again," one NWP member sadly concluded.[70]

Paul's leadership style was ill-suited to the tasks ahead.[71] The National Woman's Party would transform over time into a far smaller corps of Washington-based lobbyists.[72] Its legalist agenda—a federal Equal Rights Amendment to guarantee formal equality in the law—failed to arouse grass-roots support. The NWP had become "bogged down in legal formalism," Doris Stevens dourly concluded in 1946.[73] What had at one time been a unified sisterhood struggling together to win suffrage had in the decades that followed become a far more fractious sisterhood struggling among themselves, their efficacy greatly diminished by bitter in-fighting, attempted leadership "coups," and a suspicious resentment of fresh ideas or new recruits.

Paul's limited vision, which took equal treatment in the law as *the* feminist goal, was linked to her outmoded belief that an effective strategy must provide one cause around which women as a class could unite. A more radical agenda to address women's subordination would require addressing all sorts of issues—labor rights, racial discrimination, health and welfare support, sexual freedom—which Paul considered either diversions (not truly *women's* issues) or distasteful. For many women, the limits of Paul's strategic vision were all too apparent in the post-suffrage era, yet she never lost faith in her task. She lobbied on behalf of the ERA for the remainder of her life.[74] As a strategic thinker and leader, she never comprehended that her most powerful traits—her unflagging belief in the righteousness of her cause, her defiance and persistence in the face of opposition—could serve at one time as a source of enormous strength but at other times be her greatest weakness. Strategic capacity requires far more, if it is to endure.

NOTES

1. For a more extensive analysis of Paul's contributions to the suffrage campaign, see Lynda G. Dodd, *Parades, Pickets, and Prison: Alice Paul and the Virtues of Unruly Constitutionalism*, 24 J. Law & Pol. 339 (2008).

2. Eleanor Flexner & Ellen Fitzpatrick, Century of Struggle: The Women's Rights Movement in the United States 317 (rev. ed. 1975).

3. Dodd, 340–43.

4. Anne Firor Scott, *A New-Model Woman*, 8 Rev. Am. Hist. 442, 446 (1980). For a sampling of this work, see Ellen Carol Dubois, Harriot Stanton Blatch and the Winning of Woman Suffrage (1997); Candace Falk, Love, Anarchy, and Emma Goldman (1984); Marjorie N. Feld, Lillian Wald: A Biography (2009); Paula J. Giddings, Ida: A Sword among Lions: Ida B. Wells and the Campaign Against Lynching (2008); Louise W. Knight, Citizen: Jane Addams and the Struggle of Democracy (2005); Ann J. Lane, To "Herland" and Beyond: The Life and Work of Charlotte Perkins Gilman (1990); Kathryn Kish Sklar, Florence Kelley and the Nation's Work: The Rise of Women's Political Culture, 1830–1900 (1997); Judith Schwarz, Radical Feminists of Heterodoxy: Greenwich Village, 1912–1940 (1986); Jacqueline Van Voris, Carrie Chapman Catt: A Public Life (1987); Beverly Washington Jones, Quest for Equality: The Life of Mary Eliza Church Terrell, 1863–1954 (Oct. 1980) (unpublished Ph.D. dissertation, University of North Carolina at Chapel Hill).

5. Richard Hofstadter, The Age of Reform (1960). For a review of suffrage historiography, see Dodd, 346–53.

6. *See, e.g.,* Marshall Ganz, *Why David Sometimes Wins: Strategic Capacity in Social Movements, in* Rethinking Social Movements: Structure, Meaning, and Emotion 177 (Jeff Goodwin & James M. Jasper, eds. 2004); Elisabeth S. Clemens, *Organizational Repertoires and Institutional Change: Women's Groups and the Transformation of U.S. Politics, 1880–1920,* 98 Am. J. of Soc. 755, 757–59 (1993); Elisabeth S. Clemens, *Two Kinds of Stuff: The Current Encounter of Social Movements and Organizations, in* Social Movements and Organization Theory 351–65 (Gerald E. Davis et al., eds. 2005).

7. Dodd, 359–64.

8. Rheta Childe Dorr, A Woman of Fifty 281 (1924).

9. *See* Amelia R. Fry, Conversations with Alice Paul: Woman Suffrage and the Equal Rights Amendment, Suffragists Oral History Project, Bancroft Library, University of California at Berkeley 32–34 (1976).

10. Emmeline Pankhurst, My Own Story 49 (1914).

11. On the WSPU's campaign, *see, e.g.,* Laura E. Nym Mayhall, The Militant Suffrage Movement: Citizenship and Resistance in Britain, 1860–1930 (2003); Lisa Tickner, The Spectacle of Women: Imagery of the Suffrage Campaign, 1907–1914 (1988).

12. Inez Haynes Irwin, The Story of the Woman's Party 100 (1921).

13. Dubois, 149–55; Margaret Finnegan, Selling Suffrage: Consumer Culture & Votes for Women 45–75 (1999); Katharine H. Adams & Michael L. Keene, Alice Paul & the American Suffrage Campaign xvi, 42–75 (2008).

14. Jean H. Baker, Sisters: The Lives of America's Suffragists 191 (2005); Linda J. Lumsden, Rampant Women: Suffragists and the Right of Assembly 77 (1997); Michael McGerr, *Political Style and Women's Power, 1839–1930,* 77 J. Am. Hist. 864, 877–78 (1990).

15. *Parade Protest Arouses Ire in the Senate*, N.Y. Times, Mar. 5, 1913, at 8; *Woman's Beauty, Grace, and Art Bewilder the Capital*, Wash. Post, Mar. 4, 1913, at 3; *100 Are in Hospital*, Wash. Post, Mar. 4, 1913, at 10.

16. Dodd, 364–72.

17. *See* Photographs from the Records of the National Woman's Party, *available at* http://rs6.loc.gov/ammem/collections/suffrage/nwp/ (accessed Dec. 8, 2009).

18. Dorr, 287–88.

19. On the break with NAWSA, see Dodd, 377–79.

20. For the most thorough coverage of this dispute, see Loretta Ellen Zimmerman, Alice Paul and the National Woman's Party, 1912–1920, at 92–99 (1964) (unpublished Ph.D. dissertation, Tulane University).

21. Social movement scholar William Gamson uses the term "combat readiness" to describe this trait of hierarchical reform organizations. William Gamson, The Strategy of Social Protest, ch. 7 (2d ed. 1990).

22. Letter from Alice Paul to Eunice R. Oberly (Mar. 6, 1914), *microformed on* NWP Papers, Reel 1; Christine A. Lunardini, From Equal Suffrage to Equal Rights: Alice Paul and the National Woman's Party, 1910–1928, 51 (2000); *see also* Aileen S. Kraditor, The Ideas of the Woman Suffrage Movement, 1890–1920, 5 (1965).

23. *See also* Dodd, 381–82.

24. Clemens, 762 (examining California, Wisconsin, and Washington).

25. Ganz, 178–91.

26. *Id.* at 185.

27. Doris Stevens, Jailed for Freedom 16 (1920).

28. Irwin, 15.

29. *Id.* at 16.

30. Stevens, 15–16.

31. *See, e.g.*, Paul Interview, 83–84, 356–57.

32. On the role of collective memory in culture and politics, *see, e.g.*, Iwona Irwin-Zarecka, Frames of Remembrance: The Dynamics of Collective Memory (1994); Francesca Polletta & James M. Jasper, *Collective Identity and Social Movements* 27 Ann. Rev. Sociol. 283 (2001); *see also* Reva Siegel, *She the People: The Nineteenth Amendment, Sex Equality, Federalism, and the Family*, 115 Harv. L. Rev. 947 (2002); Reva B. Siegel, *Collective Memory and the Nineteenth Amendment: Reasoning about the "Woman Question" in Sex Discrimination Discourse, in* History, Memory, and the Law 131 (Austin Sarat & Thomas R. Kearns, eds. 2002).

33. Paul Interview, 65–66.

34. *Id.* at 113.

35. Suffragist, Jan. 19, 1918, at 8.

36. Paul Interview, 351–54.

37. Crystal Eastman, *Alice Paul's Convention, in* Crystal Eastman: On Women and Revolution 59–60 (Blanche Wiesen Cook, ed. 1978).

38. *See* Anita Pollitzer and Alice Paul at Susan B. Anthony gravesite, July 1923, Photographs from the Records of the National Woman's Party, *supra*. On Harriot Stanton Blatch's indignant objections to Paul's focus on Anthony's importance and the consequent diminishing role of Elizabeth Cady Stanton, see Dubois, 246–50.

39. Caroline Katzenstein, *Alice Paul, the Pankhurst of the Potomac: Her Personality and Characteristics*, Phil. Record, Nov. 4, 1917 (on file with the Schlesinger Library, Alice Paul Papers, Box 17, Folder 252).

40. Irwin, 180.

41. Dodd 416 n. 354; 418 n. 362; 420 n. 373.

42. *Id.* at 373–74, 385.

43. Baker, 183–230; *see also* Dodd, 396–416.

44. *See* Letter from Alice Paul to State Chairmen, Feb. 8, 1917 (Paul Papers, Box 17, Folder 252).

45. *Suffragists Girdle White House in Rain*, N.Y. Times, Mar. 5, 1917, at 3; *Rain Soaked, 500 Suffragists Parade Four Times around White House as 5,000 Cheer*, Wash. Post, Mar. 5, 1917, at 1; *President Asked to Open Second Term with Action on Suffrage, Refuses to See Delegation which Waits Two Hours in Rain*, Suffragist, Mar. 10, 1917, at 7–9.

46. *Cf. Pickets Delay Legislation, Mrs. Catt Tells Miss Paul*, Wash. Post, May 26, 1917, at 2; *Suffrage "Pickets" Remain on Guard, Miss Paul Says Party Will Not Heed Mrs. Catt's Protest*, Wash. Post, May 27, 1917, at 12.

47. The NWP may have lost up to one-sixth of its membership during the war. See Adams & Keene, 172.

48. Paul Interview, 93, 212, 214, 338–39; Nancy F. Cott, The Grounding of Modern Feminism 303 n. 11 (1987).

49. *See, e.g.,* Letters from July and August 1917, *microformed on* NWP Papers, Reels 45–47. Although the NWP initially lost some support, this rhetorical strategy succeeded in keeping the suffrage cause at the center of public debate. *See* Letter from Katharine R. Fisher to Lucy Burns (July 14, 1917), *microformed on* NWP Papers, Reel 45 ("It is better to make people mad than not to have them know you are around. . . . What a pity we cannot have a perfectly ladylike organization to raise funds and another to raise hell!").

50. Paul Interview, 216, 219–20.

51. *See* Photograph of Virginia Arnold (holding Kaiser Wilson Banner), Records of the National Woman's Party. *See Rioters Storm Women Pickets' Headquarters*, Chi. Daily Trib., Aug. 15, 1917, at 1; *Washington Crowd Eggs Suffragettes*, N.Y. Times, Aug. 15, 1917, at 3; *All-Day Suffrage Riots*, N.Y. Times, Aug.16, 1917, at 22; *Anti-Picketers Attack Women and Ex-Envoy*, Chic. Daily Trib., Aug. 17, 1917, at 3; *Suffrage Banners Seized by Throng*, Wash. Post, Aug. 17, 1917, at 7; *President Onlooker at Mob Attack on Suffragists*, Suffragist, Aug. 18, 1917, at 7.

52. *Sixteen Militants Begin 60-Day Term*, Wash. Post, July 18, 1917, at 1; *see also* Kraditor, 207 n.32.

53. Cott, 55; *see also* Paul Interview, 222.

54. For more information about the suffrage prisoners, see Linda G. Ford, Iron-Jawed Angels: The Suffrage Militancy of the National Woman's Party, 1912–1920, 197–223 (1991); Stevens, 354–371.

55. Louisine Waldron Havemeyer, *The Prison Special: Memories of a Militant*, 71 Scribner's 661–64, 672–73 (June 1922).

56. *Comments of the Press*, Suffragist, Sept. 1, 1917, at 11 (quoting Boston Journal, Aug. 18, 1917); Ford, 169. While the picketing continued, Paul characteristically sought to capitalize on the controversy, sending six of the NWP's most experienced organizers on a speaking tour "to every large city in every State in the Union." *The National Woman's Party Goes before the People*, Suffragist, Sept. 29, 1917, at 8.

57. *Pickets Bring Charges, Accuse Whittaker of Cruelty to Occoquan Prisoners,* Wash. Post, Aug. 30, 1917, at 5; *Asks Occoquan Probe, Board of Charities Acts upon Charges by the Woman's Party,* Wash. Post, Sept. 27, 1917, at 1.

58. Flexner, 279; Irwin, 305–6.

59. 55 Cong. Rec. 7369–85 (1917); *House Aids Suffrage,* Wash. Post, Sept. 24, 1917, at 2; *House Moves for Suffrage,* N.Y. Times, Sept. 25, 1917, at 11.

60. *Pickets in "Solitary,"* Wash. Post, Oct. 23, 1917, at 14; *Alice Paul Sentenced,* N.Y. Times, Oct. 23, 1917, at 12.

61. *Pickets to Be Punished,* Wash. Post, Oct. 20, 1917, at 5.

62. *Miss Alice Paul on Hunger Strike,* N.Y. Times, Nov. 7, 1917, at 13; *Miss Paul, Picket, Declines to Feast,* Wash. Post, Nov. 7, 1917, at 7; *Force Yard of Jail to Cheer Miss Paul,* N.Y. Times, Nov. 12, 1917, at 8.

63. The NWP referred to this event as "The Night of Terror." *Accuse Jailors of Suffragists,* N.Y. Times, Nov. 17, 1917, at 1; *Mrs. Brannan Tells of Treatment,* N.Y. Times, Nov. 29, 1917, at 11; *The Night of Terror,* Suffragist, Dec. 1, 1917, at 7; *A Week of the Women's Revolution,* Suffragist, Nov. 24, 1917, at 4. *See also* Lumsden, 134.

64. *Move Militants from Workhouse, Confinement There Illegal, Judge Waddill Holds,* N.Y. Times, Nov. 25, 1917, at 6; *Suffrage Pickets Freed from Prison,* N.Y. Times, Nov. 28, 1917, at 13; *Jail is Calm and Peaceful Again, as 22 Suffragettes are Released,* Wash. Post, Nov. 28, 1917, at 2; *Judge Releases 8 More Pickets,* Wash. Post, Nov. 29, 1917, at 5. On November 23 Judge Edmund Waddill had ruled that the suffragists had been illegally imprisoned at Occoquan (rather than the District Jail) and that they could be paroled on bail or finish their terms at the District Jail. Twenty-two women chose to finish their terms at the jail, and they were released on November 27 and 28. On March 4, 1918, the D.C. Court of Appeals invalidated all of the picketers' convictions and original arrests. Hunter v. District of Columbia, 47 App. D.C. 406, 409 WL 18180 (1918).

65. *Give Vote to Women Is Advice by Wilson,* Wash. Post, Jan. 10, 1918, at 1; 56 Cong. Rec. 762–810 (1918); *House for Suffrage,* N.Y. Times, Jan. 11, 1918, at 1; *Woman Suffrage Wins in House by One Vote,* Wash. Post, Jan. 11, 1918, at 1.

66. Dodd, 416–24.

67. Cott, 66 (quoting a letter from Harriot Stanton Blatch to Anne Martin, May 14, 1918).

68. *See, e.g.,* Amy E. Butler, Two Paths to Equality: Alice Paul and Ethel M. Smith in the ERA Debate, 1921–1929 (2002); Cott, 117–42; Alice Kessler-Harris, Out to Work: A History of Wage-Earning Women in the United States 181–214 (1982).

69. On the 1921 Convention, see Cott, 67–73; Eastman, 57, 61; Freda Kirchwey, *Alice Paul Pulls the Strings,* The Nation, Mar. 2, 1921, at 332–33.

70. Cott, 72 (quoting a letter from Mabel Putnam to Anita L. Pollitzer, Apr. 14, 1921).

71. Eastman, 62. On the work of the NWP in the 1920s and 1930s, when Paul retained her influence even after giving up her official position, see, e.g., Susan D. Becker, The Origins of the Equal Rights Amendment: American Feminism between the Wars (1981); Gretchen Ritter, The Constitution as Social Design: Gender and Civic Membership in the American Constitutional Order (2006); Cott, ch. 4; Nancy F. Cott, *Feminist Politics in the 1920s: The National Woman's Party,* 71 J. Am. Hist. 43 (1984).

72. On the work of the NWP from World War II to the 1960s, see Cynthia Harrison, On Account of Sex: The Politics of Women's Issues, 1945–1968 (1989): Leila J. Rupp & Verta Taylor, Survival in the Doldrums: The American Woman's Rights Movement, 1945 to the 1960s (1987).

73. Cott, 67 (quoting a letter from Doris Stevens to Betty Gram Swing, Jan. 8, 1946).

74. *Alice Paul, a Leader for Suffrage and Women's Rights, Dies at 92*, N.Y. Times, July 10, 1977.

11

"Feminizing" Courts

Lay Volunteers and the Integration of
Social Work in Progressive Reform

MAE C. QUINN

Anna Moscowitz Kross was one of New York's first women judges and the country's first judicial innovators. On the bench from 1934 to 1953 in New York City's Magistrates' Court, a trial-level police court that handled criminal matters, Kross engaged in a variety of experiments to transform criminal law and practice. She sought to use the coercive power of the justice system to engage in social engineering. From prostitution to domestic violence to unruliness in youths, Kross attempted to resolve the root causes of social problems from the bench. Her goal was not to punish but to improve the lives of the defendants and prevent them from returning to the criminal justice system.

Recognizing that New York City's Magistrates' Court lacked the necessary resources to intervene in the lives of the thousands who passed through its doors, Judge Kross took matters into her own hands. Reaching out to widows of influential New Yorkers and other women, many in her own social network, she built an army of private volunteers to assist in court-based therapeutic and rehabilitation efforts. The two entities she established—the Magistrates' Court Social Services Bureau in 1935 and the Home Advisory Council in 1946—supplemented services provided by professional court probation staff.

Private, nonprofit agencies that worked side-by-side with the court, the Social Services Bureau and the Home Advisory Council provided casework and other services to court litigants as Kross directed. Their volunteers served as Kross's eyes and ears, keeping tabs in the community and reporting back, sometimes *ex parte*, when defendants appeared resistant to change. They also shaped and served as her voice, taking public positions on various social justice issues. Despite Kross's benevolent intentions, her volunteer troops were often scrutinized and criticized—indeed at one point becoming the focus of a New York City Department of Investigation probe.

Yet with her use of lay court staff, Kross was returning to a long-abandoned practice that had been established in this country nearly a century before by the father of modern probation, John Augustus. Probation as an alternative to incarceration was reportedly born of his volunteer efforts in Boston, Massachusetts, in the 1840s, involving community-based supervision and training for offenders. Kross embraced this approach, making it her own. Her resurrection of court-based volunteerism, albeit in an arguably feminized form, laid the foundation for a transformative court volunteerism movement that ultimately swept the country during the 1960s and 1970s and is now finding new support in the problem-solving court movement of the twenty-first century. Surprisingly Kross has been given almost no credit for her groundbreaking work that helped sparked this phenomenon.

This chapter recounts the development and workings of Kross's unique volunteer forces. It examines how Kross sought to rethink the role and goals of criminal courts, to expand their boundaries and permit community involvement in their workings. It warns, however, that social engineering efforts in criminal courts at the hands of lay counselors—both then and now—raise important questions worthy of further exploration. This chapter further suggests that today's criminal justice reformers might learn important lessons from Kross's attempts at judicial innovations that relied on private funding and citizen involvement in criminal court operations.

Kross's Social Services Bureau

Anna Moscowitz Kross, one of the first women to graduate from New York University School of Law and enter into active legal practice,[1] was appointed to New York City's Magistrates' Court bench in 1934.[2] The Magistrates' Court was New York City's Police Court system, which primarily handled prosecution of low-level criminal charges. It was one of the country's busiest courts, processing more than half a million cases annually the year Kross took the bench. Given the number of people who passed through the institution each day, Kross claimed it was "the greatest social force for the correcting of individual maladjustments and the prevention of crime in our civilization."[3]

At the time Kross was appointed, the Magistrates' system had various individualized parts, some organized around neighborhoods and others focused on particular kinds of cases. Examples of the former included the Bronx Magistrates' Court and the Essex Market Court in Manhattan; perhaps the most famous of the latter was the New York City Women's Court.[4]

The Women's Court sought to address prostitution and related crimes allegedly committed by women defendants. Prior to her appointment, Kross spent years seeking to abolish the Women's Court. She and others believed it ensnared innocent women with undercover anti-vice practices, was controlled by corrupt bondsmen, and failed to provide real assistance to the women it prosecuted. Once on the bench, realizing she would not be able to close the Women's Court, she did what she could to infuse it with support for the women brought before it.[5] Most, she believed, presented "social" rather than criminal problems.

Kross was never entirely clear about what she meant by problems being "social" in nature.[6] However, her work suggests that she was concerned not only with prostitution's impact on society's "moral fabric," as were other reformers of the day, but that she wished to help address the forces that may have caused such women to turn to prostitution. For her, these included the breakdown of social and familial structures, as well as unmet mental health and other women's needs.

The Magistrates' Court did have its own probation staff, but it was ill-equipped to deal with the volume of cases handled by the institution, supervising less than 3 percent of the defendants convicted in the Magistrates' Court system in 1936. Probation officers were also legally prohibited from supervising defendants whose matters were not formally adjudicated. Pending cases were not eligible for formal oversight. Kross sought to fill this gap by creating her own experimental auxiliary social work service group.[7]

With the blessing of Mayor Fiorello LaGuardia and Chief Magistrate Jacob Gould Schurman Jr., Kross established the Magistrates' Court Social Services Bureau in 1935. The Bureau started when Kross called together a group of women interested in volunteering within the Magistrates' Courts. Their first task was to raise funds, which they hoped would support court-based social workers, doctors, and psychologists. The group also elected a Board of Directors and hired both an office manager and professional social worker to oversee the work of its volunteers.[8]

Most volunteers were assigned to a new specialty area created by Kross, the Wayward Minors' Part for girls. This specialized court dealt with the cases of young women sixteen to twenty-one years of age who ordinarily would have been processed in the adult Women's Court. The Wayward Minors' Court employed relaxed legal standards to focus on the rehabilitation of young "sex delinquents." The Social Service Bureau provided social services referrals and other assistance to defendants before they were found guilty. Using a "carrot and stick" approach, Kross often promised young defendants that by voluntarily participating in the court-sponsored programs they could avoid formal prosecution and a criminal record. Kross saw her Social Service Bureau volunteers as integral components to the Wayward Minors' Court.[9]

Although these rehabilitative plans were seen as informal, defendants had to return to court for monitoring. And some plans involved women being placed outside their homes in hospitals or reformatories. Prior to status hearings Kross conferred with her volunteer to determine how the young women were doing in treatment. Successful defendants were rewarded with the dismissal of their case. Those who did not comply or appeared to have "no prospect of an adjustment pursuant to the plans suggested" could be brought to trial, adjudicated, and immediately sentenced to an institution.[10]

Kross passionately believed that the innovations of the Wayward Minors' Part should be replicated and expanded. In 1936 the Bureau hired its first secretary and commandeered a room in the City's West Side Court Building to use, rent-free. In December 1936 the group held its first Annual Tea and fundraiser at the Hotel Plaza to "review the accomplishments of the bureau since its foundation."[11] Prominent citizens including Reverend Robert W. Searle, general secretary of the Greater New York Federation of Churches, Madeline Borg, wife of Sidney Borg and chairperson of the Jewish Big Sisters, and Frieda Schiff, wife of the famous banker and philanthropist Felix Warburg, were invited as Kross's special guests.

As she drew more interest and volunteers for the Bureau, Kross expanded its work to other parts of the Magistrates' system. Kross believed that most cases of the Magistrates' Courts system–disorderly conduct, assault, and other low-level offenses—were also rooted in social problems of the day. In these matters, too, her volunteers augmented the work of the Probation Department, for instance, by interviewing defendants before trial and providing magistrates with detailed case histories. As Kross explained, "[The Bureau's] purpose is to do something about the tens of thousands of cases which present, not criminal, but social problems. In appropriate cases it supplements, in a scientific manner, the kindly advice of well-meaning judges who must form their conclusions as to underlying social difficulties from the hurried presentation of strictly legal evidence in the courtroom."[12]

Despite the Bureau's well-meaning intentions, others criticized its work. For instance, in 1936 the New York State Division of Probation issued a report questioning the propriety of the Bureau on a number of levels. For instance, it challenged the qualifications of the volunteers, pointing out that of the thirty-five part-time social work counselors, only nine had some previous social work experience. The others came from all walks of life—lawyers, teachers, housewives, factory workers, and salespeople—and lacked sufficient training or knowledge to undertake a probation officer's role.[13]

Kross was also criticized for creating a private working group that confused the public and operated outside formal court procedures. Indeed, the New York State Probation Department maligned the "privately financed project" which, it believed, illustrated that "any judge who so desires, may with little difficulty organize his or her own particular investigative body to work independently of the Probation Bureau." Such rogue activity, it warned, resulted in unequal treatment among defendants and "discrimination in the dispensation of justice" based upon which magistrate handled a case.[14]

Nevertheless, Kross persisted in her efforts to expand the Bureau, which was formally incorporated as a nonprofit organization in July 1937.[15] Kross used the press to spread word of the project and generate additional financial support.[16] In a December 1937 *New York Times* article authored by Kross, she praised her Social Services Bureau volunteers and called for others to join their ranks.[17] Announcing the Bureau's second Annual Tea, Kross invited teachers, clergy, and others to join her project. Participating in this event were such notables as Fannie Hurst and Anna Rosenberg, then Regional Director of the Social Security Board and later the first woman to serve as Assistant Secretary of Defense.

By the following year, 1938, Kross expanded her volunteer-based court work to Harlem, where she opened a branch office in the Washington Heights Court. There, three "colored" volunteer social workers were chosen to lead a unique campaign against venereal disease. The Harlem program, described as a "special experiment of helping colored women discharged from the Women's Court and Kingston Avenue Hospital," was supported in part by a $1,000 grant from Mayor LaGuardia's Special Welfare Fund.[18]

The women targeted by this project were accused prostitutes, many of whom had their cases dismissed for lack of evidence.[19] Despite the dismissal, if they tested positive for venereal disease, the women were automatically sent to the Kingston Avenue Hospital for medical attention. Kross worried that this process was insufficient. Once declared noninfectious by Kingston Hospital the women were released "still diseased and in need of treatment," and referrals for aftercare were seldom followed. Thus, under the Harlem experiment, Kross's Social Services Bureau volunteers "assumed responsibility of investigating and following up these cases in cooperation with the Board of Health."

For instance, the volunteers might arrange for housing, clothing, and other aid for women released from the hospital. In exchange, the women agreed to see one of several area physicians who volunteered to help Kross with her Harlem venereal disease campaign. These physicians, working in conjunction with the Magistrates' Court, shared the women's treatment information with Social Services Bureau volunteers. The volunteers, in turn, shared this information with the Board of Health and, in some instances, the women's family members. In a number of cases the women's family members or sexual partners, or both, were also referred to the Board of Health for the detection of sexually transmitted diseases.[20]

In a report outlining the work of the Bureau's Harlem Project and urging its continued support, Kross noted:

> It must be borne in mind that these social workers are not highly trained and are volunteers, nevertheless, the results are most encouraging. With the proper staff, much could be done not only for the benefit of the community, but also for the rehabilitation of the unfortunate individual. . . . It is recognized that this type of service is and should be the function of the Probation Department. Unfortunately, however, our probation staff is neither qualitatively nor quantitatively equipped to handle this work.[21]

By the end of 1938 Kross had secured sufficient funds to hire an executive director for the Bureau, Miss A. Y. Yeghenian. Yeghenian, a Yale Law School graduate with some background in social services work, supervised the Court's volunteer workers and attempted to formalize its volunteer training program. With Yeghenian in place the existing board members soon resigned, allowing Kross's longtime supporters—Searle, Borg, and Rosenberg—to step in to take "complete charge of policy, procedure and finances of the Bureau" and work to expand its budget.[22]

Despite the group's expansion, with nine paid staff members, countless volunteers serving an estimated 1,275 defendants in 1939, and its continued solicitation of funds, the private, nonprofit operated without a proper Board of Directors for more than a year. Ultimately, in January 1940, Reverend Searle became President of the Board, and Kross was one of its members. Thereafter Searle suspended the organization's by-laws, and the new board did not meet again until October 1940.[23]

During this time criticism of the Bureau mounted; Chief Magistrate Henry Curran even questioned the organization's very existence. Although Curran had once used the services of the Bureau's volunteers for his cases, once he became Chief Judge he claimed that the unofficial group impeded the proper administration of justice and misled the public. In a letter of January 3, 1941, to Reverend Searle, Judge Curran urged the discontinuation of any business cards with the name "Magistrates' Court Social Services Bureau." Reverend Searle responded that he had already stopped using them and that the Board was in the process of shortening the name of the organization to the "Social Service Bureau" to meet his approval.[24]

Yet, just a few days later, Judge Kross was apparently summoned before the New York City Department of Investigations to be questioned. During the probe she was asked to account for, and justify, the Bureau's various operations. The investigator expressed particular concern with the Bureau's occupation, without charge, of three rooms at the 54th Street Courthouse and four rooms in Harlem Court. He also questioned the group's distribution of pamphlets to solicit funds, as the materials erroneously suggested that the Bureau was an official feature of the court system.

Kross took full responsibility for the Bureau's actions, which she argued were wholly appropriate and necessary in light of the legal restrictions on, and shortcomings of, the official Probation Department of the Magistrates' Court. The space occupied by the Bureau had been donated by the City's Real Estate Office under the direction of Mayor LaGuardia. As for the Bureau's written materials, Kross insisted that they all referred to the Bureau as a private agency supported by private funds. She conceded, however, that she hoped the Bureau would be formally incorporated into the court system and supported with an official government budget in the future. Kross brazenly suggested that Judge Curran was the problem, given his failure to integrate the Bureau into the formal structure of the Magistrates' Court.[25]

Following the inquiry Chief Judge Curran urged Judge Kross to resign from the Social Service Bureau's various committees and "desist from taking part in any other way in raising money for this organization." He further shared with her various "letters and resolutions" supporting his position. Kross, however, refused to heed his admonitions. In her written response to Curran, Kross explained:

> As I told you yesterday, I really regret that I feel I can't comply with your request as a matter of principle but rest assured that I am fully aware of the proprieties that you are so solicitously calling to my attention. . . . You will however find on looking into the entire question and the origin of these resolutions that my remaining a member of the Board of Directors of the Social Service Bureau is not in conflict with the spirit or the letter of these resolutions.

Let's take this up further as the matter develops but do please be assured of my sincere regard and appreciation for the spirit in which you are approaching this.[26]

Indeed, Kross continued her work with the Bureau quite publicly, the next month sponsoring a special benefit performance of George Bernard Shaw's *The Doctor's Dilemma* at the Shubert Theater to support the Bureau's programs. The *New York Times* reported that tickets were available for purchase at the headquarters of the Social Service Bureau, at the 54th Street Courthouse, and named numerous noteworthy New Yorkers—including Kross—who were affiliated with the event and the Bureau.[27] By 1941 the organization's letterhead now referred to the group only as the "Social Service Bureau," but Kross was clearly listed on the stationery as one of its nearly forty board members.[28]

During this time, as the impact of World War II hit New York City, Kross and the Bureau's volunteers reached beyond the courthouse doors into the community to address the national emergency through social intervention efforts. For instance, although defense industries provided jobs in many communities, it excluded Harlem's African American population from such work. As a result, Harlem parents often were forced to work long hours at other jobs and take in boarders to pay rent. Their sons and daughters reportedly became "door-key children" who carried keys to school to let themselves back in their homes at the end of the day. According to Kross's supporters, these conditions resulted in the youths of Harlem running the streets unsupervised and becoming either the victims or perpetrators of crimes.[29]

On the day the United States Naval Base in Pearl Harbor was bombed, the *New York Times* announced the Social Service Bureau's campaign to increase its budget from $14,000 to $60,000 a year. This was to meet increased social service needs, particularly in Harlem, in light of the war. Reverend Robert Searle conveyed the Bureau's message:

The social service bureau . . . is preparing an immediate expansion of all its facilities to meet the new social problems of the national emergency; the problems born of boon times, shifting populations, popular confusion.

The present plan calls for an increase in personnel and an enlarging of the bureau's facilities to cover all of the district courts in Manhattan and the Bronx . . . In lieu of the procedure of arrest, trial and imprisonment, the bureau calls for the handling of the entire problem on a medical-sociological basis, through the services of medical officers, psychiatrists and social workers.

In this time of emergency, the community must be rallied to face its problems honestly, to unite its resources to safeguard its youth, protect the public health, and demonstrate in terms of concrete achievement that the social welfare of its people is, even in times of stress and emergency, the chief concern of a democracy. A sound, healthy social structure is the best justification for national defense.[30]

The Bureau's volunteers, he insisted, had an "important role to play in fortifying the moral fibre of the community and in restoring to social balance many of those who have been shocked by the impact of the defense mobilization."

Finally, the Women's Court Committee of the Social Service Bureau, chaired by Borg, used the war as an opportunity to take up Kross's earlier cause of trying to close the Women's Court. With so many men being drafted into the military and visiting New York while on leave, the Bureau's Women's Court Committee warned that prostitution and venereal disease would spread. As criminal prosecution was not a deterrent, it again called for the abolition of the Women's Court and its replacement with socialized health efforts.[31] When this proposal was rejected once again, the Women's Court Committee submitted a report to the mayor "to explore what can be done in the [existing] Women's Court in the war emergency to promote the war effort, (a) by reducing the hazards of prostitution and venereal disease; (b) by social rehabilitation of the prostitute."[32]

Among its recommendations was modification of the physical setup of the courtroom and its hallways to prevent collusion between bondsmen, lawyers, and witnesses prior to hearings. The report explained:

It is the opinion of the court workers and others familiar with the Women's Court that the physical setup of this hall makes it altogether too easy to *fix* cases before trial, that bribery can and does take place there, that this situation is unfair to the police and the defendants, and that it is very difficult indeed to supervise those who are forced to use this hall.[33]

The mayor, offended by the public allegations of corruption in the courts, referred the entire matter to the Commissioner of Investigation, William Herlands. Members of the Bureau's Women's Court Committee were asked to appear before the commissioner,[34] who found the Bureau's allegations of bribery and wrongdoing without basis.[35] Thus Kross and her Bureau again found themselves amid public controversy and press scrutiny—this time at the hands of one of the group's strongest supporters, Mayor LaGuardia.

Kross's Home Advisory Council

As the group recovered from this challenge and the war drew to an end, Judge Kross saw another emerging social problem that needed to be addressed through volunteer intervention at the criminal courts, namely, increasing family violence.[36] As soldiers returned from abroad, the number of assault, disorderly conduct, and drunkenness cases filed in the Magistrates' Court increased. Kross believed that the increase stemmed from the former military members cracking under the strain of economic, housing, and other difficulties encountered upon their return from war. In other instances partners had wed hastily before the soldiers' deployment and simply had not yet developed strong relationships. Social work intervention, she believed, was more appropriate in these cases than criminal prosecution.

Thus, a decade after the Wayward Minors' Court was created, Kross established another, specialized part of the Magistrates' Court, called the Home Term Court.[37] Like the Wayward Minors' Part, Home Term attempted to foster change through an informal diversionary form of justice—urging parties to participate in treatment to avoid further prosecution or formal adjudication.[38] To assist in Home Term, Kross created another independent volunteer agency under the leadership of many of the same individuals who helped run the Magistrates' Court Social Services Bureau. Reverend Robert Searle was tapped to serve as executive director of this group, dubbed the Home Advisory and Service Council of New York.[39]

The Home Advisory Council included representatives from religious and benevolent organizations like the Jewish Family Service, Catholic Charities, and the Lutheran Welfare Council, as well as lay volunteers.[40] Like the Social Services Bureau, it was an incorporated, independent nonprofit organization but was considered an "adjunct" of the court.[41] Maintaining office space within the 300 Mulberry Street courthouse, the group had a dual role—both to develop cooperation between the court and private social services, and to provide direct casework services to those who came to the court.[42]

Home Advisory Council lay counselors worked to keep cases from needing formal adjudication or probation adjustment.[43] Kross, kept abreast of problems that arose during the informal supervision period, remained ready to intervene if necessary.[44] The Magistrates' Courts new chief judge Edgar Bromberger was supportive of Kross's use of volunteer staff to provide counseling and social service attention in such cases.[45] So, too, at least for a time, was the next chief judge John M. Murtagh.[46] Indeed, Judge Murtagh described the court and its social services in this way:

Home Term Court . . . is designed to offer more adequate assistance to persons whose family difficulties previously brought them before the District Courts. It provides a centralized socio-legal facility for the study and treatment of family cases, with emphasis on the offender and his family rather than the offense that brings him into court. Home Term recognizes that the individual, rather than his delinquencies, requires and merits the greater study. Its main objective is to effect lasting adjustments of family difficulties in applying the techniques and principles of social casework, in an authoritarian setting. By helping members of the family to reach practical and realistic solution of their problems, this court tries to keep families from being broken.[47]

Such help often involved informal supervision and marital counseling,[48] sometimes offered by the Home Advisory Council's lay volunteers.[49] Many of these individuals were recruited from Kross's own social strata—"mature women" whose own children had already left home and whose "native endowment" for family life would allow them to serve as role models in addition to counselors.[50] The group was described as including "wives of physicians, lawyers . . . business[men], newspaper and social work executives," as well as widows.[51] Most Home Term litigants, who were indigent, came from a decidedly different world.[52]

In addition, at the beginning of its operations, Home Term counselors met with clients not only at the court complex but also in the community. Because the Court believed marital breakdown was caused by a variety of contributing factors, both partners were usually asked to participate in programming run by the Home Advisory Council,[53] along with other family members.[54]

Over time, however, the Home Advisory Council's services began to fall short of initial ambitious plans. For instance, given limited resources, home visits became more infrequent.[55] Home Term's innovative in-house Alcoholism Clinic, run by the Home Advisory Council, faltered.[56] And its unique Psychiatric Unit, staffed by Bellevue Hospital doctors who studied the litigants and in some instances committed them, became overwhelmed with referrals.[57]

Beyond this, leading contemporary commentators like criminologist Paul Tappan argued that the psychological and mental health intervention attempted by the Wayward Minor's Part and Home Term, was not the kind of work that should take place within the criminal justice system. As a general matter, he warned, criminal courts and their correctional features were not yet sufficiently competent to determine which offenders presented legitimate mental health issues and to provide these defendants with effective individualized treatment and care.[58]

Tappan also feared that carrying out "comprehensive social work" plans with "unskilled or partially trained probation officer[s]" was "sheer folly."[59] These individuals were ill-equipped to address "problems of domestic relations, psychological pathology, occupational maladjustments," and the like. He argued that experimental "socialized" courts were too often instruments of the personal biases and individual views than science.[60] "However benevolent the motivation" behind the actions of individuals like Kross and her auxiliaries, he argued that "the expansive drive . . . toward problem-solving for all-comers has resulted in attenuated, inexact, and ineffectual service" when such service generally should be provided outside criminal courts.[61]

Kross's Court Volunteers: Borrowing from the Past while Shaping Courts of the Future

It was this kind of inexact but well-intended, volunteer-based intervention that served as the very genesis for the modern probation model. Indeed, with her use of lay court staff, Kross was merely returning to a long-abandoned practice that had been established nearly a century before by John Augustus, widely recognized as the father of probation in this country.[62] Augustus, a shoemaker, was a religious man who, during the 1800s, convinced judges in Boston to release offenders to his care rather than incarcerate them. During the course of his life, he provided supervision, job training, and other assistance for more than one thousand offenders while they remained under the court's jurisdiction.[63] Even Tappan acknowledged Augustus's "important role" in the development of the modern probation movement through his volunteer efforts.[64] Perhaps, without knowing it, Kross simply unearthed this concept, making it her own in the process.

Moreover, despite strong criticisms, Kross's resurrection of court-based volunteerism in an arguably feminized form laid the groundwork for a significant and transformative legal movement. It began a ground-swell of court reliance on volunteer support that swept the country during the 1960s and 1970s.[65] With the advent of the modern problem-solving court movement, this phenomenon of criminal court volunteerism is again gaining momentum in the twenty-first century. Yet Kross has been given surprisingly little credit for her role in (re)imagining these important, arguably controversial, criminal justice innovations. And surprisingly little attention is being paid to our contemporary return to her previously abandoned criminal court reform efforts.

During the 1960s New York's court system was fundamentally reorganized.[66] This restructuring resulted in the abolition of the Magistrates' Court system and the establishment of more generalized criminal courts. The reorganization also led to the creation of a new Family Court system in 1962, which embraced many of the cases previously heard in the Magistrates' Courts. For instance, most young women charged in the Wayward Minors' Court with crimes relating to unruliness and promiscuity now had their cases handled through the Family Court as "persons in need of supervision."[67] Similarly domestic violence matters previously seen in the Home Term were redirected to the Family Court's Family Offenses Part. Thus Kross's volunteer army shifted its efforts to a non-criminal setting. Ultimately, much as Kross had hoped, the volunteers became formally acknowledged as an important part of the services offered by the justice system—except now in family courts.[68]

At the very moment Kross's volunteer counselors moved from the criminal to the civil side of the justice system, other courts across the country began to try their hand with volunteer probation officers. Remarkably judges undertaking these later efforts have been the ones credited with the reemergence of volunteer rehabilitation of criminal offenders.

For instance, some claim that Judge Keith J. Leenhouts in Royal Oak, Michigan, was the first to revisit the practice of using volunteer probation officers in 1960.[69] Others assert that Judge Horace B. Holmes invoked the "ghost of John Augustus" by creating a volunteer probation force in his Juvenile Court in Boulder, Colorado, in 1961.[70] In any event, by the mid-1960s it was clear that the "court volunteer movement" had firmly "take[n] hold." The federal government provided funding and other support for these programs through the Department of Health, Education, and Welfare,[71] and trainings for volunteer court workers were held across the country.[72] By the 1970s more than 125 cities were using volunteer-supported probation programs, where such lay officials served both as friends to the offenders and officers of the court. As in Kross's model, the volunteers assisted defendants in their efforts to adjust in the community while providing written and other progress reports to the supervising judges.[73]

Although volunteerism in the courts continued during the latter part of the last century, as in Kross's New York, its focus again seemed to shift to the civil sphere with its less onerous due process and procedural protections for litigants. For instance, the Court Appointed Special Advocate (CASA) program emerged as the dominant court volunteer model in the 1980s, pairing interested lay advocates with children who were the subject of family court abuse and neglect proceedings. Such volunteers have been called upon to "speak exclusively for the best interests of the child until the case is permanently resolved or until a final decree is ordered by the court."[74]

During the 1990s, however, as interest in specialized criminal courts in this country again grew, so, too, did community involvement in criminal court processes. Indeed, in 1994, Judge Leenhouts, now retired from the bench, was named the executive director of the National Judicial College's Court Volunteer Services Program. In that role he again sought to encourage volunteer-based probation supervision. Similarly, in 1996, Chief Justice Shirley Abrahamson established the Volunteers in Courts initiative throughout the state of Wisconsin, which encouraged community involvement in all workings of the court—including criminal cases.[75]

Today a particularly striking parallel to Kross's work can be seen in the Community Court movement, which uses volunteers to play a role in both rehabilitating individual defendants and shaping court policy.[76] Lay community members may help direct offenders to social services, at the same time sharing their views with the court about the impact of offender behavior on the larger community.[77] This kind of privatization allowing private individuals to inform judicial decision making and criminal court agendas is once again considered innovative. As in Kross's day it is again drawing sharp criticisms.[78]

Unfortunately, while history is (again) repeating itself, Kross's role as the pioneer of such community involvement in criminal court processes has been largely forgotten. Conversations about the efficacy and appropriateness of volunteerism and private individual involvement in criminal court proceedings are taking place without reference to her similar experimentation more than fifty years ago. Thus modern criminal justice reformers could learn significant lessons from Kross's work and the efforts of her "lady vols" as they attempt to build another army of auxiliaries to engage in court-based social engineering efforts.[79] By placing these "old questions in a new light" history can serve as an important guide not just for academics but also for this most recent generation of criminal court innovators.[80]

NOTES

1. For more on Kross's early life and career, see Mae C. Quinn, *Revisiting Anna Moscowitz Kross's Critique of the New York City Women's Court: The Problem of Solving the "Problem" of Prostitution with Specialized Criminal Courts*, 33 Fordham Urb. L.J. 665, 669–70 (2006); Mae C. Quinn, *Anna Moscowitz Kross and the Home Term Part: A Second Look at the Nation's First Criminal Domestic Violence Court*, 41 Akron L. Rev. 733, 737 (2008).

2. Quinn, *Home Term*, at 739; Leah N. Neurer, *New York Woman Judge Attained High Goal through Sacrifice, Struggle and Determination*, 25 Women Law. J. 52, 52 (1938–39).

3. Anna Moscowitz Kross and Howard M. Grossman, *Magistrates' Courts of the City of New York: Jurisdiction, Powers and Duties of Magistrates,* 7 Brooklyn L. Rev. 295 (1937–38); Anna Moscowitz Kross and Howard M. Grossman, *Magistrates' Courts of the City of New York: Suggested Improvements,* 7 Brooklyn L. Rev. 411, 415 (1937–38).

4. *Suggested Improvements,* 423–24; Anna M. Kross and Harold M. Grossman, *Magistrates' Courts of the City of New York: History and Organization,* 7 Brooklyn L. Rev. 133 (1937).

5. See Quinn, *Women's Court,* 670.

6. *Women Organized to Assist Court,* N.Y. Times, Dec. 15, 1935, at 41.

7. *Suggested Improvements,* 434–35, 449–54; Magistrates' Courts Social Service Bureau, Statement of Organization, Aims and Purposes 1 (1939).

8. Quinn, *Women's Court,* 688-91; Zelda Popkin, *Social Service in Courts,* N.Y. Times, Jan. 5, 1936, at X13; A. Y. Yeghenian, Synopsis of History and Progress: Magistrates' Courts Social Service Bureau 1935 to Date (Oct. 1, 1940); *Women Organized,* 41; *Powers and Duties,* 451.

9. Yeghenian, 1; Quinn, *Women's Court,* 690; see also Anna M. Kross, U.S. Works Progress Admin., Procedures for Dealing with Wayward Minors in New York City 23, 26 (1936); *Suggested Improvements,* 439–41, 450–54; Anna M. Kross, *Hypocrisy Scored in Penal Methods,* N.Y. Times, Dec. 12, 1937, at 5.

10. Kross, 14–15, 30–31; *Suggested Improvements,* 441; see also Bernard C. Fisher, Justice for Youth: The Courts for Wayward Youth in New York City 21–30 (1955).

11. Kross, *Hypocrisy,* 5; *Welfare Bureau Will Meet at Tea,* N.Y. Times, Dec. 13, 1936, at D6.

12. *Suggested Improvements,* 450; Statement, 19–20, 451–52; Kross, *Hypocrisy,* 99.

13. *Suggested Improvements,* 99.

14. *Id.* at 451–52.

15. Yeghenian, 1.

16. See, e.g., *Expand Social Service Work,* N. Y. Times, Oct. 12, 1938, at 21.

17. Kross, *Hypocrisy,* 99.

18. Yeghenian, 1–2.

19. Report, Harlem Division of Magistrates' Courts Social Service Bureau 5 (1938).

20. *Id.* at 5–6.

21. *Id.* at 6–7.

22. Yeghenian, 2.

23. *Id.* at 4; *Welfare Project Is Reorganized,* N.Y. Times, Apr. 20, 1940, at 31.

24. Correspondence between Chief Magistrate Henry H. Curran and Rev. Dr. Robert W. Searle, Jan. 1941.

25. See *Questions by Mr. Sala Answered by Judge Kross,* January 21, 1941, Kross Papers, American Jewish Archives.

26. Letter from Henry H. Curran, Chief Magistrate, to Anna M. Kross, Magistrate, Feb. 18, 1941.

27. *Charity Will Gain by Theatre Party,* N.Y. Times, Mar. 10, 1941, at 14.

28. See Form Letter from A. Y. Yeghenian, June 20, 1941.

29. *Clinic to Study Crime in Harlem,* N.Y. Times, Nov. 11, 1941, at 25.

30. *Crime in Harlem Spurs Fund Drive,* N.Y. Times, Dec. 7, 1941, at 80.

31. Memorandum, Mrs. Sidney Borg, *Proposed Plan for a Social Service Program in the Women's Court as Related to the Problem of Prostitution and the National Emergency.*

32. Report, Women's Court Committee of the Social Service Bureau, June 8, 1942.

33. *Id.* at 1.

34. Letter of Rev. Searle to Mayor Fiorello H. LaGuardia, July 31, 1942.

35. See, e.g., *Deny Case Fixing in Women's Court*, N.Y. Times, July 21, 1942, at 21; *Women's Court Data Held Unconvincing*, N.Y. Times, July 22, 1942, at 11. See *Court Bribe Charges Termed Unfounded*, N.Y. Times, Aug. 3, 1942, at 15; *Mrs. Field Defends "Opinion" on Bribery*, N.Y. Times, Aug. 4, 1942, at 36.

36. See Quinn, *Home Term*, 743.

37. *Id.*; see also Walter Gellhorn, Children and Families in the Courts of New York City 217–38 (1954).

38. Quinn, *Home Term*, at 743.

39. *Robert Searle, Religious Leader: Head of Home Advisory and Service Council Dies*, N.Y. Times, June 18, 1967, at 76.

40. Quinn, *Home Term*, 745; see also Raymond I. Parnas, *Judicial Response to Intra-Family Violence*, 54 Minn. L. Rev. 585, 623–625 (1969–70).

41. Quinn, *Home Term*, 746; An Appeal in Behalf of the Home Term Advisory Council of New York—The Voluntary Auxiliary of the Family Offenses Part of the Family Court of New York City (1963).

42. Quinn, *Home Terms*, 746; Dorris Clarke & Alice W. Field, Home Term: A Socialized Court for Family Problems in the New York City Magistrates' Court System 23 (1948); see also Richard Maisel & June Christ, Families in Conflict 1 (1954).

43. Maisel & Christ, 40.

44. *Id.* at 9; see also Gertrude Samuels, *Court of First Resort for the Family*, N.Y. Times, Jan. 6, 1952, at 20.

45. Walter Gellhorn, Children and Families in the Courts of New York City 217–18 (1954).

46. See Quinn, *Women's Court*, 693.

47. John M. Murtagh, Functions of the Magistrates' Courts (1953).

48. Quinn, *Home Term*, at 749; Clarke & Field, 23.

49. *New Court to Run on $50,000 Budget*, N.Y. Times, May 15, 1946, at 18; Advisory Council Appeal, 2–5.

50. Advisory Council Appeal, 2–5; Maisel & Christ, 5. see also Quinn, *Home Term*, 749 n. 104.

51. Maisel & Christ, 7; see *Family: 4 Upstate Counties to Get Volunteer Counselors under Ford Grant*, N.Y. Times, Mar. 13, 1968; see also Quinn, *Home Term*, 749 n. 105.

52. Quinn, *Home Term*, 749 n. 102; see also Maisel & Christ, 14.

53. Clarke & Field, 6.

54. *Id.* at 7–25; see also Gellhorn, 224.

55. Gellhorn, 226.

56. Maisel & Christ, 12–13; see also *Alcoholics' Clinic for Court Formed*, N.Y. Times, Dec. 16, 1952, at FB64.

57. Clarke & Field, 19, 22–23; Gellhorn, 227–31.

58. Paul W. Tappan, Crime, Justice and Correction 59–61, 506–38 (1960).

59. Paul W. Tappan, *The Adolescent in Court*, 37 J. Crim. L. & Criminology 216, 223 (1946–47); see also Paul W. Tappan, *Prevention and Treatment of Delinquency*, in Social Problems 256 (1950).

60. Paul W. Tappan, *Treatment without Trial*, 24 Social Forces 306, 309 (1945–46).

61. *Id.*; see also Paul W. Tappan, *Unofficial Delinquency*, 29 Neb. L. Rev. 547, 552 (1949–50).

62. See John Petrisilia, *Probation in the United States,* 22 Crime & Just. 149, 155–57 (1997); see also Judge Horace B. Holmes, *The Volunteer Returns to the Court,* 18 Juv. Ct. Judges 133 (1967–68); William H. Burnett, *The Volunteer Probation Counselor,* 52 Judicature 286 (1968–69).

63. See Petrisilia, 155–57 (1997).

64. See Tappan, Crime, Justice and Correction, 543–45.

65. See, e.g., Judge Horace B. Holmes, *The Volunteer Returns to the Court,* 18 Juv. Ct. Judges 134 (1967–68).

66. See Quinn, *Women's Court,* 695.

67. See Paul W. Tappan, Delinquent Girls in Court (1947); see also Anonymous v. People, 20 A.D.2d 395 (N.Y. App. 1964).

68. See The Origin and History of the Home Advisory and Service Council of New York, Inc., at 2; see also Appeal of Advisory Council, 1.

69. William H. Burnett, *The Volunteer Probation Counselor,* 52 Judicature 286 (1968–69).

70. Ivan H. Scheier, *The Professional and the Volunteer in Probation: An Emerging Relationship,* 34 Federal Probation at 12 (1970); see also Judge Horace B. Holmes, *The Volunteer Returns to the Court,* 18 Juv. Ct. Judges 134 (1967–68).

71. Max Raskin, *Volunteer Probation Counselors: A New Dimension in Sentencing Youthful Offenders,* 54 Marq. L. Rev. 41 (1971); see also Judge Michael Corrigan, *The Juvenile Court and Community Involvement,* 10 Osgoode Hall L.J. 221, 222 (1972).

72. See, e.g., *Volunteer Workshop Planned,* 20 Juv. Ct. Judges J. 27 (1969).

73. See Raskin, 44–47.

74. Jennifer Wynne Bolden, *Comment, In Re: The Court Appointed Special Advocate (CASA) Volunteers Providing the Missing Link in "The Best Interests of the Child,"* 19 S.U. L. Rev. 421, 427 (1992).

75. See Ann Walsh Bradley, *With Courage and Passion: The Inspired Leadership of Chief Justice Shirley S. Abrahamson,* 67 Albany L. Rev. 641, 643 (2003–4).

76. See, e.g., Quinn, *Women's Court,* 701–3; Paul W. Shapiro, *Volunteers Are Vital to the Success of the Collaborative Courts,* Orange County Lawyer 10, 11 (Feb. 2008); see also Jeffrey Fagan & Victoria Malkin, *Theorizing Community Justice through Community Court,* 30 Fordham Urb. L.J. 897 (2003).

77. See Shapiro, 11–12.

78. See Adriaan Lanni, *The Future of Community Justice,* 40 Harv. C.R.-C.L. Rev. 359, 380 (2005); Sudip Kundu, *Privately Funded Courts and the Homeless: A Critical Look at Community Courts,* 14-WTR J. Affordable Housing & Community Dev. L. 170 (2005); Fagan & Malkin, 897.

79. See, e.g., Veronica Simmons McBeth & Shelley M. Stump, *Reclaiming the Courts' Historic Role: Judges as Leaders in Their Communities,* 38 Judges J. 19 (1999); see also ABA Formal Opinion 08-452: Judges Soliciting Contributions for "Therapeutic" or "Problem-solving" Courts.

80. Arthur M. Schlesinger Jr., *Folly's Antidote,* N.Y. Times, Jan. 1, 2007.

12

Sexual Harassment

Law for Women, by Women

CARRIE N. BAKER

In March 1975 a group of feminist activists in Ithaca, New York, coined the term "sexual harassment" to name something they had all experienced but rarely discussed—unwanted sexual demands, comments, looks, or sexual touching in the workplace. The experience they wanted to uncover was one that women in North America had faced since colonial times. Seventeenth-century indentured servants, eighteenth-century black slaves, nineteenth-century factory workers, and twentieth-century office workers all shared the experience of having fended off the sexual demands of those wielding economic power over their lives—masters, overseers, foremen, and supervisors.

Historically women responded to workplace sexual coercion in a myriad of ways, often submitting, but also resisting. Some escaped the situation, others tried using official channels to stop the abuse or seek relief from its effects, and still others joined together to protest sexual coercion by their employers. Escape was the only option for many female slaves, who had little power to resist their owner's sexual advances, no legal recourse, and no home away from their owner's reach. In her 1861 autobiography, *Incidents in the Life of a Slave Girl*, Harriet Jacobs described her escape from a master who "began to whisper foul words in [her] ear" when she was fifteen.[1] Domestic servants who could afford to do so escaped the sexual abuse of employers by leaving their jobs. In 1874 Louisa May Alcott published an account of how at the age of eighteen she had left a job as a domestic servant because her employer assigned her backbreaking work after she refused his sexual advances.[2] Women sometimes turned to governmental authorities for help. Although colonial courts heard charges against masters for "violating" female servants, making "forcible attempts" on their chastity, and exhibiting "lewd behavior," victims rarely gained relief.[3] In cases when a servant ended up pregnant, courts sometimes required masters to pay a fine or give security to maintain the child.[4] However, indentured servants did not have easy access to the judicial system, and their direct dependence on those who assaulted them often dissuaded them from taking action. After the Civil War, when former slaves registered charges of sexual abuse by white men with the Freeman's Bureau, an agency set up after emancipation to assist blacks, they seldom obtained relief.[5] In the early twentieth century women sometimes sued their employers for assault or for monetary damages when they became pregnant.[6] In 1908 a young immigrant woman sued her employer, a saloon-keeper, because he "abused her shamefully and then turned her out when he found that she was to become the mother of his illegitimate child," but she lost her case.[7]

Women also collectively resisted sexual coercion in the workplace. In Chicago, at the turn of the twentieth century, Grace Abbot formed an immigrant protective organization with the primary goal of protecting immigrant girls from lecherous employers.[8] Later tradeswomen formed groups to fight sexual abuse in the workplace. In 1914 a group of women in the needle trades formed the Young Ladies Educational Society to support one another in resisting their employers' sexual advances.[9] A major goal of the Working Women's Society, a forerunner of the Women's Trade Union League, was to protect working women from unwanted sexual advances by supervisors.[10] Sexual abuse of workers sometimes became an issue that sent unions out on strike. One of the issues in a 1937 strike at the Chevrolet-Flint Plant in Michigan was sexual abuse, after a large number of female workers had to go to the county hospital to be treated for venereal disease traced to a single foreman. A worker recalled, "Those were the conditions that young women had to accept in order to support their families. Sometimes they earned just enough to provide food for the family and they couldn't lose their jobs because nobody else in the family had a job."[11]

During the second wave of the women's movement in the 1970s, a grassroots movement against sexual harassment emerged in the United States, which challenged workplace sexual abuse in new ways. Relying on existing antidiscrimination law and civil rights precedents on racial harassment, women asked courts to adopt a revolutionary interpretation of the law—that sexual harassment was sex discrimination in violation of Title VII of the Civil Rights Act of 1964, thereby creating legal prohibitions of sexual coercion in the workplace for the first time in history. This chapter charts the evolution of sexual harassment from a private indignity women most often suffered silently to an issue of public concern and debate. Feminists were able to convince courts and policy makers that sexual coercion in the workplace, which had previously been understood to be an isolated, personal problem, was, in fact, a serious barrier to women's equal employment opportunity. This chapter documents how women individually and collectively acted to create this new law, and how their creative advocacy in the courts fundamentally rewrote the rules of the workplace, thereby altering social norms. Sexual harassment law is a uniquely powerful example of how women used the law and legal processes to empower themselves and exercise agency individually and collectively.

Early Lawsuits

Two strands of activism—lawsuits brought by diverse women around the country and collective organizing among feminists to raise awareness of sexual coercion in the workplace—came together to convince courts to rule that sexual harassment in the workplace and in schools was sex discrimination in violation of federal law. Resistance to sexual harassment first emerged in the early 1970s in the form of several lawsuits filed around the country under Title VII, which prohibited sex and race discrimination in employment. Six cases, filed between 1971 and 1975, led the legal effort against sexual harassment and set the framework for the movement against sexual harassment.[12] These cases heavily influenced the development of the law and of public opinion, as they were widely discussed in the media and among legal scholars and feminists. The women in these cases made the novel argument that a male employer who fires a woman for refusing his sexual advances has discriminated against her based on sex and therefore, has violated her civil rights guaranteed by Title VII. At the time these women filed their cases there were no legal precedents for this interpretation of Title VII. Sexual harassment litigation was a battleground on which traditional notions that women belonged in the private sphere and entered the public sphere at their own risk struggled with feminist notions that women were entitled to participate fully in the public sphere.

A diverse group of women from around the country working for both public and private employers brought these lawsuits. Plaintiffs in three of the six cases were young African American women, two of whom were harassed by African American men while working for federal agencies in Washington, D.C., that addressed race discrimination issues. These women were familiar with discrimination law and the mechanisms for legal redress because of their backgrounds in the civil rights movement. Two of the African American women initially filed their complaints as race and sex discrimination claims. All six cases involved a male supervisor firing or forcing out a female subordinate employee after she rejected his sexual advances. With no obvious avenues for recourse, these women reached out to what seemed their only option—Equal Employment Offices (EEO). When they lost their EEO complaints, they found civil rights and feminist attorneys in their communities to file lawsuits in federal courts.

In all cases except one, the judges denied relief, concluding that the alleged misconduct was a private matter, neither employment-related nor sex discrimination for which employers should be liable. One judge described the case as a "controversy underpinned by subtleties of an inharmonious personal relationship," perhaps "inexcusable" but not "an arbitrary barrier to continued employment based on sex."[13] Another described the harasser's conduct as "nothing more than a personal proclivity, peculiarity, or mannerism . . . satisfying a personal urge . . . [with] no relationship to the nature of the employment."[14] By portraying the conduct as natural, personal, sexually motivated behavior, the judges obscured the underlying power dynamics of the behavior—the abuse of authority and the economic coercion involved. The judges also argued that the behavior was not motivated by gender. One judge reasoned that the plaintiff "was discriminated against not because she was a woman but because she refused to engage in a sexual affair with her supervisor."[15] Finally, the judges argued that treating sexual harassment as sex discrimination would "open the floodgates of litigation," overwhelming the court system and inviting a lawsuit for every sexual indiscretion in the workplace. One judge expressed concern that there "would be a potential federal lawsuit every time any employee made amorous or sexually oriented advances toward another."[16]

The early cases denying relief showed that women faced an uphill battle to convince people that sexual harassment was a serious problem. But these cases laid the groundwork for the emerging movement against sexual harassment by framing the issue of sexual harassment as an issue of employment discrimination and a violation of Title VII of the Civil Rights Act. The individual women who brought these early sexual harassment cases tapped into resources developed by the civil rights and women's movements—the theories and precedents of employment discrimination law, as well as the networks of attorneys knowledgeable about and willing to take on these cases. These cases broke new ground by focusing on the economic consequences of sexual coercion in the workplace and linking these consequences to discriminatory attitudes of male supervisors, who treated female employees like wives, lovers, or even prostitutes rather than workers. Even before feminist activists had coined the term "sexual harassment," the courageous women who brought these suits conceived of sexual coercion in the workplace as sex discrimination and brought lawsuits, despite terrible odds. When they lost them, they appealed.

Collective Action

The lawsuits brought by individual women around the country framed the issue of sexual coercion in the workplace as sex discrimination, but it was collective feminist action that gave a name to the phenomenon and raised awareness that eventually convinced courts to take the issue seriously. Collective activism against sexual harassment was rooted in the women's movement, emerging at the intersection of activism against employment discrimination and feminist opposition to violence against women. The issue of sexual harassment brought together two of contemporary women's deepest, most troubling concerns—their desires for an unbiased workplace and their fears of male sexual aggression. Activists within the women's movement formed two organizations that focused primarily on sexual harassment in employment and that were heavily responsible for generating public awareness of sexual harassment in the 1970s—Working Women United (WWU) in Ithaca, New York, and the Alliance Against Sexual Coercion (AASC) in Cambridge, Massachusetts. The founders of these organizations were influenced by the early lawsuits, and, in turn, their success in raising awareness of sexual harassment buttressed the appeals in these cases. These new organizations not only relied on existing organizations and networks but also generated new networks and framed the issue of sexual harassment as an important feminist issue.

The founders of WWU coined the term "sexual harassment" for the first speak-out on sexual harassment that they sponsored in May 1975. At the speak-out, they conducted the first survey showing that many women had experienced sexual harassment. The speak-out led to the first national press coverage of sexual harassment in August 1975, when the *New York Times* published an article that was syndicated nationally, appearing in more than a dozen newspapers around the country, including the *Philadelphia Bulletin* and the *Chicago Tribune*.[17] WWU members Susan Meyer and Karen Sauvigné later founded the Working Women's Institute (WWI), which relocated to New York City and continued the work of researching and publicizing the issue of sexual harassment. After co-sponsoring a speak-out in New York City with *Ms.* magazine, Meyer and Sauvigné began to appear regularly on television and radio shows, including *Good Morning America*, the *Phil Donahue Show*, and the *Mike Douglas Show*, and generated regular newspaper coverage on the issue as well.[18] WWI also began to provide legal referral services to women, and became a national clearinghouse for information on legal cases and research related to sexual harassment.[19]

The Alliance Against Sexual Coercion (AASC) was the other organization formed in the mid-1970s that made pioneering efforts to help victims of
sexual harassment and raise public awareness of the issue. AASC was a grass-
roots, service-oriented organization that grew out of the rape crisis movement and characterized sexual harassment as an issue of violence against
women. AASC was founded in Cambridge, Massachusetts, in June 1976, by
Freada Klein, Lynn Wehrli, and Elizabeth Cohn-Stuntz, each of whom had
extensive experience working on the issue of rape. AASC members published
prolifically on sexual harassment, including both resource materials and theoretical analyses. Many of the publications of AASC members placed sexual
harassment within a broader critique of capitalism, patriarchy, and racism.[20]

The groundbreaking efforts of WWU and AASC spurred a movement
that by the end of the 1970s would proliferate around the country and would
challenge sexual exploitation in the workplace. Feminist activism in the mid-
1970s created physical and intellectual spaces for women to speak out about
sexual coercion on the job. Similar to abortion, rape, and domestic violence,
speaking out about sexual harassment legitimized women's feelings of violation. Naming "sexual harassment" created a cognitive category that made
the conduct visible, enabling women to share their pain and express their
outrage. Activists drew upon the theories of various social movements of the
day to analyze sexual coercion in the workplace and to articulate the phenomenon as an important feminist issue. Using feminist theories on rape,
legal theories of race and sex discrimination in employment, as well as feminist critiques of patriarchy, racism, and capitalism, they argued that sexual
harassment was a form of male domination and amounted to sex discrimination in the workplace. They also drew upon feminist theory advocating for
women's sexual autonomy and right to control their bodies.

The issue resonated with women because it spoke to the changing reality
of women's lives. Women were more likely to find themselves in the workplace and more likely to be dependent on their income for survival because of
the changing economic and demographic landscape. The country was shifting from a manufacturing-based economy that could provide jobs paying a
family wage to a service-based economy with many lower-paying jobs and
opportunities for women. Demographic factors also contributed to women's
increasing participation in the workplace—older age at first marriage, fewer
children, increasing likelihood of divorce, and higher rates of single parenthood. These factors, paired with an increasing standard of living and greater
consumption expectations, meant that women were more likely to be in the
workplace and were more likely to depend on their income from their par-

ticipation in the labor force. This new reality of women's lives directly conflicted with traditional attitudes toward women in the workplace—that they were working for pin money and not supporting a family—as well as attitudes that sexualized women. In the context of the civil rights and women's movements of the day, which advocated for justice and equal opportunities for all, as well as the sexual revolution that affirmed the right of an individual to sexual autonomy, the issue of sexual harassment in the workplace resonated deeply with women. For women of color, whose experiences of racism had often been sexualized, the new civil rights framework became an opportunity to resist both racism and sexism in the workplace.

The strength of this emerging movement grew from its diversity, which provided a range of resources to the effort. Women working in different parts of the women's movements participated—feminists with backgrounds in radical feminism and the lesbian rights movement, the more liberal National Organization of Women, the anti-rape movement and socialist feminism, as well as the civil rights movement. Bringing to the issue a rich mix of backgrounds, perspectives, skills, and resources, these activists crafted a solid foundation for the movement against sexual harassment. Activists used the resources of the women's movements, publishing articles in feminist newsletters and magazines and using the growing network of rape crisis centers to spread the word. They used women's movement strategies, such as speak-outs, surveys, myth/fact sheets, and media work. They also used the fruits of the civil rights movement—civil rights law, racial harassment precedents, and equal employment opportunity offices. This combination of efforts proved to be a very effective means of legitimating the issue, motivating collective action, and raising awareness about sexual harassment. Increased awareness of the issue began to change public attitudes, and the attitudes of judges, about sexual coercion in the workplace. In the appeals of the early sexual harassment cases, feminist attorneys would build upon this increased awareness as they would attempt to convince judges that sexual harassment was illegal sex discrimination.

Legal Change

By the late 1970s, when federal circuit courts were hearing the appeals of the early cases denying sexual harassment claims, the climate was right for a change in court opinion. By then, feminists had succeeded in raising awareness of sexual harassment, developing stronger networks, and generating influential research and analysis of the issue, all of which contributed significantly to convincing courts that sexual harassment was a serious violation of women's civil rights. Feminist attorneys and activists had developed a network that could now support the women appealing their cases. The plaintiffs turned to feminist attorneys to represent them on appeal. Feminist attorneys working on these early cases and activists against sexual harassment shared information, discussed strategy, exchanged briefs, and gave one another moral support. The challenge for this informal network of feminist attorneys and activists was to convince courts that sexual harassment was not a personal problem but a serious barrier to women's equal employment opportunity. To do so, feminists made not only legal arguments but also economic, sociological, and historical arguments in their appellate briefs. Their arguments drew upon feminist research showing that sexual harassment was a widespread and devastating phenomenon that denied women equal employment opportunity. They also drew upon feminist theory, arguing that sexual harassment was not merely an individual injury but group-based discrimination that harmed all women by reinforcing women's subordinate status in the workplace. Catharine MacKinnon, for example, argued that sex segregation in the workplace and male control of hiring and firing made women systematically vulnerable to sexual harassment and was a mechanism by which men retained dominance over women in the workplace.[21] Another important strategy that plaintiffs used to frame sexual harassment as sex discrimination was to analogize sexual harassment to racial harassment.

Feminists' efforts, growing media coverage of the issue, and the more progressive makeup of the appellate courts ultimately led to victory for each of the plaintiffs of the early sexual harassment cases. In overturning every case that denied relief and ruling in favor of the sexually harassed women, appellate courts agreed that Title VII prohibited *quid pro quo* sexual harassment, where a supervisor fires a subordinate employee for refusing to comply with sexual advances. In addition to the workplace cases, a district court ruled for the first time in *Alexander v. Yale*[22] that federal law prohibited *quid pro quo* sexual harassment at educational institutions. These landmark rulings resulted from the joint efforts of individual women filing suits and collective activism against sexual harassment.

Feminist arguments convinced the courts to take the issue seriously and treat workplace sexual harassment as sex discrimination. With several federal circuit courts of appeals having affirmed the basic principle that sexual harassment was sex discrimination, no further courts ruled against sexual harassment plaintiffs on this basic principle. In just a few years feminists had overcome significant negative precedent on the issue of sexual harassment. By the end of the 1970s, while the Supreme Court had yet to rule on the issue, courts across the country had established the basic principle that Title VII held employers responsible if they tolerated sexual demands made by supervisory employees of their subordinates who then suffered tangible harm, such as termination or denial of a promotion.

The scope of the early sexual harassment decisions, however, was narrow. They covered only *quid pro quo* sexual harassment—where a supervisor fires a subordinate employee who has refused his sexual advances. Several courts held that harassment resulting in intangible harm, such as a hostile working atmosphere, was not sex discrimination. This narrow definition of sexual harassment was soon challenged by women working in nontraditional, blue-collar fields. Women working in construction, mining, and other traditionally male occupations began to raise concerns about what came to be known as hostile environment sexual harassment, the new frontier of sexual harassment activism.

Expanding Definitions of Sexual Harassment

In the late 1970s, while feminist activism was raising public awareness of sexual harassment and appellate courts were ruling in favor of victims, women were breaking down occupational barriers. Antidiscrimination laws and the resulting affirmative action programs encouraged more women to enter traditionally male-dominated workplaces and occupations. As women began breaking into these masculine domains, they experienced a range of harassing behavior. Much of the harassment consisted of sexual graffiti, dirty jokes, repeated propositioning, and even sexual assault. But often the harassment experienced by women in nontraditional occupations had nothing to do with sexual behavior but was an attempt to discourage women from staying in the trades because they were taking a "man's" job. Women were subject to isolation, work sabotage, severe verbal abuse, and physical violence.

In response, women working in construction, coal mining, fire fighting, law enforcement, and other nontraditional occupations across the country organized against sexual harassment. As with the African American women who brought many of the first sexual harassment cases, the working environments, backgrounds, and identities of blue-collar women in male-dominated fields shaped their experiences of sexual harassment and their strategies and resources for addressing the problem. Through unions and employee associations, blue-collar women urged courts and policy makers to broaden their definitions of sexual harassment to include not just sexual demands by a supervisor of a subordinate employee but also hostile environment harassment—when supervisors or coworkers create a hostile working environment through sexual or nonsexual behavior aimed at creating an intimidating or offensive environment for women. This activism occurred simultaneously, but usually independently, from other anti-sexual harassment activism until the very end of the 1970s, when activists converged in Washington to testify about sexual harassment before Congress.

When blue-collar women joined the growing chorus of voices speaking out against sexual harassment, they spoke with a distinct voice and made a distinct contribution to the growing movement against sexual harassment. Building on feminist understandings of sexual harassment, blue-collar women articulated their experiences of harassment—coworkers' misogynist, often violent, behavior designed to push women out of traditionally male fields. They reframed this behavior as a form of sexual harassment, arguing that this behavior violated women's civil rights. Blue-collar women urged courts and federal policy makers to broaden their understanding of sexual harassment beyond *quid pro quo* sexual harassment to include sexual harassment arising from a hostile environment. They also urged feminist activists to include the issue of hostile environment harassment in their advocacy work. Working individually, or in local and regional groups such as Women in Trades in Seattle, Women Working in Construction in Washington D.C., the Coal Employment Project in Oak Ridge, Tennessee, the Chicana Service Action Center in Los Angeles, and in unions, grass-roots activists collaborated with feminist attorneys in national organizations such as the League of Women Voters in Washington D.C., Equal Rights Advocates in San Francisco, and NOW Legal Defense and Education Fund in New York City. Although working-class women did not always share the same concerns as middle-class feminists, sexual harassment was an issue of cross-class concern that generated collaborative activism among women.[23]

To combat sexual harassment, blue-collar women engaged in many of the same strategies used by activists in Ithaca, Cambridge, and Washington, D.C., such as surveys, newsletters, speak-outs, and support groups. But working-class women were able to draw upon other resources available to them as a result of their status as members of unions and employee associations, and they used the resources of these organizations to advance their agendas. They also took advantage of the political opportunities provided by newly formed governmental agencies to protect civil rights, such as the Kentucky Human Rights Commission, or progressive Carter appointees in the Department of Labor who were committed to advancing affirmative action and sympathetic individuals in the federal government, like Alexis Herman of the Women's

Bureau. In these ways, blue-collar women working in male-dominated fields influenced the development of public policy on sexual harassment. Their activism led to the first federal regulations on sexual harassment in 1977.[24] Blue-collar women won several precedent-setting hostile environment sexual harassment lawsuits, thereby establishing legal prohibitions against this conduct.[25] By sharing stories that clearly demonstrated the fundamentally abusive nature of sexual harassment, blue-collar women significantly enhanced public understanding of sexual harassment—that it was motivated not by sexual desire but by men's desire to keep women subordinate in the workplace, and therefore was a serious problem that harmed women on the job. By raising the issue in new contexts and pushing to broaden the scope of sexual harassment, blue-collar women contributed significantly to building a persuasive argument that sexual harassment was a serious civil rights issue that government policy makers should address. This broader articulation of the issue also contributed toward expanding participation in the movement. More and more women around the country were working on the issue of sexual harassment.

By 1979 this groundswell of concern caught the attention of Congressman James Hanley, Chairman of the Subcommittee on Investigations of the House Post Office and Civil Service Committee, who called the first congressional hearings on sexual harassment in the federal workplace, hearings that would lead to several powerful government initiatives against sexual harassment. A broad array of women's organizations, including feminist groups, labor unions, and organizations representing women of color and blue-collar women, participated in public hearings and submitted comments on policy proposals. These activists helped shape the public discussion and developing government policy on sexual harassment. Government officials usually took the issue seriously, expressing strong disapproval and developing remedies for victims of sexual harassment. As a result of the hearings, the Equal Employment Opportunity Commission (EEOC) proposed and passed sweeping guidelines prohibiting both *quid pro quo* and hostile environment sexual harassment, setting a high standard by which the issue would be framed in the coming years.

The movement was also able to mobilize the resources of the Merit System Protection Board and the Office of Personnel and Management to conduct the first large-scale scientific study of sexual harassment as well as develop and disseminate model sexual harassment policies and training curriculum to public and private employers around the country. Activists also successfully lobbied state and local governmental bodies to act on the issue.

Throughout the 1980s feminist activists were integrally involved in the development of sexual harassment jurisprudence, participating in all the precedent-setting sexual harassment cases. The powerful collaboration of diverse constituencies working against sexual harassment peaked at two points in the 1980s—in efforts to preserve the EEOC guidelines in 1981 when the Reagan administration tried to overturn them and in broad support of the plaintiff Mechelle Vinson in the first Supreme Court sexual harassment case. In 1980, when Reagan took office, his attempt to deregulate business included efforts to overturn or weaken the EEOC sexual harassment guidelines. Feminists organized a public outcry in opposition to changing the guidelines, which successfully thwarted these attempts.

In 1986 the Supreme Court finally spoke on the issue of sexual harassment in the case of *Meritor Savings Bank v. Vinson*. Feminist organizations filed many *amicus curiae* briefs in the case, urging the court to adopt broad prohibitions of sexual harassment. The plaintiff in the case, Mechelle Vinson, was an African American woman who accused an African American man of sexually harassing and abusing her when she worked for him as a teller in a bank where he was the manager. Notably the EEOC, chaired at the time by Clarence Thomas, supported the defendant in the case, reversing the agency's previous support for broad protections against sexual harassment. A few years later, in 1991, when Thomas was nominated to the Supreme Court, he was accused of sexual harassment by Anita Hill, who had been an employee of his at the EEOC in the early 1980s. The televised confirmation hearings of Thomas contributed significantly to public awareness of sexual harassment and led to an explosion of sexual harassment claims at the EEOC in the 1990s. The Supreme Court, in *Vinson*, ruled against Thomas's position, holding that Title VII prohibited sexual harassment, including both *quid pro quo* and hostile environment harassment. The Court, however, erected several obstacles to obtaining relief, most notably rejecting the lower court's ruling that employers were strictly liable for sexual harassment by supervisors. As sexual harassment increasingly came to dominate the headlines in the 1990s, the courts continued to struggle with an array of legal questions left open by this decision.[26]

Conclusion: Victories and Remaining Battles

The victory in *Meritor Savings Bank v. Vinson* was the crowning achievement of the early movement against sexual harassment. Whereas at the beginning of the 1980s only a few lower courts had ruled in women's favor on cases involving the most extreme factual scenarios, by the end of the 1980s federal law had significantly developed, and employers and educational institutions paid serious attention to the issue. Courts expanded the definition of sexual harassment to include hostile environment harassment and held employers liable for tolerating coworker harassment. By the end of the 1980s women had significantly more legal protection against sexual harassment than they had had at the beginning of the 1980s, and the movement had achieved victory before the highest court in the land. The Supreme Court's decision in *Meritor Savings Bank v. Vinson* paved the way for sexual harassment to become the high-profile issue that repeatedly brandished newspaper headlines in the 1990s. The decision was a turning point for the movement against sexual harassment. With a Supreme Court stamp of approval, the movement shifted from localized struggles in a variety of arenas to a more specialized, legalized, national effort with new women's organizations and actors joining the movement. Sexual harassment advocacy became a mainstay of the women's movement, nestled into the leading feminist organizations as one of the core issues, and fully integrated into the agendas of equal employment opportunity agencies and offices of federal and state governments, as well as private employers.

The strength of the movement against sexual harassment stemmed from its racial and economic diversity. We hear a lot about the participation of white middle-class women in the second wave of the women's movement, but less appreciated is the activism of women of color and working-class women who made critical contributions to women's expanding rights, especially in the fight for laws prohibiting sexual harassment. African American women were critical contributors to the movement against sexual harassment, acting both individually and collectively to combat sexual coercion on the job and at educational institutions. Racist and sexist stereotypes melded in the harassment directed toward African American women, giving them a particularly clear understanding of the discriminatory nature of sexual overtures in the workplace. Informed by a history of race discrimination and sexual abuse, these women did not mistake sexual harassment for harmless flirtation. Drawing on the ideas and resources of the civil rights community, African American women filed the first precedent-setting cases under Title VII, thereby setting the prevailing framework within which sexual harassment law developed. Sexual harassment law also grew out of the activism of people of color by building on racial harassment precedent in the law. Similarly the background and identities of working-class women, both white and black, shaped their experiences of sexual harassment and their activism. Women working in male-dominated, blue-collar fields like mining and construction experienced male hostility to their presence that often took the form not only of sexual abuse but also of physical violence in order to push them out of male-dominated workplaces. Working through unions and employee associations, these women urged courts and policymakers to broaden their definitions of sexual harassment beyond a supervisor's sexual demands of a subordinate employee to include hostile environment harassment. The activism of women of color and working-class women fundamentally shaped public policy on sexual harassment in the United States.

Prohibitions on sexual harassment led to sexual harassment training in workplaces across the country, raising the issue with thousands of people in a broad range of occupations. These training workshops provided a forum to discuss women's status in the workplace, gender roles, and sexual stereotypes. In this training women's right to participate in the workplace on an equal footing with men was assumed, challenging traditional and persisting notions that women were not serious participants in the workplace. By the 1990s most employers had policies against harassment, and many offered training to sensitize workers. Women were challenging sexual harassment across the country in a broad range of occupations and sometimes even winning large verdicts in sexual harassment cases. Through these successes, the movement had come a long way in achieving its goal of claiming the right of women to enter the public sphere, both political spaces as well as workplaces and schools. The movement achieved social change not only by achieving legal changes through court houses and legislatures, but also by achieving cultural changes in workplaces and educational institutions. The movement raised consciousness about women's right to enter the workplace and function there free from sexual coercion and molestation. Women are no longer outsiders or interlopers but have a central place in these institutions—a shift for which the movement against sexual harassment deserves significant credit.

This success, however, is tempered by the continuing high rates of sexual harassment and the persisting stereotypes used against women who resist harassment. Rates of sexual harassment are similar to what they were twenty-five years ago when reliable studies of the phenomenon first appeared.[27] The public/private sphere ideology that historically justified and reinforced male dominance and that undergirded courts' early denials of sexual harassment claims continues to shape public discussion of sexual harassment. For example, both Clarence Thomas and Bill Clinton refused to answer questions in sexual harassment investigations by claiming their right to privacy.[28] The issue is often still seen as a matter of private sexual conduct, not abuse of power. Long-standing stereotypes blaming women for sexual harassment or accusing them of lying about it, existing from the earliest days of this country's history, still plague women who bring accusations of sexual harassment.

According to political science professor Gwendolyn Mink, women com-plaining of sexual harassment face a "regime of disbelief."[29] Powerful biases against women continued to shape public opinion and court opinions on sexual harassment.

Furthermore, the conceptualization of sexual harassment primarily as a legal claim, and, in particular, as a claim of sex discrimination, placed the issue squarely within a highly contentious adversarial framework that often has not led to satisfactory solutions to the problem, especially for women who do not have the resources to use the legal system. The bureaucratic and legalistic procedures for addressing sexual harassment are often slow, costly, and contentious, and women have often felt victimized again by these pro-cesses. Although employers are providing training on sexual harassment, many are motivated more out of concerns for liability rather than the integra-tion of women into the workplace. Some employers use the fear of litigation to justify draconian policies that control workers' behavior.[30] Workers often resent the threat of lawsuits and the close oversight of employers seeking to avoid liability. The framing of the issue as a legal question narrowed the stra-tegic options available to women resisting sexual coercion in the workplace, leaving many women without recourse.

Early feminist activists did not achieve their larger goal of undermining the system of dominance that produced sexual harassment. The founders of WWI and AASC had viewed sexual harassment as part of a larger struggle against sexism, classism, and racism, and they understood sexual harass-ment to be symptomatic of a deeply flawed patriarchal, capitalist, and racist system. They hoped to use the issue to inspire collective action to fight the root causes of injustice and transform society. In arguing that sexual harass-ment was sex discrimination, they conceptualized sexual harassment as a group harm. They argued that sexual harassment harmed not just individual women but women as a class by reinforcing sex segregation and subordina-tion of women in the workforce. By focusing on employer liability for sexual harassment, feminists attempted to address this harm to women.

Despite this approach, individualized solutions to sexual harassment came to dominate the movement's agenda. As has been true in other areas, the legal remedies were a valuable tool for individuals seeking relief from sexual harassment, but they undermined collective efforts that might have led to deeper societal transformation and reached the root causes of sexual harassment in society. Despite feminist hopes to challenge broader injustices in America, liberal legal gains eclipsed these radical hopes in the 1980s. The movement against sexual harassment shifted away from collective protest and toward individual legal solutions to sexual harassment. Although legal solutions have offered much, and the possibility of class action suits is promising,[31] they have left in place the basic societal structure that allows sexual harassment to continue. Nevertheless, sexual harassment law did challenge social norms and has provided an avenue of relief for many women who have experienced unwanted sexual behavior in the workplace and in educational settings. By transforming what was considered a private indignity into a federal civil rights violation, sexual harassment activism is an important example of how women exercised agency and created social change through the law.

NOTES

This essay is drawn from Carrie N. Baker, The Women's Movement against Sexual Harassment (2008).

1. Harriet Jacobs, Incidents in the Life of a Slave Girl 27 (Jean Fagan Yellin ed. 1987).

2. Louisa May Alcott, *How I Went Out to Service*, The Independent, June 4, 1874, at 1.

3. John D'Emilio and Estelle B. Freedman, Intimate Matters: A History of Sexuality in America 12–13 (1988); *see also* Julia Cherry Spruill, Women's Life and Work in the Southern Colonies 321–22 (1972).

4. Spruill, 322.

5. Kerry Segrave, The Sexual Harassment of Women in the Workplace, 1600–1993, 20–21 (1994); Herbert G. Gutman, The Black Family in Slavery and Freedom, 1750–1925, 393, 399 (1976).

6. Martin v. Jansen, 193 P. 674 (Wash. 1920).

7. Mary Bularzik, *Sexual Harassment at the Workplace*, Radical America, June–July 1978, at 36.

8. *Id.*

9. 4 Life and Labor, Aug. 1914, at 242 (publication of the National Women's Trade Union League).

10. Maud Nathan, The Story of an Epoch-Making Movement 15–16 (1926).

11. *Striking Flint: Genora Dollinger Remembers the 1937 Sitdown* (oral history interview by Susan Rosenthal in February 1995), *in* Sol Dollinger and Genora Johnson Dollinger, Not Automatic: Women and the Left in the Forging of the Auto Workers' Union 124 (2000).

12. Barnes v. Train, 13 Fed. Empl. Prac. Cas. 123 (D.D.C. 1974), *rev'd sub nom*, Barnes v. Costle, 561 F.2d 983 (D.C. Cir. 1977); Corne v. Bausch and Lomb, 390 F. Supp. 161 (D. Ariz. 1975), *vacated and remanded*, 562 F.2d 55 (9th Cir. 1977), *cert. denied*, 434 U.S. 956 (1977); Garber v. Saxon Business Products, 14 Empl. Prac. Dec. 7587 (E.D. Va. 1976), *rev'd and remanded*, 552 F.2d 1032 (4th Cir. 1977); Williams v. Saxbe, 413 F. Supp. 654 (D.D.C. 1976), *rev'd in part and vacated in part, sub nom.* Williams v. Bell, 587 F.2d 1240 (D.C. Cir. 1978); Miller v. Bank of America, 418 F. Supp. 233 (N.D. Cal. 1976), *rev'd*, 600 F.2d 211 (9th Cir. 1979); Tompkins v. Public Service Electric and Gas Company, 422 F. Supp. 553 (D.N.J. 1976), *rev'd*, 568 F.2d 1044 (3rd Cir. 1977).

13. *Barnes*, 13 FEP at 124.

14. *Corne*, 390 F. Supp. at 163.

15. *Barnes*, 13 FEP at 124.

16. *Corne*, 390 F. Supp. at 163.

17. Enid Nemy, *Women Begin to Speak Out against Sexual Harassment at Work*, N.Y. Times, Aug. 19, 1975, at 38.

18. 1979 Annual Program Report and Audited Financial Statement, *Sauvigné Papers*; *Phil Donahue Show: Sexual Harassment on the Job* (with Susan Meyer and Karen Sauvigné 1977) (Films for the Humanities and Sciences, Princeton, N.J., 1988); telephone interview with Susan Meyer, Feb. 17, 2001.

19. Working Women's Institute Archives, Barnard Center for Research on Women, New York); telephone interview with Karen Sauvigné (Feb. 4, 2001); Speak-out on Sexual Harassment of Women at Work, May 4, 1975, Ithaca, N.Y., *in* Karen Sauvigné Papers, Brooklyn, N.Y. Private Collection.

20. Lynn Wehrli, *Sexual Harassment at the Workplace: A Feminist Analysis and Strategy for Social Change* (Master's thesis, Massachusetts Institute of Technology, 1976); *Rochelle Lefkowitz, Help for the Sexually Harassed: A Grass-Roots Model*, Ms., Nov. 1977, at 49; Alliance Against Sexual Coercion, *Sexual Harassment at the Workplace* (1977); Martha Hooven & Freada Klein, *Is Sexual arassment Legal?* Aegis, Sept.–Oct. 1978, at 28.

21. Catharine MacKinnon, Sexual Harassment of Working Women 156–58, 174–92 (1979).

22. Alexander v. Yale University, 631 F.2d 178 (2d Cir. 1980).

23. Susan M. Hartmann, The Other Feminists: Activists in the Liberal Establishment 46–52 (2000).

24. Public Contracts and Property Management, 42 Fed. Reg. 41381 (1977) (codified at 41 C.F.R. pt. 60) (proposed on Aug. 16, 1977).

25. *See, e.g.* Continental Can Company v. Minnesota, 297 N.W.2d 241, 246 (Minn. 1980); Bundy v. Jackson, 641 F.2d 934 (D.C. Cir. 1981).

26. 477 U.S. 57 (1986).

27. See Darius Chan et al., *Examining the Job-related, Psychological, and Physical Outcomes of Workplace Sexual Harassment: A Meta-analytic Review*, 32 Psych. of Women Q. 362, 362–76 (Dec. 2008).

28. Mary F. Rogers, *Clarence Thomas, Patriarchal Discourse and Public/Private Spheres*, 39 Soc. Q. 289, 289–308 (1998).

29. Gwendolyn Mink, Hostile Environment: The Political Betrayal of Sexually Harassed Women 77, 115 (2000).

30. *See* Vicki Schultz, *The Sanitized Workplace*, 112 Yale L.J. 2061, 2063–93 (2003).

31. Jenson v. Eveleth Taconite, 842 F. Supp. 847 (1993), 130 F.3d 1287 (8th Cir. 1997).

13

Ledbetter's Continuum

Race, Gender, and Pay Discrimination

EILEEN BORIS

She became the living embodiment of the slogan "equal pay for equal work," campaigning across America during the 2009 presidential election to ensure that other women never would experience wage discrimination without legal remedy. For nearly twenty years Lilly Ledbetter received less pay than men who held the same floor manager job for the Gadsden, Alabama, branch of Goodyear Tire and Rubber Company. Wages depended on performance ratings, and she had long suspected prejudicial evaluations because of her sex, but she only discovered the gap between her monthly earnings and those of the lowest compensated man when she saw the pay stub of another in the late 1990s. Ledbetter sought a determination of discrimination from the Equal Employment Opportunity Commission (EEOC) in 1998 and, a year later, brought suit in federal district court under Title VII of the Civil Rights Act. Offering compelling evidence that merit evaluations could not account for the gap between her pay and that of male managers, she won $360,000 in compensatory damages as well as court costs. On appeal, the Eleventh Circuit sided with Goodyear and the Supreme Court affirmed its reasoning: Lilly Ledbetter waited too long to seek redress by filing her complaint more than 180 days after the initial discriminatory act.[1]

The subject of *Ledbetter* was sex discrimination but, in narrowly construing the rules for bringing charges to EEOC, the Court potentially restricted antidiscrimination law as a whole and in ways with consequences for suits involving race. That a case involving unfair treatment because of sex upended restitution against harms on the basis of race represents just the latest twist in the tangled relation between race and sex in law and social policy. For even when law addresses only race or gender, the other category exists as a ghostly other, impacted even if silent, though not necessarily affected in the same way. An intersectional perspective—one that considers identity as a composite of multiple characteristics whose interaction with one another produces a whole distinct from a mere addition of one identity to another—suggests that we must look at race, gender, and discrimination together. The standard story of antidiscrimination in the workplace moves from the Fair Employment Practices Commission (FEPC) of the World War II era to Title VII of the Civil Rights Act of 1964. Sex discrimination stands as an afterthought to the main action, while discrimination in hiring and promotion represents the central focus. Rather than a component of fair employment, equal pay had its own trajectory. As a narrow alternative to the Equal Rights Amendment (ERA), it became part of the Fair Labor Standards Act in 1963. In this chapter *Ledbetter v. Goodyear Tire and Rubber Co.*, and its subsequent legislative redress through the 2009 Lilly Ledbetter Fair Pay Act, are contextualized by revisiting the history of fair employment and equal pay. Turning back to World War II, it is clear that equal pay, like fair employment, belonged to an understanding of civil rights that included labor standards: worker rights were civil rights. Equal pay was a component of labor law, part of the social rights central to the welfare state.

What constituted fairness or equality was hardly self-evident. Did equality mean identical labor, or might it refer to comparable labor? How would performance on a job be measured and by whose standards? What constituted comparable worth between jobs in a world of occupational segmentation by race and gender or, to conceptualize in an intersectional way, by racialized gender? When it came to equal pay for women, race served as the subaltern category: under the radar but present from its absence. Sex, in turn, was the silent, if not suppressed, category in race-based fair employment. The embodiment of workers provided rationales for lower pay scales for those not classified as white or male, or both. This identitarian framework also shaped evaluation of the worth of labor that both crept into standardized measurements of the job and offered objectivity in light of the racialized gendered organization of social life—reproduction as well as production—coloring such evaluations.[2]

Development of Fair Employment and Sex-Based Equal Pay

In their World War II origins fair employment and equal pay stood apart in relation to the problem of discrimination. During the war a pattern developed that divided race from sex discrimination, with the FEPC taking cases related to the first, and women workers left to plead through the federal Women's Bureau. Fair employment came out of the freedom struggle of African Americans to end Jim Crow practices, using federal contracts as the basis to oppose white exclusion of black workers from jobs in the better-paying defense industries. Sex-based equal pay developed from efforts to maintain the rate for the job for white male industrial workers, though women in the labor movement and the Women's Bureau embraced this measure to gain equity in the workplace. The first offered relief to women not as women but only if they faced exclusion from employment on the basis of their race, religion, or nationality. The second focused on the plight of industrial workers, from which most black women were excluded.[3]

As a response to the March on Washington movement and its mobilization against fascism and empire abroad, and against Jim Crow at home, Franklin D. Roosevelt issued Executive Order 8802 in June 1941, creating the Fair Employment Practices Commission. This order covered African Americans and other racial minorities, Jews and other religious minorities, and non-citizens or those not of U.S. nationality—however, most cases involved African Americans.[4] Although "sex" was absent from FEPC's mandate, discrimination wore a gendered face; harms against black or Latina women on the basis of their racialized gender lay outside its purview, as did wrongs to white women.[5]

The disassociation of fair employment from women took multiple forms. Barriers stemming from the sexual division within the household lay outside the FEPC's jurisdiction. It justified refusal to investigate discriminatory hiring at a child-care center on the basis that child care was not directly part of the war effort. Yet, without child care, women were unable to hold defense jobs. Consider this an early example of "family responsibilities discrimination," the foundation to problems that women like Ledbetter would face into our own day.[6] When black men gained positions over black women, there was no racial discrimination and so no redress. Assumptions about womanhood with racial overtones pervaded discriminatory placements on the job but also remained outside FEPC's mandate. Drawing upon the stereotype of the fat black woman, for example, a Kaiser personnel manager explained, "that black women were too large to climb, walk around, and get into difficult positions and places."[7] The reasoning of FEPC examiners could be circuitous: "the Union was actually concerned because of the job assignment, and in this instance, there was no discrimination between white and colored women" because the job became "racial only to the extent that only Negro women worked" in the janitorial department.[8] Such reasoning separated fair employment doctrine from sex discrimination.

White male–dominated trade unions created obstacles to fair employment but sought to use equal pay for their own advantage. During World War I "equal pay for equal work" stood along with the prohibition of night work, the safeguarding of state labor laws for women, and protection from hazardous occupations as ways to enhance the war effort while protecting women in industry.[9] Efficiency, along with the need to maintain wages, shaped support for equal pay. Equal pay would maintain "standards" established by unions. It would protect men, their jobs, and wage structure—and disproportionately these men were white industrial workers. Equal pay might not break down occupational segmentation by sex or race, and it offered employers an excuse to reject hiring women if those employers doubted women's worth. It was fair, not just.[10]

World War II advanced the idea of equal pay. Here the activism of white labor feminists paid off. They had fought for equal pay since the 1910s and gained an entry into government with the establishment of the U.S. Women's Bureau in 1920. The Women's Bureau's Mary Anderson took credit for shaping the National War Labor Board's (NWLB) determinations on equal pay, including General Order No. 16 of November 1943, which promulgated "equal pay for comparable quantity and quality of work on comparable operations."[11] This order was more narrowly construed then those ringing words suggest: it applied to jobs currently performed by both sexes, to those previously done by men, for which employers were apt to lower the piece rate when assigned to women, and to jobs that employers rearranged when women took them over in order to downgrade the jobs' worth. It did not extend to wage setting between plants or jobs within a plant and thus could not address low rates on "women's work."[12] Most women actually labored at sex-segmented occupations that never came under any equal pay mandate. For the first half of 1943 a demonstrable gap existed between the presence of corporate equal pay policy and the hiring of women at the same entry rate as equally inexperienced men.[13]

Employers claimed that differences in the environment of production justified varying rates for the job, citing welfare capitalist amenities as well as protective labor laws.[14] In the 1943 *Bendix* case, the NWLB held that "sex differentials in wage rates could be allowed where women took over men's jobs and were given rest periods which men had not been given."[15] Leading war contractor General Motors considered the provision of "a hot plate, a cot, several rocking chairs, and a mirror" in the women's bathroom as factors increasing production costs. Some employers removed women from a building rather than install separate facilities, and others indirectly took the cost out of women's paychecks by lowering the rate for jobs performed by women.[16]

The corporate imagination fixated on toilets—those sites of physicality, bodily functions, and dirt—as did Southern opponents of fair employment who objected to black and white women sharing the same bathroom facilities. In separating blacks from whites, black women could no longer appear as women but became classified as black, thus degrading their womanhood. In such cases, as at one Midwestern plant, black men and women, who composed the janitorial staff, used the same single toilet and sink. At other companies, white women refused to share toilets with black women, whom they rejected as dirty and diseased. Sometimes management drew upon such prejudices to explain hiring patterns; telephone companies justified judging black women as unsuitable operators "because of the intimate nature of the work, the close cooperation necessitated by the crews on the switch boards." Enough incidents occurred when white women actually stopped production over the toilet question to lend credibility to such claims.[17]

In defending equal pay, Michigan circuit judge Charles Hayden rejected the politics of the toilet. In a May 1942 case that awarded the first back pay under Michigan's equal pay statute, he rejected the argument that "the operation of statute is to be avoided by any difference in the appointment of toilets."[18] Neither did he find that the differential provision of rest breaks changed the nature of the work, because "the women had to turn out the same quantity and quality of work as the men." Indeed, they trained the men. At the Oldsmobile plant under contention, management attached quotas to machines, no matter whether a woman or a man ran them. At issue was whether the work was "substantially alike." Judge Hayden concluded "that any differentiation urged as between the employment of men and women upon the record as made exists only in theory, rather than in fact; in form rather than in substance," and, for all intents, equal work begot unequal pay on the basis of sex.[19]

Passed in 1931, Michigan's law was one of two at the start of the war.[20] Covering manufacturing alone, its reach extended only to production for which men were "similarly employed" or had previously performed. The law embodied biological and social understandings of female difference as manifested through the female body by demanding that women only work at tasks appropriate "to her strength" and beneficial to morals, health, and "potential capacity for motherhood."[21] In 1946 seven states had equal pay laws; none of them, however, covered agriculture or domestic service, where women of color predominated, and none had the same wording. By 1953, after a period when Congress actively considered various equal pay bills, thirteen states—including the major industrial states—had enacted some kind of statute. The number grew to twenty-two by the passage of the federal law in 1963.[22]

Like earlier protective labor laws, questions of health and physical capability pervaded the debate over equal pay. References to women's skills conveyed gender stereotypes, with labor and management alike speaking of "delicate and careful touch, manual dexterity . . . quickness of hand and brain."[23] Employers drew upon similar understandings of female bodies to argue against equal pay. GM characteristically claimed that "it is not possible to assign to a woman all the duties that over a period of time can be assigned to a male janitor because of her physical capacity."[24] Yet the NWLB rejected "the fictions and the fallacies which have arisen from certain facts of female physiology," including the notion that menstruation curtailed female efficiency.[25]

In the minds of critics, "service to their families" and engaging in "personal services for themselves" defined women, which led them, but not men, to miss work. But the Women's Bureau explained greater absenteeism from the job in the social terms of "unfavorable plant conditions" as well as home responsibilities. The single as well as the married had "household duties to perform"—"necessary work" that took longer with wartime overcrowding and transportation delays. Child care proved a major barrier, as did care for the sick, but plants that provided aid in finding child care or on-site care had lower absenteeism rates. Industry, the Bureau argued, would have to accommodate so women could meet familial responsibilities and still perform on the job. The solution was to reconfigure the workplace, not punish the worker.[26]

Purchasing power arguments also justified equal pay. The social welfare version saw equal pay as a buttress against dependency. For rates "lower than for men we set in motion the whole vicious cycle of substandard existence."[27] The macroeconomic version emphasized overall growth. Claude Pepper (D-Florida) and Wayne Morse (R-Oregon), the original sponsors of equal pay bills during the 1940s, linked "full production, full employment and full purchasing power" to equal pay.[28] In this Keynesian formulation, welfare and growth reinforced each other.

Entrance of married women into the war plants partially undermined assumptions that women workers had others to support them. But the status of wage-earning married women after the war generated a debate that was as disingenuous as some of the arguments for unequal pay. Traditionalists long had advocated "getting women out of employment when the war is over and seeing to it that the women do NOT get the same wage as a man who has a whole family of women at home to support."[29] But, as a Denver clubwoman explained in 1945, "it is a curious thing that when these issues arise, they relate only to the 'good' jobs. No one asks whether a scrub woman who cleans out offices in the middle of the night is married or single."[30] No one questioned the labor force participation of those who engaged in service work, in the occupations dominated especially by older women of color.

Industrial specialists, unionists, management, and government advocates debated how to determine wages. Would the rate follow from scientific evaluation of job components? Who would decide the value of a task? The Women's Bureau pushed for "an objective standard." It focused on "job content and not on the employees in the job," rejecting any system that separated "workers into two distinct groups, 'male' and 'female'" out of the assumption that sex had nothing to do with performance. But since women and men were rarely in the same jobs, the Bureau supported comparable work.[31]

The Women's Bureau's conclusion—"Equal pay without equal employment and job opportunities and an equitable determination of wages will not result in equal earnings"—also applied to discrimination on the basis of race.[32] The World War II Southport Petroleum Company case, which involved inequities between black and white men, saw the NWLB affirm "equal pay for equal work as 'one of the equal rights in the promise of American democracy regardless of color, race, sex, religion or national origin.'"[33] But a legacy of separation hung over the quest for equal pay. Only a few African American workers directly contacted the Bureau. For example, the Faithful Domestic Workers League of Nashville, Tennessee, a mixed-sex group of black cooks employed by a defense contractor, protested arbitrary pay rates, denial of equal pay, and other infringements of "human rights." The Women's Bureau replied with its standard form letter that reiterated the government's commitment to "the principle of Equal Pay" for all. When it came to the Maids of Dale Dormitory, who cleaned defense worker housing in Portsmouth, Virginia, the Bureau referred them to state remedies and asked the local YWCA to intervene: as domestic workers, the maids lacked federal protection even though their labor indirectly facilitated war production.[34]

Legislating Equal Pay and Fair Employment: Race and Gender

An exchange between Secretary of Labor W. Willard Wirtz and Congresswoman Edith Green (D-Oregon) at 1963 hearings on the Equal Pay Act captures the separated, albeit entwined, trajectories of race and sex in federal policy following World War II. Green was a labor feminist whose strong support of civil rights and opposition to the ERA would lead her in 1964 to vote against including "sex" in Title VII out of fear of both torpedoing the bill and toppling protective labor laws for women. But during hearings the previous year, she asked, "Why could not the word 'sex' also be written into" Executive Order 10925? That Executive Order of March 1961 created the President's Committee on Equal Employment Opportunity. Its purpose was to alleviate "discrimination because of race, creed, color, or national origin," the categories of the wartime FEPC. Green was impatient after having introduced equal pay bills for nine years and could see no reason not to amend the Executive Order while seeking the broader legislative remedy.

Wirtz's reply underscored how liberals believed, as the President's Commission on the Status of Women would report, that "discrimination on the basis of sex and the reasons for it are so different that a separate program is necessary to eliminate barriers to the employment and advancement of women."[35] He answered:

The two matters, without making any comparison between the degree of the seriousness they present, are sufficiently different that probably they warrant different treatment. . . . [T]here is more prejudice in our treatment of minority groups than there is in our treatment of women today . . . [W]e have matured in this area [treatment of women] more . . . so that we face now primarily a business matter of seeing to it that we remove a degree of discrimination which . . . is just a kind of carryover, and that it does not have the elements which are inherent in the minority situation.

Wirtz admitted, "The resultant discrimination may very well have an equivalence of effect," even if he refused to see sex discrimination as possessing "the same characteristic of . . . benightedness."[36] Modern racialism with its adherence to color blindness rejected biological difference when it came to race, but biology still distinguished women from men.[37]

The path to the 1963 Equal Pay Bill and the reenactment of FEPC through the stronger Title VII of the Civil Rights Act of 1964 rarely intermeshed. Between 1946 and 1963 Congress considered nearly twice the number of bills against employment discrimination (with only a few covering sex) than those for equal pay, 170 to 98. Both trajectories actually began with war's end. In 1944 liberals launched a campaign for a permanent FEPC, but southern congressmen filibustered even an extension of funding. Denying interference in the right of African Americans to work, supporters of states' rights insisted that a permanent FEPC meant the nationalization of business, with federal bureaucratization extending from economic to social relations.[38] Congressman Adam Clayton Powell proposed nondiscrimination in employment throughout the 1950s only to find his bills bottled up in various committees.

Sex entered the FEPC debate itself during the mid-1940s. Georgia Senator Richard Russell, a leading opponent of civil rights, suggested including age and sex in a voluntary FEPC. Most within the civil rights coalition dismissed "this chivalrous proposal." Before a major Women's Bureau conference in 1948, women from the United Auto Workers and Amalgamated Clothing Workers of America listed a sex-less FEPC among items, such as equal pay and fair labor standards, necessary for women in the postwar world. Some union women sought to ban sex as well as race discrimination in government contracts and state law, but when other supporters feared that adding "sex" would kill state FEPC legislation, they retreated. Part of the overall liberal agenda, fair employment remained identified with the industrial unions, the National Association for the Advancement of Colored People, and the American Jewish Congress.[39]

After the war the Women's Bureau closely tied the fate of equal pay to the elimination of other inequalities, especially toward "other minority groups."[40] Although alleviation of wrongs on the basis of sex remained separate from proposals to combat racial discrimination, Senator Claude Pepper modeled his proposed 1945 equal pay act "along the lines of the FEPC Bill."[41] That year the Senate Committee on Education and Labor reported out the Women's Equal Pay Act. It announced: "The status of women as citizens, whether or not they are gainfully employed, is dependent on their potential economic bargaining power." Without equal pay, women became "second class citizens."[42] In a few years the Cold War need for "womanpower" and concern with countering Soviet propaganda about "inequality of opportunity" fueled the demand for equal pay.[43]

The momentum to reward women for their contributions during World War II with equal pay dissipated quickly. Although there was no testimony against the 1945 bill, neither was there great enthusiasm within Congress. The bill was poorly drawn and had provocative provisions, like forbidding the discharge of women without cause during reconversion and placing enforcement with the Women's Bureau. These items quickly dropped out but delayed the bill's movement through the legislative process. This bill was the only one reported out of committee until 1962. Disagreements proliferated on enforcement mechanisms—the original took the quasi-judicial hearing from the National Labor Relations Act and industry committees from the Fair Labor Standards Act (FLSA), but Republicans wanted to lodge enforcement with Wage and Hour rather than establish a new division directly under the Secretary of Labor.[44]

In the late 1940s and early 1950s Robert Taft (R-Ohio) blocked the bill for expanding the federal bureaucracy. Explicit business opposition to legislative solutions, the temporary defection of the AFL, and Republican capture of the presidency with a subsequent redirection of the Women's Bureau further hampered the equal pay bill.[45] To gain passage in 1963 required narrowing coverage: the FLSA at that time excluded professional workers as well as domestic, agricultural, and many service laborers. As an African American businesswoman from Chicago complained, "I don't know why women laundry workers, etc., should continue to receive less pay than men." The final bill also spoke of "equal pay for equal work" rather than labor feminists' more expansive notion of "comparable work."[46]

Along the way opponents raised the old objections, for example, that women were more costly to employ because of their bodily limits or family needs and, in any case, their place was in the home. The century-long upward trajectory in women's participation in the labor force belied such a gender imaginary, while other social changes challenged, though hardly vanquished, the sexual division of labor. "Automation will invite women of relatively feeble physical strength into the labor market who will be able to do as well as any man no matter how muscular and even though he conforms to the Mr. Atlas type," predicted the AFL-CIO (American Federation of Labor and Congress of Industrial Organizations).[47] "Men and women should have full partnership in our economy, including equal job opportunities," Esther Peterson, the Assistant Secretary of Labor and Director of the Women's Bureau asserted in 1963.[48]

Supporters of equal pay had long drawn upon fair employment in mounting their case, despite liberal differentiation of race from sex discrimination, as we have seen. A few, like New York's powerful Democratic congressman Emanuel Celler, asserted that "distinctions based on sex have never been considered within the purview of [the] prohibition[s of] . . . the 14th amendment."[49] Nonetheless, in 1962, equal pay was initially part of that year's fair employment practices bill (HR 10144), which outlawed discrimination on the basis of race, religion, color, national origin, ancestry, age, and sex. The House Education and Labor Committee then removed sex discrimination to present a separate sex-based equal pay bill. While Southern opposition in the House Rules Committee blocked the fair employment bill, equal pay bills passed in both chambers, though the session ended before Congress could reconcile the different versions.[50]

Despite this uncoupling, supporters of equal pay still analogized their efforts with those used to combat racial discrimination. During the 1962 hearings, the CIO's James B. Carey discussed Truman's Committee on Civil Rights, while in 1963 Green scoffed at business witnesses who provided a gendered equivalent to "some of my best friends are Jews or some of my best friends are Negro"; she spoke of "Jane Doe" laws that paralleled Jim Crow laws. For Sonia Pressman of the American Civil Liberties Union the equal pay bill attempted "to give to women who constitute the majority of our population some of the rights already enjoyed by our various minority groups."[51]

Other women had expressed the same sentiment, but in a more invidious manner that harkened back [and we might say forward] to feminists who defended women's rights at the expense of racial equality. In 1948 a twenty-year employee of Boston Edison complained, "We have a [state] fair employment act that takes care of color, race and creed, but nothing is done for the fair employment of married women. Are we less than they?"[52] Citing the unequal pay and unhelpful union at her workplace, a Virginian wrote to Women's Bureau head Esther Peterson in 1961, "Not only are the colored held back but we white women also." The secretary of the Independent Women Voters of Philadelphia sent an accusatory telegram to John F. Kennedy: "We all know the men you sponsor for Congress go all out for the Negro block vote but what is their position on equal pay for white women."[53]

Title VII of the 1964 Civil Rights Act appeared to bring sex and race together. It prohibited workplace discrimination on the basis of race, color, religion, sex, or national origin.[54] Popular accounts, along with older scholarly ones, portray the addition of "sex" as a decoy, though we now know that amender Howard K. Smith, a conservative Virginia Democrat, was a staunch proponent of the ERA. Many liberals at the time felt that the act was really about race and that Southern legislators introduced "sex" merely to obstruct its passage.[55] Certainly the EEOC, Title VII's enforcement agency, acted from that belief, pursuing race cases more vigorously than sex cases.[56] The statute's "bona fide occupational qualification" provided a greater loophole for sex discrimination on the basis of female difference, and so did the question of when a classification was sex-based, as with pregnancy. After 1964 courts deployed the Fourteenth Amendment to subject race to a stricter scrutiny than sex, allowing a lower threshold for the government to prove the necessity for distinctions on the basis of sex. Pregnancy and privacy thus justified different treatment, whereas there was nearly no excuse for discrimination on the basis of race.[57]

Congressional debate over Title VII reveals how gender was racialized in the process of a discussion centered on race or sex, making the whiteness of the female referent to equal pay more apparent. Feminist Martha Griffiths of Michigan argued that the omission of sex would place "white women . . . last at the hiring gate."[58] After Title VII linked sex and race discrimination, most feminists rejected such overt racism. Even the racialist National Women's

Party defended the amendment and signed onto a dual strategy of promoting constitutional change and litigation under the Fourteenth Amendment.[59] To their credit, after gaining coverage in 1972, professional women continued to push for inclusion of private household workers under the FLSA, finally won in 1974.[60] But when administration of equal pay shifted from Labor to the EEOC in 1978, the ability to initiate cases to build a legal basis for comparable worth suffered; complainants no longer could count on a predisposed administrator to guide their case.

Ledbetter *and the Antidiscrimination Continuum*

With *Ledbetter,* the Supreme Court treated race discrimination in pay differently from sex discrimination but ultimately hurt plaintiffs in both kinds of suits. *Ledbetter* began as a common enough kind of pay discrimination case, but its plaintiff, as we have seen, pursued her complaint under Title VII (rather than under the Equal Pay Act). The EEOC certified her to go to court under its "paycheck accrual" rule that subsequent paychecks maintain the initial discrimination, restarting the 180-day period in which Title VII restricts the filing of a suit.[61] During the years of discrimination, Ledbetter's salary grew to be 40 percent lower than her male counterparts. Before the Supreme Court, *Ledbetter's* lawyers relied on *Bazemore v. Friday,* which addressed relief from inequalities from separate pay scales developed prior to Title VII that persisted in lower pay for African Americans after a new integrated pay scale.[62] *Bazemore* held against "exempting from liability those employers who were historically the greatest offenders of the rights of blacks." Justice Alito rejected this precedent in holding that Goodyear's system was "facially non-discriminatory."[63]

Justice Ginsburg's dissent relied on *Bazemore* for an opposite lesson: to ignore prior acts of discrimination that each paycheck perpetuates means to let employers who have historically offended the rights of women off the hook. Ginsburg emphasized that "pay disparities" differed from other "adverse acts," like lay-offs, because they remained hidden. Rather than a one-time event, pay discrimination was cumulative. Ginsburg brought the real world into the law, a basis upon which the EEOC had proceeded: "Having received a pay increase, the female employee is unlikely to discern at once that she has experienced an adverse employment decision" from larger raises being given to men. Drawing from feminist concepts of hostile work environment, she argued that management must know of its existence and such environment can stem from the kind of degrading of performance that

Ledbetter experienced. Congress did not intend to perpetuate such discrimination, she reasoned.[64]

Tellingly Ginsburg chided the majority in suggesting that Ledbetter could have pursued a case under the EPA, which allows only for limited back pay and "provides no relief when the pay discrimination charged is based on race, religion, national origin, age, or disability." That lacuna would have widened the gap between sex and race in the law. Essentially women still could gain redress under the EPA, but minorities only could use the newly time-restricted Title VII.[65] Discrimination on the basis of race and other Title VII categories now came under a rule generated by a sex discrimination case that bore the old prejudices against women out of place at work. In less than two years federal courts applied *Ledbetter* to some three hundred cases involving not only Title VII but also the Age Discrimination in Employment Act, the Fair Housing Act, Title IX, and the Eighth Amendment. They exonerated employers from the continuing consequences of discrimination by throwing out cases presented after the 180-day deadline following a "discrete" act of harm.[66]

Ginsburg's dissent deserves the praise of feminist commentators. But shortly afterward she joined the other Justices in upholding a Department of Labor ruling that exempted home-care workers employed by third-party agencies from the FLSA. This case, *Long Island Care at Home v. Coke*, illuminates the dilemma of discussing race and gender separately and suggests the inadequacy of individualized equal pay suits when so much wage discrimination rests on occupational segregation. It further illustrates how dualistic categories forced by history and law obscure racialized gendered issues, especially those involving low-waged immigrant women of color. Ginsburg suggested during oral argument that a legislative remedy was appropriate, but in doing so was willing to retain a disproportionate harm on one group of women workers. That Ledbetter conformed to the model woman of liberal feminism, a trailblazer in a male job, whereas the Jamaican immigrant home-care aide Evelyn Coke engaged in work conflated with unpaid labor of wives and mothers, and long associated with servile status, highlights the problem of which work and which women count in equity discourse.[67]

Ginsburg's different actions—a scorching dissent and near silent agreement—remind us of (in)equities that equal pay by itself fails to address: the home as a workplace, intimate labor involving bodies, the devaluing of the domestic, and the lower status of immigrant and women of color. As if to underscore these priorities, while the Fair Home Health Care Act, introduced in 2007 to correct the Coke case, remained on the backburner, the first bill that President Barack Obama signed was the Lilly Ledbetter Fair Pay Act, which restores the filing clock to 180 days after the last, rather than the first, act of discrimination.[68]

Lilly Ledbetter will never receive financial restitution from Goodyear. Still, at the signing ceremony of her Fair Pay Act, she noted, "with the president's signature today I have an even richer reward."[69] She continued lobbying for stronger state equal pay laws and promoted the Paycheck Fairness Act that would make the EPA comparable to other antidiscrimination measures through the ability to award compensatory and punitive damages and close procedural loopholes. As Ledbetter declared in June 2009, "We owe it to our daughters, our granddaughters and ourselves to get this act signed into law."[70]

NOTES

1. Derrick A. Bell Jr., *Nineteenth Annual Supreme Court Review: Ledbetter v. Goodyear Tire & Rubber Co.*, 23 Touro L. Rev. 843, 845–47 (2008).

2. Serena Mayeri, *Reconstructing the Race-Sex Analogy*, 49 Wm. & Mary L. Rev. 1789 (2008).

3. Nancy MacLean, Freedom Is Not Enough (2006).

4. Merl E. Reed, Seedtime for the Modern Civil Rights Movement (1991).

5. Eileen Boris, *The Gender of Discrimination: Race, Sex, and Fair Employment*, in Women and the U.S. Constitution: History, Interpretation, and Practice 273–91 (Sibyl Schwarzenbach & Patricia Smith, eds. 2004).

6. Hastings College of Law, Center for WorkLife Law, http://www.worklifelaw.org (accessed Aug. 17, 2010).

7. Reed, 306.

8. Final Disposition Report, 5-BR-1328, June 19, 1944 (FEPC Papers, Reel 59F, National Archives).

9. Reports of the Department of Labor: 1918, 119–120, 123 (1919).

10. First Annual Report, Director of the Woman in Industry Service [1919], 1146–47 (1920); *Slogan of Equal Pay for Women*, 1 Jewelry Workers' Monthly Bulletin 10 (July 1917).

11. Mary Anderson, "Equal Pay," War History of Women's Bureau (Box 385, RG86, National Archives).

12. Women's Bureau, "Equal Pay" for Women in War Industries, Bulletin of the Women's Bureau No. 196, 16 (1942).

13. Mary Anderson to Mary B. Gilson, July 8, 1943 (Box 385, RG86).

14. Tenth Reg'l War Lab. Bd., in the Matter of California Metal Trades Association and International Association of Machinists, Lodge 68, Report and Recommendation of the Panel, NWLB Case #665, May 20, 1945, 4 (Box 193, RG86).

15. Women's Bureau, Equal Pay—A Progress Report, May 1944, 2 (Box 385, RG86).

16. Report on the Application of the Principle of Equal Pay for Equal Work in the Firesafe Building Products Corporation (Box 385, RG86,).

17. Information for Committee on Seven (7) Points to be Discussed in Connection with Atlas Powder Company, in St. Louis Scrapbook, 113, Brotherhood of Sleeping Car Porter Papers, Chicago Historical Society; Harry Kingman to Clarence Mitchell on Status of Telephone Cases, Nov. 28, 1944, 2 (FEPC Papers).

18. *Women Win on Equal Pay*, Detroit News, May 28, 1942.

19. St. John v. General Motors Corp. (Mich. Cir. Ct., May 29, 1942).

20. Margaret L. Plunkett, *Women in Industry*, 63 Monthly Lab. Rev. 380, 386–87 (Sept. 1946).

21. St. John v. General Motors Corp., 13 N.W. 2d 840, 841 (Mich. 1944).

22. Plunkett, *Women in Industry*, 388; Frieda S. Miller, *Equal Pay—Its Importance to the Nation*, Indep. Woman, Nov. 1946, 3; Women's Bureau, *Handbook of Facts on Women Workers*, Bulletin No. 242, 80 (1952); Esther Peterson to Aileen Elliott, April 12, 1963 (Roll 59 Equal Pay Correspondence, Apr. –Dec. 1963, JFK Library).

23. "Equal Pay" for Women in War Industries, 3.

24. Ruth Milkman, Gender at Work: The Dynamics of Job Segregation by Sex during World War II 75 (1987).

25. Nat'l War Lab. Bd., Advance Release, for Sunday Papers, Apr. 11, 1943, 2–3.

26. Mary Elizabeth Pigeon, Chief, Research Division, to Helen Blanchard, New York Women's Trade Union League, Sept. 29, 1942; Mary Anderson to Helena O. Morgan, Dec. 22, 1942 (Box 385, RG86); John O. Louis to L. E. Mills, Dec. 7, 1943 (Box 194, RG86); "Equal Pay" for Women in War Industries, 11–14.

27. Miss Elizabeth Christman, Wage Rates for Women Workers, in 66th Convention of the American Flint Glass Workers' Union of North America 15 (1942) (Box 385, RG86).

28. *Equal Factory Pay Asked for Women*, N. Y. Times, July 3, 1947; Women's Equal Pay Act of 1945, S. Rep. No. 79-1576, at 2, 9.

29. Virginia B. to Mary Anderson, Sept. 3, 1942 (Box 385, RG86).

30. *Denver Women Give Views on Issue of Postwar Jobs*, Denver Post, May 27, 1945.

31. Cynthia Harrison, On Account of Sex: The Politics of Women's Issues, 1945–1968, 45–47 (1988); Deborah M. Figart, Ellen Mutari, & Marilyn Power, Living Wages, Equal Wages: Gender and Labor Market Policies in the United States 120–42 (2002).

32. Working Paper on Equal Pay, Sept. 1951, 2 (Box 390, RG86).

33. George F. Addes to All Regional Directors, International Representatives and Local Union Presidents (UAW), 6/10/1943 (Box 385, RG86).

34. Newt McClain to FEPC, October 2, 1942; Mary Anderson to Newt McClain, October 14, 1942 (Box 350, RG86); Mrs. Della Wilkins to Frances Perkins, May 15, 1943; Mary Anderson to the Maids of Dale Dormitory, May 21, 1943 (Box 350, RG86).

35. Presidential Comm. on the Status of Women, Report of the Committee on Private Employment 8 (1963).

36. Equal Pay Act, Hearings on H.R. 3861 & Related Bills before the Spec. Subcomm. on Lab. of the Comm. on Educ. & Lab., 88th Cong. 58–59 (1963), 58–59; Harrison, 100, 179.

37. Peggy Pascoe, *Miscegenation Law, Court Cases, and Ideologies of "Race" in Twentieth-Century America*, 83 J. Am. Hist. 44 (June 1996).

38. 79 Cong. Rec. 805–06 (daily ed. Feb. 4, 1946) (statements of Sen. Tom Stewart & Sen. James Eastland).

39. Jo Freeman, *How "Sex" Got into Title VII: Persistent Opportunism as a Maker of Public Policy*, 9 Law & Ineq 163, 170 (1991); Herbert R. Northrup, *Progress without Federal Compulsion: Arguing the Case for Compromise Methods*, Commentary, Sept. 10, 1952, at 207; *Women's Bureau Conference: The American Woman, Her Changing Role*, Women's Bureau Bulletin No.224, 104, 151 (1948).

40. Notes: Williams, Weissbrodt, Bagwell, Hammerle, Beyer meeting (Box 250, RG86).

41. U.S. Senate Comm. on Education and Labor, Press Release, June 21, 1945 (Box 390, RG86).

42. Women's Equal Pay Act of 1945, S. Rep. No. 79-1576, at 5 (1946).

43. Women's Equal Pay Act of 1950, Rep. of the Comm. on Lab. & Pub. Welfare on S.706, S. Rep. No. 81-22263, at 2–3 (1950); Spec. Subcomm. to the Comm. on Educ. & Lab., 81st Cong., Report on H.R. 1584, Women's Equal Pay Act of 1949, 2,6 (1950).

44. Harrison, 42–47; Alice Kessler-Harris, *The Double Meaning of Equal Pay, in* A Woman's Wage: Historical Meanings & Social Consequences 85–90, 101–2 (1990).

45. Individual Views of Mr. Taft, in United States Senate, Women's Equal Pay Act of 1950, 14; Harrison, 89–105.

46. Edna M. Johnson to Esther Peterson, June 11, 1963 (Roll 58, JFK Library); Harrison, 89–105.

47. Equal Pay Act of 1963, Hearings Before the Subcommittee, Committee on Labor and Public Welfare on S.882 and S.910, 88th Cong. 88 (1963).

48. Esther Peterson to Orville Kirking, June 6, 1963 (Roll 58, JFK Library).

49. Freeman, 172.

50. C. Fast, On Equal Rights, Equal Pay, Cong. Q., Dec. 26, 1962.

51. Equal Pay Act of 1962, Hearing before the Subcommittee, Committee on Labor and Public Welfare on S. 2494 and HR 11677, 87th Cong. 80–81 (1962); Equal Pay Act, Hearings before the Special Subcommittee, Committee on Education and Labor on HR 3861 and Related Bills, 88th Cong. 173, 204 (1963); Equal Pay Act of 1963, Hearings on S. 882 and S.910, 169.

52. Letter to the Editor from M. L. M. Newton, *FEPC Wanted for Married Women,* Boston Traveler, July 7, 1948.

53. Elizabeth Walsh to Esther Peterson, Feb. 28, 1961; Ann Walsh to the President, Nov. 6, 1962 (WB Papers, JFK Library).

54. Civil Rights Act of 1964, § 703(a), 42 U.S.C.A. §2000e-2(a).

55. Smith investigated the FEPC during World War II. See Report of Proceedings, Hearing held before Special Committee to Investigate Executive Agencies, Feb. 25, 1944 (1944). For the deliberate addition of "sex," see Freeman, *supra.*

56. Harrison, 187–91; Hugh D. Graham, The Civil Rights Era: Origins and Development of National Policy 205–32 (1990).

57. Cynthia Harrison, *Constitutional Equality for Women: Losing the Battle but Winning the War, in* Constitutionalism and American Culture: Writing the New Constitutional History 174–210 (Sandra VanBurkleo et al., eds. 2002).

58. 88 Cong. Rec. 2578 (daily ed. Feb. 8, 1964).

59. Serena Mayeri, *Constitutional Choices: Legal Feminism and the Historical Dynamics of Change,* 92 Cal. L. Rev. 755, 774 (2004).

60. Phyllis Palmer, *Outside the Law: Agricultural and Domestic Workers under the Fair Labor Standards Act,* 7 J. Pol'y Hist. 428 (1995).

61. Linda Greenhouse, *Justices' Ruling Limits Lawsuits on Pay Disparity,* N.Y. Times, May 30, 2007.

62. 478 U.S. 387 (1986).

63. Ledbetter v. Goodyear Tire & Rubber Co., 550 U.S. 618 (2007).

64. *Id.* at 649, 654.

65. *Id.* at 658.

66. Robert Pear, *Justices' Ruling in Discrimination Case May Draw Quick Action by Obama*, N.Y. Times, Jan. 4, 2009.

67. Long Island Care at Home v. Coke, 551 U.S. 158 (2007).

68. Occupational Health & Safety, Home Care Bill Would Undo DOL's "Casual Basis" Interpretation, Sept. 24, 2007; Robert Pear, *House Passes 2 Measures on Job Bias*, N.Y. Times, Jan. 10, 2009; Jim Abrams, *Senate Passes Wage Discrimination Bill*, AP, Jan. 23, 2009.

69. Katharine Mieszkowski, *All Hail Lilly Ledbetter*, http://www.Salon.com, Jan. 29, 2009.

70. Letter to the Editor, *Promoting Equal Pay: Lilly Ledbetter States Her Case*, N.Y. Times, June 30, 2009; Nat'l Org. for Women, *The Paycheck Fairness Act: The Next Step in the Fight for Fair Pay*, http://www.now.org, Sept., 7, 2009.

Selected Bibliography

Baker, Carrie N. *The Women's Movement against Sexual Harassment*. Cambridge: Cambridge University Press, 2008.

Basch, Norma. *In the Eyes of the Law: Women, Marriage, and Property in Nineteenth-Century New York*. Ithaca, N.Y.: Cornell University Press, 1982.

Batlan, Felice. "Engendering Legal History." *Law & Social Inquiry* 30 (2005): 834.

———. "Law and the Fabric of the Everyday: The Settlement Houses, Sociological Jurisprudence, and the Gendering of Urban Legal Culture." *Southern California Interdisciplinary Law Journal* 15 (2006): 236.

Becker, Mary, Cynthia Grant Bowman, and Morrison Torrey, eds. *Feminist Jurisprudence: Taking Women Seriously*. 2d ed. West, 2001.

Blair, Karen J. *The Clubwoman as Feminist: True Womanhood Redefined, 1868–1914*. New York: Holmes & Meier, 1980.

Blumkin, Rada. "Rosalie Loew Whitney: The Early Years as Advocate for the Poor." Women's Legal History Biography Project. Robert Crown Law Library, Stanford Law School, 2001. http://www.law.stanford.edu/library/womenslegalhistory/ papers0203/WhitneyR-Blumkin01.pdf (accessed Jan. 5, 2010).

Bordin, Ruth Birgitta Anderson. *Woman and Temperance: The Quest for Power and Liberty, 1873–1900*. Piscataway, N.J.: Rutgers University Press, 1990.

Boris, Eileen. "The Gender of Discrimination: Race, Sex, and Fair Employment." In *Women and the U.S. Constitution: History, Interpretation, and Practice*. Edited by Sibyl Schwarzenbach & Patricia Smith, 273–91. New York: Columbia University Press, 2004.

Bredbenner, Candice Lewis. *A Nationality of Her Own: Women, Marriage, and the Law of Citizenship*. Berkeley: University of California Press, 1998.

Cain, Patricia. "Feminist Jurisprudence: Grounding the Theories." *Berkeley Women's Law Journal* 4 (1989–90): 191.

Chamallas, Martha. *Introduction to Feminist Legal Theory*. 2d ed. Aspen, 2003.

Chused, Richard. "Married Women's Property Law, 1800-1850." *Georgetown Law Journal* 71 (1983): 1359–1425.

Clapp, Elizabeth J. *Mothers of all Children: Women Reformers and the Rise of Juvenile Courts in Progressive Era America*. University Park: Pennsylvania State University Press, 1998.

Cott, Nancy. *The Grounding of Modern Feminism*. New Haven, Conn.: Yale University Press, 1987.

———. *The Bonds of Womanhood*. New Haven, Conn.: Yale University Press, 1982.

———. "Marriage and Women's Citizenship in the United States, 1830–1934." *American Historical Review* (1998): 1140–74.

Drachman, Virginia G. *Sisters in Law: Women Lawyers in Modern American History*. Cambridge, Mass.: Harvard University Press, 2001.

———. *Women Lawyers and the Origins of Professional Identity in America: The Letters of the Equity Club, 1887 to 1890*. Ann Arbor: University of Michigan Press, 1993.

Dubler, Ariela R. "Wifely Behavior: A Legal History of Acting Married." *Columbia Law Review* 100 (2000): 964.

Dubois, Ellen Carol. *Feminism and Suffrage: The Emergence of an Independent Women's Movement in America, 1848–1869*. Ithaca, N.Y.: Cornell University Press, 1999.

Fineman, Martha. "Feminist Theory in Law: The Difference it Makes." *Columbia Journal of Gender & Law* 2 (1992): 171.

———. "Gender and Law: Feminist Legal Theory's Role in New Legal Realism." *Wisconsin Law Review* (2005): 405–31.

———. "Challenging Law, Establishing Differences: The Future of Feminist Legal Scholarship." *Florida Law Review* 42 (1990): 25–43.

Flexner, Eleanor, and Ellen Fitzpatrick. *Century of Struggle: The Woman's Rights Movement in the United States*. Cambridge, Mass.: Harvard University Press, 1959.

Freeman, Jo. "How 'Sex' Got into Title VII: Persistent Opportunism as a Maker of Public Policy." *Law & Inequality* 9 (1991): 163–84.

Ginsburg, Ruth Bader, and Barbara Flagg. "Some Reflections on the Feminist Legal Thought of the 1970s." *University of Chicago Legal Forum* (1989): 16.

Gordon, Linda. *Pitied But Not Entitled: Single Mothers and the History of Welfare*. Cambridge, Mass.: Harvard University Press, 1994.

———. *The Moral Property of Women: A History of Birth Control Politics in America*. New York: Penguin, 1974.

Harrison, Cynthia. *On Account of Sex: The Politics of Women's Issues, 1945–1968*. Berkeley: University of California Press, 1988.

———. "Constitutional Equality for Women: Losing the Battle but Winning the War." In *Constitutionalism and American Culture: Writing the New Constitutional History*, ed. Sandra VanBurkleo et al., 174–210. Lawrence: University of Kansas Press: 2002.

Hasday, Jill. "Contest and Consent: A Legal History of Marital Rape." *California Law Review* 88 (2000): 1373–1505.

Helly, Dorothy O., and Susan M. Reverby, eds. *Gendered Domains: Rethinking Public and Private in Women's History*. Ithaca, N.Y.: Cornell University Press, 1992.

Hoff, Joan. *Law, Gender and Injustice: A Legal History of U.S. Women*. 2d ed. New York: New York University Press, 1994.

Holland, Patricia G., and Ann Gordon, eds. *The Papers of Elizabeth Cady Stanton and Susan B. Anthony*. Microfilm. Wilmington, Del.: Scholarly Resources, 1991.

Jones, Bernie D. "Southern Free Women of Color in the Antebellum North: Race, Class, and a 'New Women's Legal History.'" *Akron Law Review* 41 (2008): 763–98.

Jordan, Gwen Hoerr. "Agents of (Incremental) Change: From Myra Bradwell to Hillary Clinton." *Nevada Law Journal* 9 (2009): 580–645.

Kerber, Linda K. *No Constitutional Right to Be Ladies: Women and the Obligations of Citizenship*. New York: Hill and Wang, 1998.

———. *Women of the Republic: Intellect and Ideology in Revolutionary America*. Chapel Hill: University of North Carolina Press, 1980.

———. "Separate Spheres, Female Worlds, Woman's Place: The Rhetoric of Women's History." *Journal of American History* 75 (1988): 9–39.

Kerber, Linda K., and Jane Sherron De Hart. "Gender and the New Women's History." In *Women's America: Refocusing the Past*, 6th ed. Oxford: Oxford University Press, 2004.

Kessler-Harris, Alice. *Out to Work: A History of Wage-Earning Women in the United States.* 20th ed. New York: Oxford University Press, 2003.

Larson, Jane E. "'Even a Worm Will Turn at Last': Rape Reform in Late Nineteenth-Century America." *Yale Journal of Law & the Humanities* 9 (1997): 1–71.

Lerner, Gerda. *The Majority Finds Its Past: Placing Women in History*, 145–59. New York: Oxford University Press, 1979.

Levit, Nancy, and Robert R. M. Verchick. *Feminist Legal Theory: A Primer.* New York: New York University Press, 2006.

MacKinnon, Catharine. *Sexual Harassment of Working Women.* New Haven, Conn.: Yale University Press, 1979.

———. *Toward a Feminist Theory of the State.* Cambridge, Mass.: Harvard University Press, 1989.

———. *Only Words.* Cambridge, Mass.: Harvard University Press, 1993.

MacKinnon, Catharine, and Andrea Dworkin, eds. *In Harm's Way: The Pornography Civil Rights Hearings.* Cambridge, Mass.: Harvard University Press, 1997.

———. *Pornography and Civil Rights: A New Day for Women's Equality.* Minneapolis: Organizing against Pornography, 1988.

Mayeri, Serena. "Reconstructing the Race-Sex Analogy." *William & Mary Law Review* 49 (2008): 1789–1857.

———. "Constitutional Choices: Legal Feminism and the Historical Dynamics of Change." *California Law Review* 92 (2004): 774.

Milkman, Ruth. *Gender at Work: The Dynamics of Job Segregation by Sex during World War II.* Champaign: University of Illinois Press, 1987.

Murray, Pauli, and Mary O. Eastwood. "Jane Crow and the Law: Sex Discrimination and Title VII." *George Washington Law Review* 34 (1965): 232–56.

Novkov, Julie Lavonne. *Constituting Workers, Protecting Women: Gender, Law, and Labor in the Progressive Era and New Deal Years.* Ann Arbor: University of Michigan, 2004.

Offen, Karen. "Defining Feminism: A Comparative Historical Approach." *Signs* 14 (1988): 119–57.

Rhode, Deborah L. "Feminist Critical Theories." *Stanford Law Review* 42 (1990): 617–38.

Segrave, Kerry. *The Sexual Harassment of Women in the Workplace, 1600–1993.* Jefferson, N.C.: McFarland, 1994.

Siegel, Reva. "'The Rule of Love': Wife Beating as Prerogative and Privacy." *Yale Law Journal* 105 (1996): 2117–2207.

———. "The Right's Reasons: Constitutional Conflict and the Spread of Woman-Protective Antiabortion Argument." *Duke Law Journal* 57 (2008): 1688.

———. "The New Politics of Abortion: An Equality Analysis of 'Woman-Protective' Abortion Restrictions." *University of Illinois Law Review* (2007): 991–94.

———. "She the People: The Nineteenth Amendment, Sex Equality, Federalism, and the Family." *Harvard Law Review* 115 (2002): 947–1046.

———. "The Modernization of Marital Status Law: Adjudicating Wives' Rights to Earnings, 1860–1930." *Georgetown Law Journal* 82 (1995): 2127–2211.

———. "Home as Work: The First Woman's Rights Claims Concerning Wives' Household Labor, 1850–1880." *Yale Law Journal* 103 (1994): 1073–1217.

———. "Reasoning From the Body: An Historical Perspective on Abortion Regulation and Questions of Equal Protection." *Stanford Law Review* 44 (1992): 261–381.

Sklar, Kathryn Kish. *Florence Kelley and the Nation's Work: The Rise of Women's Political Culture, 1830–1900.* New Haven, Conn.: Yale University Press, 1995.

Stanley, Amy Dru. *From Bondage to Contract: Wage Labor, Marriage, and the Market in the Age of Slave Emancipation.* Cambridge: Cambridge University Press, 1998.

Stansell, Christine. *City of Women: Sex and Class in New York, 1789–1860.* Champaign: University of Illinois Press, 1987.

Stanton, Elizabeth Cady, Susan B. Anthony, and Matilda Josyln Gage. *History of Woman Suffrage.* Vol. 1. New York: Fowler & Wells, 1870.

Strebeigh, Fred. *Equal: Women Reshape American Law.* New York: Norton, 2009.

Warbasse, Elizabeth B. *The Changing Legal Rights of Married Women, 1800–1861.* Edited by Harold Hyman and Stuart Burchey. London: Taylor & Francis, 1987.

Welke, Barbara Young. *Recasting American Liberty: Gender, Race, Law, and the Railroad Revolution, 1865–1920.* Cambridge: Cambridge University Press, 2001.

———. "Unreasonable Women: Gender and the Law of Accidental Injury, 1870–1920." *Law & Social Inquiry* 19 (1994): 400–402.

———. "When All the Women Were White, and All the Blacks Were Men: Gender, Class, Race, and the Road to Plessy, 1855–1914." *Law & History Review* 13 (1995): 261–316.

Welter, Barbara. "The Cult of True Womanhood: 1820–1860." *American Quarterly* 18 (1966): 152.

Wollstonecraft, Mary. *Vindication of the Rights of Woman.* Boston: Peter Edes, 1792.

CASES

Bradwell v. Illinois, 83 U.S. (16 Wall.) 130 (1873).

Craig v. Boren, 429 U.S. 190 (1976).

Frontiero v. Richardson, 411 U.S. 677 (1973).

General Elec. Co. v. Gilbert, 429 U.S. 125 (1976).

Gedulig v. Aiello, 417 U.S. 484 (1974).

Goesaert v. Cleary, 335 U.S. 464 (1948).

Gonzales v. Carhart, 550 U.S. 124 (2007).

Hoyt v. Florida, 368 U.S. 57 (1961).

J.E.B. v. Alabama, 511 U.S. 127 (1984).

Ledbetter v. Goodyear Tire & Rubber Co., 550 U.S. 618 (2007).

Meritor Sav. Bank v. Vinson, 477 U.S. 57 (1986).

Minor v. Happersett, 88 U.S. (21 Wall.) 162 (1874).

Muller v. Oregon, 208 U.S. 412 (1908).

Personnel Adm'r of Mass. v. Feeney, 442 U.S. 256 (1979).

Reed v. Reed, 404 U.S. 71 (1971).

Roe v. Wade, 410 U.S. 113 (1973).

Rostker v. Goldberg, 453 U.S. 57 (1981).

United States v. Virginia, 518 U.S. 515 (1996).

Contributors

CARRIE N. BAKER is Associate Professor in the Department of Sociology and Anthropology at Berry College in Georgia. She is the author of *The Women's Movement Against Sexual Harassment in the United States* (Cambridge University Press, 2008).

FELICE BATLAN is Associate Professor of Law at the Chicago-Kent College of Law in Illinois. Before entering the academy, she practiced law for nine years. Her writings on feminist jurisprudence, women's legal history, and the gendered origins of public interest law appear in numerous law reviews, history journals, and in edited books focusing on women and legal history.

TRACEY JEAN BOISSEAU is Associate Professor of Gender and Cultural History at The University of Akron in Ohio. She is the author of *White Queen: The Imperial Origins of American Feminist Identity* and co-editor, with Abigail Markwyn, of *Gendering the Fair: Histories of Women and Gender at World's Fairs.* Her research exploring feminist production of self and identity in popular culture has appeared in *Signs, Gender and History, NWSA Journal, thirdspace,* and *Women's History Review.*

EILEEN BORIS is Hull Professor and Chair of the Department of Feminist Studies at the University of California, Santa Barbara, where she holds affiliate appointments in History and Black Studies and directs the Center for Research on Women and Social Justice. Among her books are the prizewinning *Home to Work: Motherhood and the Politics of Industrial Homework in the United States; Intimate Labors: Cultures, Technologies, and the Politics of Care,* co-edited with Rhacel Parreñas; and, with Jennifer Klein, *Caring for America: Home Health Workers in the Shadow of the Welfare State.*

RICHARD H. CHUSED is Professor of Law at New York Law School and, previously, was Professor of Law at Georgetown Law School in Washington, D.C. His writings explore married women's property laws, nineteenth-century federal land grants, divorce, Myra Bradwell's *Chicago Legal News*, the idea of gendered spaces, and the history of marital status.

LYNDA DODD is the Joseph H. Flom Professor of Legal Studies at the City College of New York. She teaches in the Skadden Arps Honors Program in Legal Studies and specializes in constitutional law and theory, constitutional tort litigation, and jurisprudence.

JILL ELAINE HASDAY is the Julius E. Davis Professor of Law at the University of Minnesota Law School. Her work on constitutional law, family law, and legal history has appeared in the *Harvard Law Review, Stanford Law Review, New York University Law Review, Michigan Law Review, Georgetown Law Journal, California Law Review, UCLA Law Review,* and *Minnesota Law Review.*

GWEN HOERR JORDAN is Assistant Professor of Legal Studies at the University of Illinois, Springfield. She is a former J. Willard Hurst Legal History Fellow at the University of Wisconsin Law School. Jordan has published studies on women lawyers' local and transnational law reform campaigns for gender justice.

MAYA MANIAN is Associate Professor of Law at the University of San Francisco in California. After law school, she served as a Fulbright scholar in India, studying India's domestic violence laws. She practiced civil rights litigation as a Blackmun Fellowship Attorney at the Center for Reproductive Rights in New York City.

MELISSA MURRAY is Assistant Professor of Law at the University of California, Berkeley. Her articles on constitutional law and women's legal history have appeared in the *Virginia Law Review,* the *California Law Review,* and the *Michigan Journal of Gender and the Law.*

MAE C. QUINN is Professor of Law at Washington University School of Law in St. Louis, Missouri, where she co-directs the law school's Civil Justice Clinic. Her past work has focused largely on ethical, legal, and other issues facing accused persons and their lawyers.

MARGO SCHLANGER is Professor of Law and Director of the Civil Rights Litigation Clearinghouse at the University of Michigan Law School. Schlanger served as a judicial law clerk to Justice Ruth Bader Ginsburg. Her research focuses on torts, civil rights, and litigation dynamics.

REVA SIEGEL is the Nicholas deB. Katzenbach Professor of Law at Yale University. Her research on the history of abortion and marital property laws was some of the earliest work from legal scholars to explore the interactions of women's legal history. Her recent publications include *Before Roe v. Wade: Voices That Shaped the Abortion Debate Before the Supreme Court's Ruling* (with Linda Greenhouse); *The Constitution in 2020* (edited with Jack Balkin); and *Directions in Sexual Harassment Law* (edited with Catharine A. MacKinnon).

TRACY A. THOMAS is Professor of Law at The University of Akron School of Law. Her most recent publication on women's legal history is "Sex v. Race, Again," in *Who Should Be First? Feminists Debate the 2008 Presidential Campaign*. Prior to teaching she was a litigation attorney for Covington & Burling in Washington, D.C.

LETI VOLPP is Professor of Law at the University of California, Berkeley. Her study of law in the context of the humanities focuses on immigration, citizenship, culture, and identity. Most recently she co-edited, with Mary L. Dudziak, the collection of essays *Legal Borderlands: Law and the Construction of American Borders*. Prior to teaching, she worked as a public interest lawyer in immigration, employment, and voting rights.

Index

Vaughan, Hester, 148–49
Vaughn v. Menlove, 52
Veterans' education, 93–94. See also GI Bill
Vindication of the Rights of Women (Wollstonecraft), 142
Vinson, Mechelle, 234–35
Volpp, Leti, 13–14, 68–83
Voting: citizenship and, 72, 76–77; marital expatriation and, 72. See also Paul, Alice; Suffrage movement

Waldo, Alice, 183
Warner, John, 109, 110
Wayward Minors' Court, 208–9, 218
Weber, Fanny, 177
Wehrli, Lynn, 228
Welke, Barbara, 52
Welter, Barbara, 4
West Coast Hotel v. Parrish, 8
White, Rore Carl, 74
White women: citizenship of, 73–74, 76–77; republicanism of, 76–77. See also Race
Willard, Francis, 49
Williams, Joan, 152
Wilson, Woodrow, 6; NWP and, 195–96, 203n49; Paul and, 191
Wirtz, W. Willard, 246–47
Wives: expatriation of, 68–69; under GI Bill, 87–88; imputed negligence of, 58–60; in tort cases, 53–54. See also Coverture
Wollstonecraft, Mary, 142
Woman's Advocate, 42
The Woman's Bible (Stanton), 145
Woman's Christian Temperance Union (WCTU), 5–6; age of consent and, 163; founding of, 33; PAWC and, 163; suffrage movement and, 47; Willard and, 49. See also Prohibition; Temperance
Women drivers, 54–57. See also Daniels v. Clegg; Fox v. Town of Glastenbury
Women lawyers, 6, 37, 80–81, 159; as lay lawyers, 173, 176–77, 180, 185n1; for legal aid, 177–79; at NYLAS, 178–79; PAWC and, 157; Smith, R. H., against, 182–83; Supreme Court against, 7

Women of the Republic: Intellect and Ideology in Revolutionary America (Kerber), 4
Women's Armed Services Integration Act, 104
Women's Army Auxiliary Corps (WAAC), 86
Women's Bureau: equal pay and, 248; fair employment and, 241–42; NWLB and, 243; for workplace reconfiguration, 245
Women's Court, 208, 214
Women's Legal Education Society, 177–78
Women's military conscription: combat positions and, 107–8; sex-based state action and, 111–12. See also Rostker v. Goldberg
Women's military legal status, 111–13, 116–17. See also Rostker v. Goldberg
Women's military registration, 100–102, 104–15. See also Rostker v. Goldberg
Women's military service: civilian jobs and, 88, 104–5; in combat, 101, 104–8, 109; current levels of, 98, 101; draft, abolition of, 104; Eisenhower on, 104; ERA and, 104–10; ERA supporters for, 105–6; fears about, 86–87; "home front" and, 88; limitations on, 87–88, 100, 104–7; recruiting for, 104–5; requirements for, 89; status of, 100, 106; as support, 87, 104–5, 107; traditional gender roles and, 85–88, 100–101, 104–9; WAAC for, 86
Women's rights movement: first-wave, 3; second-wave, 3; sexual harassment and, 229–30. See also Feminism
Women's Social and Political Union (WSPU), 190–91
Working women, 10–11; demographics of, 228–29; prostitution and, 174–75; protection for, 175; race and, 243–44; Stanton on, 147–49. See also Employment; Sexual harassment; specific cases, organizations
Working Women's Institute (WWI), 227, 237